Families in Classical and Hellenistic Greece

Representations and Realities

SARAH B. POMEROY

CLARENDON PRESS · OXFORD

Oxford University Press, Great Clarendon Street, Oxford OX2 6DP
Oxford New York
Athens Auckland Bangkok Bogota Bombay Buenos Aires
Calcutta Cape Town Dar es Salaam Delhi
Florence Hong Kong Istanbul Karachi
Kuala Lumpur Madras Madrid Melbourne
Mexico City Nairobi Paris Singapore
Taipei Tokyo Toronto Warsaw

and associated companies in
Berlin Ibadan

Oxford is a trade mark of Oxford University Press

Published in the United States
by Oxford University Press Inc. New York

First published in paperback 1998

British Library Cataloguing in Publication Data
Data available

Library of Congress Cataloging in Publication Data
Families in classical and Hellenistic Greece: representations and realities/Sarah B. Pomeroy.
Includes bibliographical references and index.
1. Family—Greece—History. I. Title.
HQ510.P66 1996 306.85'09495'20 9633592

ISBN 0-19-815260-4

1 3 5 7 9 10 8 6 4 2

Printed in Great Britain on acid-free paper by
Bookcraft (Bath) Ltd., Midsomer Norton

Families in Classical and Hellenistic Greece

*To Jordana, Jeremy,
and Alexandra*

Preface

While writing a commentary on Xenophon's *Oeconomicus*,[1] a fourth-century treatise on the management of the *oikos* ('household', 'family', or 'estate'), I realized that there was a need for a comprehensive history of the Greek family covering the classical and Hellenistic periods. Although the generally accepted scholarly opinion was that Xenophon was conservative and old-fashioned, in his view of the family I found him to be radical, often advocating and anticipating changes that occurred in the Hellenistic period. Thus, the controversy over Xenophon inspired me to write the present book. Whereas my commentary on the *Oeconomicus* necessarily concentrated on the views of one classical Athenian author, this book exploits a wider variety of primary sources, and covers a broader geographical area and chronological span. Because I was trained as a papyrologist, I do not regard the study of the Greek diaspora as irrelevant to social history; nor do I consider the Hellenistic period as less worthy of study than the classical period. The chronological focus of this book is classical and Hellenistic (500–30 BC): as is common among papyrologists, I define the Hellenistic period as terminating with the death of Cleopatra VII.

It is a pleasure to have an opportunity to thank the Rockefeller Foundation for a Fellowship to the Bellagio Study and Conference Center in spring 1991, which provided a tranquil setting in which to plan this book. I am also grateful to the Institute for the Humanities of the University of Michigan, Ann Arbor, for a Visiting Fellowship in fall 1991, during which I used the papyrology collection and drafted Chapter 6, and to the Netherlands Institute for Advanced Study for a Fellowship in spring 1994. The following friends deserve thanks for reading and commenting on the entire manuscript: Stanley M. Burstein, Keith Bradley, Jo Ann McNamara, Barbara McManus, Jorgen

[1] Sarah B. Pomeroy, *Xenophon Oeconomicus, A Social and Historical Commentary* (Oxford, 1994).

Mejer, and H. A. Shapiro. I wish to thank Klaas Worp for his comments on Chapter 6. I am indebted to my Family History reading group who urged me to write a book that professional family historians who were not specialists in ancient history could understand. I am also grateful to the participants in the National Endowment for the Humanities Summer Seminars for College Teachers on 'The Family in Classical and Hellenistic Greece', which I directed in 1987 and 1989. During the past decade I have participated in several scholarly conferences on the family in classical antiquity. I would like to thank in particular the other panelists and audiences at the round table discussion on 'Ancient History and the "New" Social History', at the annual meeting of the Association of Ancient Historians, Brown University, 5 May 1989; at the seminar on 'The Demography of Roman Egypt' at the annual meeting of the American Philological Association, New Orleans, 29 December 1992; and at the seminar on 'Ethnicity and the Macedonian Conquest' sponsored by the Friends of Ancient History at the annual meeting of the American Philological Association, Atlanta, 28 December 1994.

'Pseudo-' preceding an author's name indicates that scholars have cast doubt upon the attribution of a literary work to a particular author; it does not imply a post-classical forgery. Thus a work attributed to Pseudo-Demosthenes was probably written by one of Demosthenes' less gifted contemporaries, and one attributed to Pseudo-Plutarch written by a Hellenistic author other than Plutarch. Except in Chapter 6, Greek names have usually been Latinized.

The manuscript of this book was completed in August 1995, and I have been able to refer to only a few works published after that date.

Contents

List of Plates

List of Figures

Abbreviations

AAWW	Anzeiger der Österreichischen Akademie der Wissenschaften in Wien
ABSA	Annual of the British School at Athens
AC	L'Antiquité Classique
AE	*Αρχαιολογικὴ ἐφημερίς*
AION	Annali dell'Istituto universitario orientale di Napoli, Dipartimento di Studi del mondo classico e del Mediterraneo antico
AJA	American Journal of Archaeology
AJAH	American Journal of Ancient History
AJP	American Journal of Philology
Anc. Soc.	Ancient Society
ASAA	Annuario della Scuola Archeologica di Atene e delle Missioni Italiane in Oriente
BASP	Bulletin of the American Society of Papyrologists
BCH	Bulletin de Correspondance Hellénique
BICS	Bulletin of the Institute of Classical Studies of the University of London
BSAA	Bulletin de la Société d'Archéologie d'Alexandrie
C&M	Classica & Mediaevalia. Revue danoise d'Histoire et de Philologie
CE	Chronique d'Égypte
CJ	The Classical Journal
CPh	Classical Philosophy
CQ	Classical Quarterly
CR	Classical Review
CSCA	California Studies in Classical Antiquity
Dar.-Sag.	Dictionnaire des antiquités grecques et romaines, ed. C. Daremberg and E. Saglio
EAA	Enciclopedia dell'arte antica, classica e orientale
EMC	Échos du Monde Classique. Classical Views
GRBS	Greek, Roman and Byzantine Studies

HPTh	History of Political Thought
JCS	Journal of Classical Studies
JHS	Journal of Hellenic Studies
JJP	Journal of Juristic Papyrologie
JRS	Journal of Roman Studies
Mnem.	Mnemosyne. Bibliotheca Classica Batava
PAE	Problèmes d'archéologie et d'ethnologie
PCPS	Proceedings of the Cambridge Philological Society
RE	Pauly's Realencyclopädie der classischen Altertumswissenschaft
REA	Revue des Études Anciennes
REG	Revue des Études Grecques
RSA	Rivista Storica dell'Antichità
TAPhA	Transactions and Proceedings of the American Philological Association
WS	Wiener Studien. Zeitschrift für klassische Philologie und Patristik
ZPE	Zeitschrift für Papyrologie und Epigraphik
ZRG	Zeitschrift der Savigny-Stiftung für Rechtsgeschichte (Romanistische Abteilung)

Introduction

MODELS AND SOURCES

A Critical Review of the History of the Greek Family in the Modern Era

Is there a history of the Greek family? Since history studies change over time, we must ask whether there were changes in the Greek family from the classical to the Hellenistic period. Were new family shapes, structures, values, and behaviour introduced in response to the changing world? The principal historiographic question I shall pose here is whether a synchronic or a diachronic approach is most appropriate to the study of the Greek family.

Most historians in the past have believed that the family did change over large periods of time, though they did not discuss minor historical transitions such as that from the classical to the Hellenistic period. The study of the family is neither a new nor a rare phenomenon in the field of ancient history.[1] Beginning in the 1860s, H. S. Maine, J. J. Bachofen, Fustel de Coulanges, John McLennan, Friedrich Engels, and others attempted to trace the history of human family patterns.[2] Among their primary sources were Greek and Latin

[1] See review essays by Jon-Christian Billigmeier, 'Studies on the Family in the Aegean Bronze Age and in Homer', *Trends in History*, 3, 3/4 (1984), 9–18, Sarah B. Pomeroy, 'The Family in Classical and Hellenistic Greece', ibid. 19–26, and S. C. Humphreys, *The Family, Women, and Death: Comparative Studies* (London, 1983), 58–78. I presented most of the material in the first half of this essay at the session on 'Ancient History and the "New" Social History' at the annual meeting of the Association of Ancient Historians, Brown University, 5 May 1989.

[2] See e.g. H. S. Maine, *Ancient Law* (London, 1861), 121; J. J. Bachofen, *Das Mutterrecht* (Stuttgart, 1861); Numa Denis Fustel de Coulanges, *The Ancient City* (trans. from *La Cité antique* [1864]; Baltimore and London, 1980); John McLennan, *Primitive Marriage* (Edinburgh, 1865); and Friedrich Engels, *Der Ursprung der Familie des Privateigentums und des Staates* (Zurich, 1884). G. Glotz's *La Solidarité de la famille dans le droit criminel en Grèce* (Paris, 1904) builds on the groundwork laid by Fustel, but current scholarship has rejected his theory of evolution from *genos* to nuclear family: see further Ch. 2 n. 42 and Ch. 3 n. 8.

texts, legal sources, myths, and kinship terminology. They relied heavily on Herodotus's description of non-Greek societies, because implicit in their thinking was the notion that 'barbarians' were less civilized than Greeks, and thus represented an earlier stage of human evolution. Like Herodotus, who sometimes wrote about non-Greeks (such as Amazons) whom he could not possibly have seen himself, some nineteenth-century historians were not adverse to using 'armchair' anthropology in their speculations about the development of the family in prehistoric times. Some of them also treated the Old Testament as a historical text that provided information about changes both in family structure, from polygamy to monogamy, and in religious thinking, from polytheism to monotheism. They not only made free use of analogies between the Greek and Roman family, but where the Greek record was lacunose, they borrowed concepts from Roman law and domestic cult. This sort of historicism, or speculative history, starting with prehistory, is no longer fashionable among mainstream historians except for a few Marxists, and the works of the nineteenth century have been properly relegated to the category of social philosophy rather than history.

The belief in historical change, however, is still a valid model and provides the structure for the most useful general study of the Greek family published in the twentieth century: W. K. Lacey's, *The Family in Classical Greece*.[3] The arrangement of Lacey's book is chronological and regional, but it actually covers a longer time span and a more limited geographical area than the title indicates. Although Lacey discusses the family in Sparta and elsewhere in Greece, as well as in epic and utopian literature, the book is Athenocentric. As his principal sources Lacey employs Athenian private orations and laws governing kinship and inheritance, though he fails to caution the reader against assuming that there is always a direct connection between law and life. Lacey exploits the evidence of comedy because it was about 'normal human beings' (p. 10), but he uses comedy too freely perhaps, without deference to the exaggerations inherent in the genre. Lacey does not discuss sexual relationships, beyond reporting the penalties for adultery, or acts of violence, and he explicitly rejects the use of tragedy as a means of understanding the Athenian family. Although tragedy was a representative element of popular culture at Athens, the use of tragedy by ancient historians remains problematic,

[3] Ithaca and London, 1968.

perhaps because the plots were set in the mythical Bronze Age, and the heroic characters were different from the people in the fifth-century Athenian audience. The most recent large-scale attempt to use it, Bennett Simon's, *Tragic Drama and the Family: Psychoanalytic Studies from Aeschylus to Beckett*, is unsuccessful.[4] In my view, neither Simon nor anyone else has yet devised an intellectual framework which would permit the social historian to exploit tragic texts systematically.[5] Despite the title, Simon is over-cautious in employing psychoanalytic theory, and does not offer original explanations that might refer to historical reality.

Most scholars who have written about the Greek family in the last decade have preferred a synchronic approach. Mark Golden, whose *Children and Childhood in Classical Athens*[6] was published in 1990, argues provocatively, but not convincingly, against the notion of historical change in the classical Athenian family, and consequently organizes his evidence and his book not chronologically, but by family role and relationship. Unlike Lacey, Golden does occasionally introduce anecdotes from tragedy and myth and use psychoanalytic explanations and speculations. Considering the nature of our sources, I am pessimistic about our ability to discover very much about the emotional experiences of the past, and whether they changed over time. Talented historians, including Mark Golden and Barry S. Strauss, have not yet found an appropriate methodology for the recovery of private, personal feelings. Strauss, in *Fathers and Sons in Athens. Ideology and Society in the Era of the Peloponnesian War*,[7] introduces the myth of Aegeus, Theseus, and Hippolytus, a tale of the Bronze Age that was popular in classical Athenian art, to explore father–son conflict in a democratic society in which all adult male citizens were theoretically equal. The mythical cycle of accidental and premeditated infanticide and patricide is used to demonstrate that there is no change over time in affective relationships whether mythi-

[4] New Haven and London, 1988. See also my cautionary remarks on women in tragedy in 'The Study of Women in Antiquity: Past, Present, and Future', *AJP* 112 (1991), 263–8, esp. 268.

[5] Some scholars have illuminated connections between a limited number of tragedies, or parts thereof, and historical reality. See most recently Judith Maitland, 'Dynasty and Family in the Athenian City State: A View from Attic Tragedy', *CQ* 42 (1992), 26–40, and Barry S. Strauss, *Fathers and Sons in Athens. Ideology and Society in the Era of the Peloponnesian War* (Princeton, 1993).

[6] Baltimore, 1990. See further Sarah B. Pomeroy, review, *EMC* 36 (1992), 73–6.

[7] Princeton, 1993.

cal or historical fathers and sons are being considered.[8] Virginia Hunter, in *Policing Athens. Social Control in the Attic Lawsuits, 420–320 BC*,[9] also employs a synchronic approach in her study of the Athenian family and society. Citing continuities in laws and practices concerning adoption, Lene Rubinstein, in *Adoption in iv. Century Athens*,[10] also argues that the fourth century was not a period of transition. The evidence which Rubinstein relies on for the fourth century simply does not exist for the fifth, so, even if her confidence that laws did not change were justified, there would be no way of determining whether practice did not change. Furthermore, Rubinstein does not take account of the tendency of Athenians in the fourth century to attribute contemporary goals and laws to Solon and other glorious predecessors, making their own time seem to be a revival of the past. Thus they revised and invented their heritage as was flattering and expedient.[11] Although Golden, Hunter, and Rubinstein cite evidence from New Comedy, none of them explores the changes that Macedonian domination imposed on the Greek world; all discuss only the classical period in detail. Hence, they reject the diachronic perspective, and emphasize continuity and *la longue durée*.

The Demographic Model

The demographic picture is nearly always in the background in recent work on family history, and there is no doubt that significant demographic factors changed over time, generally showing an improvement in the classical period and a deterioration in the Hellenistic period. For these reasons, demography will be referred to again and again throughout this book in connection with relevant evidence, rather than isolated in a separate chapter. Among the demographic factors that affect family life are the age at marriage of both men and women, age at death, fecundity rates, rates of infant and juvenile mortality, sex ratio, and rates of adoption, divorce, and remarriage. For the Greek world, however, important information is often missing, and statistics based on large samples are few. For example, despite demographic and life-style patterns that must have produced thousands of widows in classical Athens, the activities of only forty-

[8] Ibid. 100. [9] Princeton, 1994.

[10] (Copenhagen, 1993), esp. 7–10, 15, 82. Rubinstein *et al.*, 'Adoption in Hellenistic and Roman Athens', *C&M* 42 (1991), 139–51, present data, but little historical analysis.

[11] See Ch. 1, 37–8, and Ch. 3 n. 2.

eight can be described in any detail.[12] We can be fairly certain that the factors which determined the selection were not random: the widows are usually very wealthy women known through private orations. Thus forty-eight are scarcely statistically significant. The bulk of demographic evidence comes from burials. Therefore, though it may seem odd to scholars who specialize in later historical periods to examine the life cycle in the context of death, in this book the major treatment of demographic issues appears in Chapter 3, which is on that topic.

Because a large data base for Greece is lacking, it is tempting to adopt theoretical models or comparative data from the Roman world. Roman historians have much more detailed evidence, including census records and thousands of funerary inscriptions giving age at death, duration of marriage, and other facts that are not recorded on Greek tombstones.[13] It is not clear, however, which models are appropriate, or whether the picture traced by Roman demographers is applicable to Greece completely or only in part or not at all, owing to major structural differences between the two societies.[14] For example, in a recent study of Greek demography Thomas W. Gallant uses 16–19 as the age of first marriage for Greek women.[15] Roman demographers had determined this age of marriage for Roman women.[16] The Roman evidence, however, dates mostly from the imperial period, some 600 years after the classical period in Greece. Moreover, the status of women in classical Greece was not the same as that of Roman women: this difference was due in part to the early marriage of Greek women to men who were often twice their age. The evidence I have examined points to 14–15 as the age of first marriage for most Greek girls.[17] Thus, Plutarch approves of the Spartans inasmuch as they are unusual

[12] See Virginia Hunter, 'The Athenian Widow and her Kin', *Journal of Family History*, 14/4 (1989), 291–311, and see further Chs. 5 and 6.

[13] See further Richard P. Saller, *Patriarchy, Property and Death in the Roman Family* (Cambridge, 1994), esp. 12–42, and Ch. 3 below.

[14] See above; also Ch. 3 n. 44 and Ch. 6 below.

[15] *Risk and Survival in Ancient Greece* (Stanford, Calif., 1991), ch. 2. On p. 20 Gallant states that 'the evidence from Greece resembles that from the Roman period', but he does not identify this evidence. See further Ch. 3 n. 44 below. Gallant (pp. 17–19) also ignores the distinction between between eastern and western Mediterranean marriage patterns: see below, n. 25 and 26.

[16] See below, n. 28.

[17] According to Xen. *Oec.* 3. 13, 7. 5, the wives of Critobulus and Ischomachus married before the age of 15. See further Pomeroy, *Xenophon Oeconomicus*, 3, 232, 268–9, 275. The average age of menarche was thought to be 14: Soranus, *Gynecology*, 1. 4. 20, and see D. W. Amundsen and C. J. Diers, 'The Age of Menarche in Classical Greece and Rome', *Human Biology*, 41 (1969), 125–32.

among the Greeks in delaying marriage until the women are fully mature.[18] Because there is more evidence for men, both prescriptive and descriptive, there is little disagreement that the age of first marriage for men was about 30, or slightly younger.[19] The demographic evidence for age at marriage is derived from a range of sources, including private orations, tombstones, religious practices for designated age-groups, examination of skeletal remains, and medical and historical texts. This evidence for age at marriage is not drawn exclusively from the élite; but even if it were, it would be legitimate to use it, for it would be congruous with the rest of the demographic evidence from the Greek world, which is also drawn from the élite out of proportion to their numbers in the population at large. The demographic implications of one factor, such as women's age at marriage, are enormous. A woman who married at 14 would be likely to have at least two more babies than a woman who married at 19, and would produce quite different demographic figures for the society as a whole.

The basic demographic picture for Greece (not limited to Athens) established in the pioneering studies of skeletal remains by J. Lawrence Angel has not been significantly altered, despite the accumulation of additional data and the application of more sophisticated methodologies.[20] Angel determined that the average age at death in the classical period for adult females was 36.2, and for adult males 45; the corresponding figures for the Hellenistic period were 36.5 and 42.4.[21] The average childbirth rate per woman was 4.3 in the classical period, 3.6 in the Hellenistic period, with an infant survival rate of 2.7 in the classical period, 1.6 in the Hellenistic period, and a death

[18] Ch. 1 n. 62.

[19] Hes. *Op.* 698–9; Xen. *Oec.* 7. 5; Plato, *Rep.* 460E, *Laws* 721B, 785B; Dem. 27. 4, 65; Arist. *Pol.* 1335a6; and see further Pomeroy, *Xenophon Oeconomicus*, 268–9.

[20] J. Lawrence Angel, 'The Length of Life in Ancient Greece', *Journal of Gerontology*, 2 (1947), 18–24; 'The Bases of Paleodemography', *American Journal of Physical Anthropology*, 30 (1969), 427–38; and 'Paleoecology, Paleodemography and Health', in Steven Polgar (ed.), *Population, Ecology and Social Evolution* (The Hague, 1975), 167–90. On the problems of using skeletal evidence for demographic studies, see Tim G. Parkin, *Demography and Roman Society* (Baltimore, 1992), 41–58. Gallant, *Risk and Survival*, 20–1, generally accepts Angel's figures, but (p. 20) adopts 40 as the average age at death for men, and 38 for women.

[21] In S. C. Bisel and J. L. Angel, 'Health and Nutrition in Mycenaean Greece', in N. C. Wilkie and W. D. E. Coulson (eds.), *Contributions to Aegean Archaeology. Studies in Honor of* W. A. *McDonald* (Minneapolis, 1985), 197–210, table 4, these figures were altered slightly, to adult females 36.8, adult males 44.1 for the classical period; adult females 38.0, male 41.9 for the Hellenistic period. Ian Morris, *Death-Ritual and Social Structure in Classical Antiquity* (Cambridge, 1992), 77, accepts Angel's figures.

ratio of 500 infants per 1,000 adults in the classical period, 700 in the Hellenistic period. The sex difference in longevity alone would produce a sex ratio favouring males. Selective infanticide of females exacerbated this unbalance.[22] Thomas Gallant reasonably postulates an average family of two sons and one daughter.[23] Ideal family size is connected to partible inheritance in equal shares among male descendants and to the wish to ensure the perpetuation of the patriline as well as the family's economic status.[24] If both sons survive to adulthood, perhaps only one would marry or stay in Athens. The second son might remain a bachelor, or emigrate. Certainly there is plenty of room for theory and interpretation, though, as the preceding survey of nineteenth-century views indicates, such generalizations may lead to error. Therefore in Chapters 5 and 6 I have adopted a case-study approach.

Other Models: The Mediterranean, Rome, Historicism

Historians have shifted their opinions more than once on the extent to which the Greek family was similar to or different from other families in classical antiquity. For example, as I have mentioned, social philosophers of the nineteenth century generally assumed that the Greeks were like the Romans, and could be discussed in tandem. By contrast, some modern historians emphasize the difference. Opinions have varied even concerning sameness or difference between family structures in different Greek cities. Previous historians followed their ancient texts in pointing to major differences between Athens and Sparta. Later structural interpretations suggested that this polarization was an intellectual artefact more than a historical fact (see Ch. 1).

Large geographical areas have been discussed in terms of the sameness or difference in their family patterns. In 1965 John Hajnal described the marriage practices of Western Europe, and compared them to those of Eastern Europe and non-European countries.[25] According to Hajnal and to other historians who later elaborated and refined this contrast, the Eastern pattern was characterized by endogamy, a low age of marriage for women, strict patrilineality and

[22] See Ch. 3 n. 61–3 below. [23] *Risk and Survival*, 21.

[24] See further S. C. Todd, *The Shape of Athenian Law* (Oxford, 1993), 219.

[25] John Hajnal, 'European Marriage Patterns in Perspective', in D. V. Glass and D. E. C. Eversley (eds.), *Population and History: Essays in Historical Demography* (London, 1985), 101–43.

emphasis on the agnatic group, segregation of the sexes, and exclusion of women from the public sphere.[26] The Western pattern was characterized by exogamy, delayed marriage or even celibacy for both women and men, bilineality, and less segregation of the sexes and exclusion of women from the public sphere.

Although in the 1990s anthropologists and historians have become wary of generalizations about 'the Mediterranean family',[27] Hajnal's distinction between Western and Eastern European marriages, especially in so far as it is based on women's age at first marriage, is still partially valid for the ancient Mediterranean world, though not for all times and places. On the other hand, the names the Greeks chose for their children and the ways in which they transmitted property show that Greek society was not strictly patrilineal, as postulated in the model created by Hajnal and others, but had important bilineal features. A woman's natal family retained ultimate control over her dowry and reproductive potential. In fact, in Greece, a girl who had no brothers could produce heirs for her father's estate, and the property of a man who died intestate without direct descendants would be inherited by a sister (even a married one), rather than by a male cousin (see Ch. 1). The model does appear to be correct in suggesting that girls in Italy married at a later age than they did in Athens. In Athens girls' marriage was closely linked to menarche. The purpose of marriage was declared to be reproduction, and genealogical hypotheses are properly based on the assumption that the first child was born approximately a year after the wedding (see Ch. 5).

Studies of small numbers of tombstones earlier this century had indicated that, like Greek girls, Roman girls married at about the age of 14. Pre-pubertal marriages were also attested. Hajnal had not been able to find the European marriage pattern in antiquity, and tried to link its origin to later developments in European history. In the past ten years, however, Richard Saller and Brent Shaw have shown that marriage in the Western Roman Empire conforms more closely than previously thought to Hajnal's Western pattern.[28] After a critical examination of inscriptions giving a woman's age at death and the

[26] David Herlihy and Christiane Klapisch-Zuber, *Tuscans and their Families* (New Haven), 1985, 215 (originally published as *Les Toscans et leurs familles* (Paris, 1978)), distinguish a Tuscan marriage pattern different from that found by Hajnal for northern Europe.

[27] See n. 30, below.

[28] e.g. Saller, *Patriarchy, Property*, 26–7, and Brent Shaw, 'The Age of Roman Girls at Marriage: Some Reconsiderations', *JRS* 77 (1987), 30–46.

duration of her marriage, Saller and Shaw argue that a low age of marriage for women was characteristic only of the élite and their slaves, and that outside the city of Rome women tended to marry somewhat later in their teens.

A new picture of the Roman family has emerged, partly due to the exploitation of newly discovered or freshly analysed primary sources.[29] In the past, the Roman family was seen to be extended, multi-generational, frequently broken by divorce, and dominated by a stern paterfamilias, who exercised the power of life and death over all members of the family. These ideas were culled principally from Roman law, and resulted as well from a naïve reading of historians such as Livy, who mythologized the stern and virtuous fathers and mothers of the early Roman Republic. The new view is that the history of families in the early Republic is virtually unknowable. Instead, social historians begin with the late Republic, and pay special attention to the lower classes with small conjugal families, affectionate regard for children, some stable marriages (often beginning in slavery with *contubernium*, i.e. 'cohabitation'), and others unstable (terminating in death or divorce). Roman wives exercised sufficient authority to moderate the power of the paterfamilias, and, in any event, owing to the age difference in the married couple, the paterfamilias usually predeceased his wife.

According to the new historical model, the Roman family looks more different from the Greek than it used to (see Chs. 2 and 3). For example, the Romans were exogamous, while the Greeks were endogamous (see below). Rome was generous with her citizenship, granting it to foreigners and some ex-slaves, and thus providing an incentive for fathers to free their children born in slavery; by contrast, classical Athens recognized as citizens only those descended from at least one parent who was a citizen. It is clear that analyses of European family history constructed on a grand developmental scheme placing the Greeks before the Romans as though the latter evolved from the former are misleading.

Social historians of antiquity understandably find it tempting to exploit first-hand anthropological reports of traditional Mediterranean societies, with their wealth of detail about private life. An important question is the extent to which family dynamics and

[29] See further Keith Bradley, 'Writing the History of the Roman Family', *CPh* 88 (1993), 237–50, and Tim G. Parkin, review of B. Rawson (ed.), *Marriage, Divorce and Children in Ancient Rome;* S. Dixon, *The Roman Family*; etc., *JRS* 84 (1994), 178–85.

structures in traditional Greek societies described by anthropologists in the twentieth century may be comparable to those in antiquity, perhaps through conscious imitation of ancient ideology or owing to more subtle influences. Some of the structures of everyday life and the ecology of rural Greece have not changed dramatically in the past two and a half millennia. Despite my overall preference for a historical model founded on change over time, occasionally, for example in some of my remarks on widows, I have cited modern anthropological data to supply an explanation or parallel. The classical nexus of honour and shame, connected largely with control over women's reproductive capacity, is still recognizable in certain parts of traditional Greek society.[30] On the other hand, there are many significant differences concerning the position of the married woman. Today women's status has improved, and menarche and marriage are not closely linked. As a result of the imposition of Roman law and religious strictures, the close degree of endogamy that was common in antiquity is no longer permitted. Furthermore, in Athens and elsewhere during the classical period and in the first two centuries of Ptolemaic rule in Egypt, Greek women did not own land,[31] whereas today in Greece they often do. In rural areas especially, women's ownership of land or the lack of it certainly affects the choice of spouses and the transmission of property. Although they are illegal, dowries, or their equivalent, often including land, are still found. Thus, studies of contemporary Mediterranean anthropology are certainly of use to the ancient historian, though they must be used with extreme care. Even more problematic are arguments from common sense based confidently on either the assumption that the Greeks of the classical and Hellenistic world were like ourselves or, in the light of their endogamous habits, that they were 'primitive' or different.[32] Should we assume that we understand the following two epitaphs just as their ancient readers did? How would we react if we were to discover that each of the married couples

[30] See e.g. Stanley Brandes, 'Reflections on Honor and Shame in the Mediterranean', in David D. Gilmore (ed.), *Honor and Shame and the Unity of the Mediterranean* (Washington, DC, 1987), 121–34, esp. 122.

[31] Ch. 6 n. 39 below. Women did own land in Sparta; see further Ch. 1 and Ch. 5 n. 98 below.

[32] For the view that Greeks were exotic, see e.g. E. R. Dodds, *The Greeks and the Irrational* (Berkeley and Los Angeles, 1951). For the view that they were similar to the author himself and treated their wives as English gentlemen did, see e.g. H. D. F. Kitto, *The Greeks* (Harmondsworth, 1951; rev. 1957), esp. 223–6.

were comprised of an uncle and a niece? The first is from the Athenian port of Piraeus:

Xenoclea, the good.
Leaving two unmarried girls, Xenoclea, daughter of Nicarchus, lies here, having perished. She mourned the lamentable end of her son, Phoenix, who died at sea at the age of eight.
Which mortal is so ignorant of grief, Xenoclea, that he does not pity your fate? You left behind two unmarried girls and died of longing for your son, who has a pitiless tomb where he lies in the murky sea.[33]

The second is in the form of a dialogue between husband and wife. On the stela the couple are portrayed shaking hands:

Farewell, tomb of Melite. A good wife lies here. Loving your husband Onesimus, who loved you in return, you were the very best. And so he longs for you now that you are dead, for you were a good wife.
And to you farewell, dearest of men: love my children.[34]

We cannot know whether concepts such as 'maternal instinct' or 'conjugal love' or visual depictions of family groups have an emotional content and range similar to that which such words and images provoke in the author and readers of this book. In the area of 'emotionology' our judgements are subjective and intuitive, but in my opinion, at least, familial sentiments have changed over time. For example, modern Western society finds child abuse and infanticide abhorrent, but tolerates wife abuse and even murder as a 'crime of passion'. By contrast, the Greeks practised infanticide, and regarded harsh corporal punishment as a normal component of childrearing, but there is little evidence of wife-battering or murder—even in the case of an adulteress. Nevertheless, we ought not conclude from this observation that Greek men loved their wives more than their children, for the abundance of misogynous literature prevents us from drawing such a conclusion.

[33] P. A. Hansen (ed.), *Carmina Epigraphica Graeca*, vol. 2 (Berlin, 1989), 526 = *IG* I^2 12335, *c.*360.

[34] Ibid. 530 = *IG II*^{2} 12067 = C. Clairmont, *Classical Attic Tombstones*, Introd. vol., vols. 1–6, and plates (Kilchberg, 1993), 2. 406(v), *c.*365–340.

Families in Classical and Hellenistic Greece: Representations and Realities

I believe that a chronological framework is more often appropriate for the study of the Greek family than a synchronic, topical approach. That a chronological approach is appropriate, however, does not mean that it can yield thoroughly satisfactory results. The primary sources for the study of ancient societies are few, and, in general, fewer for social than for political history (see below). The sources themselves vary over time in response to historical forces and changes in taste. Enormous problems face the historian who insists upon a chronological approach. It is indeed tempting to consolidate all the extant information from the entire Greek world, from the archaic through the Hellenistic period, garnered from disparate sources including legal texts, private oratory, epigrams, vase-paintings, and papyri, on a topic such as marriage, and to search for similarities and unchanging themes. Placing the material on a chronological grid emphasizes its pathetic meagreness. When the primary sources are especially sparse, or derive from a limited historical period, as is the case for families that were victorious in athletic competitions (see Ch. 2), it is especially difficult to demonstrate change over time. Furthermore, the standard periodization derived from political history is not always suitable for family history. Changes in social structures often come about slowly, and may or may not coincide with political events. For example in the mid-fifth century, Pericles' citizenship law and urbanization influenced the choice of spouses and emotional bonds among blood relatives.[35] Major upheavals following the Peloponnesian War and post-war migration affected family relationships. These events, however, do not serve to define the chronological limits of the classical period. On the other hand, the death of Alexander the Great and the inauguration of the Hellenistic period (323 BC) did coincide with major changes in family history. Demographic patterns for Hellenistic Greece differ significantly from those for the classical

[35] See the prosopographically based articles of Cheryl Ann Cox, 'Sibling Relationships in Classical Athens: Brother–Sister Ties', *Journal of Family History*, 13 (1988), 377–95, and 'Sisters, Daughters and the Deme of Marriage: A Note', *JHS* (1988), 185–8, where she discusses the ways in which political interests and kinship ties influenced Athenian marriage patterns. Cox also postulates that the urbanization of the last quarter of the fifth century brought women closer to their family of origin, and that matrilineal ties and women's power within the family were thereby increased.

period (see above). For Greeks in Egypt during the Ptolemaic period, infanticide vanished, but bigamy and brother–sister marriage entered the historical record (see Ch. 6). On a smaller scale, a chronological approach to the study of the family is clearly appropriate. Thus in the narratives in Chapter 5, events are presented in their order of occurrence, as, indeed, they were conceptualized by the various participants who give their versions of the stories recorded in the primary sources.

Rather than duplicating Lacey's work,[36] the present book covers a substantially different time period. Lacey wrote about archaic and classical Greece. As the title indicates, this volume concentrates on the classical and Hellenistic periods (*c.*500–30 BC) with some references to the foundation of political, legal, and social institutions in the archaic period. I also exploit a greater variety of primary sources than Lacey, as well as some sources that were not available to him: much of the archaeological evidence that I cite has been excavated or published only in the past twenty years. Furthermore, whereas Lacey used evidence from the visual arts, such as vases and funerary stelae, only as illustrations of what he already knew from written texts, I use material evidence as independent testimony (see Ch. 3). The relationship between family composition and values as they are represented, on the one hand, in cemeteries and, on the other hand, in life is not perfectly clear, but the artefacts of dead families do not confront the historian with the same opacity as the families of myth and tragedy.

The primary sources also vary in quantity according to time and location. The historian must be wary of generalizing about the rest of the Greek world on the basis of the relatively abundant evidence of certain types from classical Athens and Ptolemaic Egypt. Yet, for the most part, social historians who deal with later periods of history will be amazed at the sparsity of documents available to historians who study antiquity. The social historian must use virtually every primary source cautiously, and be constantly alert for class, gender, and other biases. Most of our evidence, including the documents that survive from Egypt, usually deals with a social and economic élite. J. K. Davies's *Athenian Propertied Families*[37] has been a tremendous spur to Greek family history through his reconstructions of wealthy

[36] *Family in Classical Greece.*

[37] Oxford, 1971. This book, subsequently abbreviated *APF*, is usually cited herein by entry number, not page number.

Athenian families. The élite have always dominated the Greek historical records out of proportion to their numbers, but they certainly did not constitute a caste apart from their less fortunate countrymen. A speech-writer like Demosthenes was born into a very wealthy family, and commanded substantial fees; nevertheless, even in his youth, his orations not only had to persuade, but had to resonate with the beliefs of the older men who were usually less wealthy than he was, and who comprised Athenian audiences and juries.

There is far more information about men than women even among the élite, and most of the sources are male-authored, or in the case of material evidence, created or purchased by men. Thus we know more about upper-class free males than about the lower classes or about women and slaves, and almost everything is presented from a male perspective. For example, in classical Athens vases of certain shapes were used specifically by women and given to them as gifts; but the historian must remember that they were created and purchased by men. Although vase-paintings may depict women's activities, they are presented through the medium of the 'male gaze'.

Women's History and Family History

Classics is an interdisciplinary field, and in the past twenty years there has been much work on women in a variety of areas, including literature, medicine, ancient history, art, and archaeology. Despite the wide range of evidence used, questions asked, and methodological approaches adopted, all who study women in classical Athens agree to the axiom that women's sphere was the family, while men's was the city. The most stark expression of this dichotomy is the formula: male is to female as *polis* ('city-state') is to *oikos* ('family, household, estate'), as public is to private. When I turned from women's history to family history, I thought that, although I would be excluding marginal women such as prostitutes, I would still concentrate on women. I assumed that the major difference was that men would be included, as they are in histories of the family in other European societies. In working on the Athenian family, however, I found that it was easy to lose track of women. I also noticed that other scholars thought that they had written about the family and children when they had actually discussed only men and boys.

The problem is the result not merely of the male perspective of past generations of ancient historians. If it had been, it would have been easier to correct. The problem is rather in the primary sources themselves. In the funeral oration which Pericles delivered to the Athenians in 430 he stated that the best women are those who are known neither for praise nor for blame.[38] When I wrote about the history of Athenian women, I dealt with all women, whether notorious or respectable. In writing a history of the Greek family, I have been restricted to respectable women and a couple who attempted to insinuate themselves into the ranks of the respectable. These women are passed from the protection of the father to the husband and then to the son. They are simultaneously hidden from the snooping eye of the historian. The history of Spartan women is also obscure, but for different reasons. Nevertheless, beginning in the fourth century, widows constitute a major exception to the pervasive obscurity of women. Epicteta, Cleobule, Archippe, and Demetria, whose guardians include sons, a son-in-law, and an irresponsible fiancé, have left their mark on the historical record (see Chs. 3, 5, and 6).

The genealogical charts in this book have typically been constructed from sources such as biographical texts, orations written in connection with legal suits in which members of the family were involved, and from the gravestones of some of them that have been excavated. Because daughters did not inherit from fathers, nor wives from husbands, women are less likely than men to be mentioned in private orations dealing with inheritance.[39] Sometimes a woman's male kin are known, though she is not identifiable by name, but only as a daughter, wife, or mother. These women are indicated on the charts by their role. I have added a wife wherever there is a child, even if the woman does not appear in any historical source. For example, in the genealogical chart of Demosthenes' family (Fig. 7) I gave a wife to Demomeles. By doing so, however, I may have inflated the number of women. The Athenian upper class was highly endogamous, with marriages between first cousins and between uncles and nieces quite common. Therefore the same unnamed woman may appear on a chart as both a daughter and a wife, and I will have counted her twice. For example, if we had not been informed that Demosthenes' sister married her cousin Laches, an extra woman might well have been added. As it is, this chart shows a total of

[38] Thuc. 2. 45. 2. It is possible that Pericles allowed that women might be known for praise or blame among other women.

[39] On inheritance see Ch. 1; on possible undercounting of dead women see Ch. 3.

twenty-three persons. There are fourteen men, and all their names are known. There are nine women, only two of whose names are known. An ancient society could scarcely reproduce itself with sex ratios like fourteen men to nine women, but it is difficult to determine how many women have been omitted from the historical sources and how much correction is necessary. It does appear that all the adult women in a family were married at an early age, which would maximize their reproductive potential. Yet even in this wealthy group not all the men had wives.

Feminists in the 1970s criticized the family, viewing it as oppressive to women, and were inspired to write women's history. I have not abandoned my commitment to women's history. Nevertheless, all the sources on the Athenian family that I have examined in the course of writing this book leave no doubt that despite the identification of women with the private sphere, the Greeks considered the family in all its manifestations too important to turn over to women. The history of the Greek family must be largely the history of an institution dominated by men.

I
Defining the Family

The family in classical and Hellenistic Greece had a far greater range of functions and manifestations than it has in the modern Western world. Consequently, the definition of the Greek family is not only broad, but protean, including in some cases people who are not related to one another by blood, marriage, or adoption, or sometimes even people who never shared a household. Because the greatest range of definitions, the most clearly articulated historical development, and the most numerous and varied primary sources appear in Athens, the Athenian family will serve as the paradigm in the first part of the following discussion. The Spartan family will then be described as 'the exception that proves the rule'. Very little is known about the family lives of Greeks of the classical period who lived in city-states other than Athens or Sparta.

This chapter is designed, in particular, to orient the reader who is unfamiliar with the basic ideas of Greek family history. It is a highly selective survey, and not intended to delve into controversial issues or to cover such topics as marriage, kinship, Greek law, or the Spartan constitution in an encyclopaedic manner. Although the focus of the present book is on the classical (*c.*500–323 BC) and Hellenistic (323–30 BC) periods, the first chapter includes family legislation of the archaic period (*c.*800–500 BC).

ATHENS

Public and Private

When used in reference to classical Athens, the words 'public' and 'private' are problematic, and do not correspond exactly to the modern conceptions of these terms. The definitions of these words are further complicated by the fact that in antiquity the state intervened in matters which many modern readers would regard as private. When the Athenian family is defined by its membership, the chief variable is whether the orientation is public or private, and the secondary variable is gender. According to this method of definition, there are three basic versions of the family. The first version, totally public, is artificial. The phratry ('brotherhood') and *genos* ('clan'), which were vital elements in the political structure of the Athenian *polis* and restricted to male citizens, were quasi- or pseudo-kin groups (see Ch. 2). The *polis* is often referred to as a 'men's club', though a more accurate description would be 'a family of men'. Evidently as part of an effort to create a cohesive, loyal group of citizens, the *polis* usurped the terminology of the family in order to appropriate its affective relationships. The metaphorical use of kinship terminology appears also in the Hellenistic period, when a younger person may address an older protector as 'father', though the two are not blood-relations, or when a husband and wife call one another 'sister' or 'brother' in private correspondence, to connote intimacy and permanent ties of affection (see Ch. 6). The failure of scholars to distinguish various manifestations of the pseudo-family has often been responsible for ambiguity and problems in interpreting political and social institutions (see Ch. 2).

The other two versions of the family are composed of women, men, and children who are related by blood, marriage, or adoption. Such families, however, may represent themselves in two ways, in which the chief variable is gender (see Ch. 3). In one type some women are included, but men predominate. This version of the family is oriented towards the public, and can be readily observed, for example, in honorary inscriptions naming male members of the family and their male forebears. Because respectable women in the classical period were generally restricted to the private sphere, their male relatives concealed not only their names, but sometimes their very existence. Thus the membership of such families seems to be largely male.

The third version of the family, more intimate and private, is most like the modern Western type. Only this private version accommodates women and children freely, though they do not predominate as men did in the previously described version. Affective relationships within this final version are often represented in vase-paintings, funerary stelae, and many genres of literature, but not in public oratory or political history.

Thus the traditional dichotomy public/private used to describe Greek life is misleading. A tripartite division is more accurate: public, domestic/public, and domestic/private. In short, an Athenian man was a member of three types of family simultaneously: one consisted of his associates in political activities, another largely of male kinsmen, and the third of all his male and female kin.

Legal and Linguistic

In law, the extended family, including all males and females, is defined by the terms *suggeneia* and *anchisteia*. *Suggeneia* connotes all relatives, but *anchisteia* (literally 'closest') is limited to relatives up to first cousins once removed, or perhaps second cousins.[1] Members of the *anchisteia* bear special responsibilities towards one another, including obligations to bury the dead and to provide dowries for needy female relatives; males on the father's side are also obliged to marry *epikleroi* ('heiresses'—i.e. fatherless, brotherless women), or to find them husbands among themselves. These obligations, obviously, are often gender-specific. Both males and females also enjoy rights of inheritance.[2] Because there was no primogeniture and inheritance was partible among male descendants in equal shares, property was divided and redistributed frequently. In the absence of direct descendants, natural or adopted, the right to succeed passed to a man's relatives in the following order: homopatric ('of the same father') brothers and their descendants, homopatric sisters and their descendants, paternal uncles and their descendants, paternal aunts and their descendants, homometric ('of the same mother') brothers and their descendants, homometric sisters and their descendants, maternal uncles and their descendants, maternal aunts and their descendants, maternal great uncles and their descendants, maternal aunts and their descendants, and lacking any of the aforementioned, to the nearest relative on the father's side. Because of the frequency of endogamy and adoption within the *anchisteia*, one person may fill multiple positions in the family tree (see Ch. 5). In such cases property is not distributed through the wider society, but rather is concentrated within the *anchisteia*. The life span of the *anchisteia* was unlimited, although the life span of the individual was short.

[1] On *anepsios* as 'cousin' see Wesley E. Thompson, 'Some Attic Kinship Terms', *Glotta*, 48 (1970), 75–81.

[2] See further A. R. W. Harrison, *The Law of Athens*, i (Oxford, 1968), 143–9, *et passim*.

The hierarchy of those who may inherit mimics the hierarchy of family relationships, with priority accorded to males within the same degree of relationship and to collaterals on the father's side (i.e. agnates), starting with brothers. Wives did not inherit from husbands, nor daughters from fathers; but sisters could inherit from brothers. Thus, unless a dowry is considered as an ante-mortem inheritance, the position of women in this legal definition of the family is ambiguous, and cannot be clarified simply by referring to the categories of marriage or blood relationship. Though women did not usually inherit, they did have opportunities to acquire property. For example, a husband could leave a legacy to his wife; moreover, as I have just suggested, a dowry could be considered a daughter's ante-mortem inheritance (see Ch. 5). The dowry passed from a woman's father to her husband, then to her sons. Thus, if the marriage is not endogamous, the dowry circulates property beyond the family network, from the maternal grandfather to his daughter's sons. The laws concerning succession, however, are complex, and open to interpretation and manipulation by clever speech-writers. Private lawsuits, which are our principal source for these laws, demonstrate that it might be difficult to establish the facts of kinship, marriage, and legitimate birth. The kinship terminology commonly used in such speeches and elsewhere in literature was limited to members of the *anchisteia*.[3]

The Oikos

A third rubric of definition is concerned with the word *oikos*. The *oikos* includes not only human beings, but property, and therefore, according to its size and to the context, it may be translated as 'family', 'household', or 'estate'.[4] The membership of the third version of the family mentioned above, the most private, all-inclusive

[3] Although there are no Linear B tablets from Athens, it is interesting to observe that in such tablets found elsewhere in the Greek world kinship terms are used only for members of the nuclear family, not for the extended family and communal structure posited by Marxist theory: Billigmeier, 'Studies on the Family', esp. 15.

[4] *Oikos* is synonymous with *oikia* in the following discussion. It is not a legal term. According to Douglas M. MacDowell, 'The *Oikos* in Athenian Law', CQ 39 (1989), 10–21, the meaning of *oikos* changed over time. In legal texts *oikos* at first denoted only house or property, but in the forensic orations of the late fifth and fourth centuries it began to refer to people as well, i.e. 'family'. But MacDowell is not persuasive. See further Pomeroy, *Xenophon Oeconomicus*, 31, 213–14 n. 2, *et passim*.

type, is the same as the free members of the *oikos*. A wife is part of her husband's *oikos*, though she is not a member of his *anchisteia*. The *oikos* refers to people related by blood, marriage, and adoption and to the property held by the family, including slaves and other movables and immovables. Thus an obvious difference between the Greek *oikos* and the modern Western family is that the former includes human and non-human possessions. Slaves are not members of the master's *oikos* in the way that Roman slaves were members of the master's or mistress's *familia*. The names of Greek slaves and freedmen do not connect them to their owners as the names of Roman slaves did. Nor does it seem that Greek slaves were buried with their masters as they were at Rome. Instead, in Greece slaves are considered part of the property of the *oikos*. Furthermore, Greek slaves did not usually have families even in the informal way that some Roman slaves did.[5]

According to Aristotle (*Pol.* 1252b10–12), who refers to Hesiod, the *oikia* consists of 'a house, and a woman (*gyne*), and an ox for the plough'. Aristotle, however, understands *gyne* as 'wife', and in so doing misrepresents Hesiod (*Op.* 405) who defines *gyne* in the following line (i.e. 406): 'a bought woman, not a wife, to follow the plough'.[6] Hesiod thus emphasizes that the productive basis of the *oikos* must be created before marriage and children. The woman who plays the role of wife cannot follow the plough, for then she would be working out of doors, the potential prey of rapists and seducers. The presence of a slave-woman ensures the wife's chastity. Seclusion of women was a solution to the problem of paternity in an open society where foreigners passed through, men were constantly vying to win honour for themselves at the expense of other men's honour, and wives were often mere adolescents. (See Introduction, and cf. below on the lack of seclusion at Sparta.) Among slaves the sexual division of labour is blurred: a female can not only work out of doors, but she can also perform personal services for the respectable wife that allow the latter to keep her distance from men who are strangers. Elsewhere Aristotle (*Pol.* 1323a5–6) states that the basic constituents of the *oikos* are the father, mother, wife, and slave, but that among the

[5] See e.g. Columella, *Rust* 12. 1–2 on the duties of a slave's 'wife', and see further P. R. C. Weaver, *Familia Caesaris* (Cambridge, 1972), and Ch. 5 below.

[6] M. L. West, *Hesiod. Works and Days* (Oxford, 1978), commentary *ad loc.*, discusses the possible interpolation of l. 406, and asks why Hesiod should want to replace the wife by a female slave. The slave, however, should come first.

poor the wife and children also play the role of slaves. The structure of the *oikos* is hierarchical. The male head of the *oikos* plays three roles: husband, father, and slave-master, and he is the authority in all three relationships. Aristotle is not interested in the relationships between other members of the *oikos*—for example, the mother to the child, or the child to the slave. He calls the yoking together of wife and husband within the *oikos* a *koinonia* ('partnership'), but the relationship is not equal in terms of power *(Pol.* 1252b10).

In the *Oeconomicus* (Discourse on the Skill of Estate Management) Xenophon describes the functioning of two upper-class families.[7] The first, that of Critobulus, is problematic: he scarcely talks to his wife, and has not shown her how to manage his *oikos*. Yet he himself has been diverted from family responsibilities by frivolous boyish interests, and has left her in charge of very serious matters. As a consequence, he is always short of funds. Xenophon then describes in great detail another family, in which, by contrast, the husband, Ischomachus, has educated his wife to be a superior administrator. His *oikos* is a financial success. The *Oeconomicus* is didactic, and the picture of Ischomachus and his wife is idealized; but the treatise conveys a great deal of information about Greek views concerning intrafamilial relations and the economic foundations of the *oikos*.

The works of Xenophon and Aristotle leave no doubt that the male head is the active citizen through whom the *oikos* is linked to the *polis*. Foundation myths of Athens variously describe the creation of its male citizens without birth from females.[8] Athenian men believed they were born from the soil ('*autochthonous*'): this notion helped to justify their claim to exclusive ownership of the land of Attica. In antiquity civic rights were often connected with land ownership. A story about Cecrops, the first king of Athens, gives the aetiology of women's exclusion from political life.[9] According to this myth, before

[7] The topics covered include sexual relations between spouses, the arranged marriage, the influence of domestic slavery on sexual behaviour, the material context of everyday life, the design of the house, and gendering of spaces. See further Pomeroy, *Xenophon Oeconomicus*.

[8] See further Nicole Loraux, *The Children of Athena. Athenian Ideas about Citizenship and the Division between the Sexes*, trans. Caroline Levine (Princeton, 1993), 9–22; *et passim*, esp. for Athena and other female figures (originally published as *Les Enfants d'Athéna: Idées athéniennes sur la citoyenneté et la division des sexes* (Paris, 1984)).

[9] August. *De civ. D.* 18. 9, citing Varro. On the ambivalent nature of women's citizenship see Cynthia Patterson, 'Hai Attikai: The Other Athenians', *Helios*, 13/2 (1987), 49–67.

the invention of marriage, women enjoyed the right to vote. In the days of Cecrops, Athena and Poseidon vied to become the principal divinity in Athens. The women voted for Athena, and the men for Poseidon; Athena was selected. Poseidon, in revenge, sent a flood to Athens, and the women were held responsible for this disaster. Because they were thought to have abused their political power, it was taken from them permanently and marriage was imposed as an additional penalty. This social charter myth explains women's exclusion from political activities: under Cecrops women became only citizen's wives instead of active participants in political institutions. Fathers, not mothers, served to link children to the larger society. Thus, in historical times, a father's recognition and acceptance of a new-born baby into his *oikos* was the first step and *sine qua non* for membership in the Athenian *polis* (see Ch. 2).

The Household

The *oikos* is permanent, but its members are not. The family is a dynamic entity that reconfigures itself over time. The residential composition of the household changes over the life cycle of the family. To begin with marriage, the conjugal unit is usually virilocal. Because women generally married at the age of 14 or 15, while men married at around 30, the bridegroom's mother (but less often his father) might still be alive and she might live with the newly married couple until she died.[10] Vase-paintings show the mother of the groom greeting the newly married couple at the door.[11] The older woman may initiate her daughter-in-law into the customs of her new home, and also serve as her chaperone. One husband recalled that at first his bride's conduct was irreproachable, but that after his son was born, his wife's seducer caught sight of her at the funeral for her mother-in-law (Lys. 1. 8). The adulterous couple enjoyed trysts in the house of the cuckolded husband, who eventually murdered the seducer *in flagrante delicto*. Such a situation could scarcely occur if the

[10] For life cycle reconstructions see Gallant, *Risk and Survival* ch. 2, but see Introduction, n. 15 above. Moreover, inexplicably Gallant (p. 23) distinguishes between data derived from a study of private orations and data in Davies, *APF*, when, in fact, both sets of data are derived from the élite, and Davies includes evidence from the orations in his genealogical reconstructions.

[11] John H. Oakley and Rebecca H. Sinos, *The Wedding in Ancient Athens* (Madison, 1993), 26, 29, 31, 33, 34, 36, 38, and figs. 70, 73, 91, and 116.

mother-in-law were still living in the house, which is described as quite small. The composition of this household changed, and the familial roles of its members simultaneously increased, as we have seen, from mother and son (bridegroom); mother (mother-in-law), son (husband), son's wife (daughter-in-law); mother (mother-in-law, grandmother), son (husband, father), son's wife (daughter-in-law, mother), baby; and husband (father), wife (mother), baby. As a result of virilocal marriage, the most permanent elements are the man, who played the role of son, husband, and father, and his domestic slaves. By contrast, the wife's position appears less stable and more contingent upon her relationship with the husband (see Ch. 2).

A sequence of three relief sculptures on a marble base that probably supported a tombstone represents one man's roles in his relationships with various members of his family (see Plate 1[12]). The central scene (*b*) shows a young man, the deceased, bidding farewell to his wife, who is seated. On the left a young girl stands with her arm draped around the woman's chair in a comforting gesture. A young boy stands on the right. The intimacy of the girl's gesture and the relaxed position of her left leg, as well as the boy's attire and brave posture, make it likely that these two represent the couple's daughter and son. The right-hand relief (*c*) portrays the young man on the right with his right arm raised to his head, lamenting his fate. His mother gazes at him. She seems at least as tall as her son: her stature probably alludes to her age. Behind the mother stand his two sisters; the one on the right is weeping copiously. In the left-hand relief (*a*) the young man's father, a standing, bearded figure on the right, reaches to shake his son's hand in a gesture of farewell. Another standing, bearded figure looks on sadly. Because of his central position between father and son and his expression, he probably is a member of the family. The other two men standing on the far left do not seem emotionally concerned about the young man's fate. They are probably colleagues or family friends. We also observe that only male members represent the family in this scene with men who are not relatives. The sculptor has been careful to place the men who are not family members as far away as possible from the women in the family: they are at the far left, where they are not able to see the women, who are around the corner. Moreover these two men are not

[12] Clairmont, *Classical Attic Tombstones*, 1. 10(v). Athens, Tsami, Ephoria Acropoleos, fourth century: photos courtesy of the Deutsches Archäologische Institut. The two small figures in front may represent slaves, but Clairmont's suggestion that they are family members seems more likely.

even looking towards the women, but rather at each other, and all the female figures face right, looking away from the two strangers. The two men are additionally separated from the women by the solid group of male family members. The series depicts an individual man and his relationships to three generations of his family. The principal figure's life cycle is expressed, for though he is beardless in all three representations, he appears older in the central relief. Thus, first he was a son to both his father and mother, and a brother to his sisters. Next, he became a husband and a father, first of a daughter, then of a son; then he died.

Demographic factors are the principal determinants of household size, composition, and dynamics, and these factors may be modified by customs, laws, and ecological influences that vary geographically[13] and over time—for example, those that dictate the treatment of elderly kinsfolk, the practice of infanticide, or the age of marriage for women. The life expectancy and mortality rates meant that, under normal circumstances, a maximum of three generations would live together in the same house,[14] as happened briefly in the households just described, when they contained paternal grandparents, a married couple, children, and a few slaves. The *oikos* is perpetuated through marriage and the production of legitimate children, preferably sons.[15] A lack of sons presents problems, for without legal remedies a lineage could become extinct. With one exception, all the lawsuits for which Isaeus wrote speeches which are extant concern estates without a natural son.[16] When there is no son, a daughter (i.e. *epikleros*, see above) can prevent the extinction of the *oikos* by producing a son, who is then considered his grandfather's heir. Adoption of an heir is an alternative strategy. The kinsman who married the *epikleros*, or the adopted heir, probably would become a member of his wife's deceased father's or his adoptive father's household. Moreover, the age difference between spouses at first marriage (approximately 14 or

[13] Vincent Rosivach, 'The Distribution of Population in Attica', *GRBS* 34 (1993), 391–407, esp. 406, points out that in the fourth century inhabitants of Attic rural demes had higher fecundity and lower mortality rates than those in urban demes.

[14] See further pp. 121–3, below. Gallant, *Risk and Survival*, 21, in an examination of the private orations, found that 74.3 per cent of parents resided with a married son.

[15] Using evidence from Davies, *APF*, Gallant, *Risk and Survival*, 23, found that 62.5 per cent of households had 0–2 children; 32.2 per cent 3–4; and 5.3 per cent more than 4.

[16] The exception is Isae. 7. As usual, the sample is limited: there are twelve substantially complete speeches.

(*a*)

(*b*)

(*c*)
PLATE 1*a–c*. Biographical tombstone base, illustrating three aspects of the dead man's family relationships

15 for women, 30 for men), the average age of death for men (45),[17] and the aversion to leaving fertile women without a husband made it likely that children would be orphaned (i.e. 'fatherless') early in life, and that a young widow would remarry, perhaps leaving her children in their father's house and becoming a mother again and/or a stepmother elsewhere (see Ch. 5). An alternative scenario would include the death of a young mother in childbirth, followed by the remarriage of the father and the introduction of a stepmother into the household. Orphaned children might move into a relative's house. Thus Alcibiades was raised by his kinsman Pericles (Plut. *Alc.* 1, Plato, *Alc.* 1. 104B; *Prt.* 320A). The ease with which divorce could be obtained also contributed to changes in household occupancy.

Marriage, of course, affected household composition. Because, as we have mentioned, marriage was usually virilocal and often patrivirilocal, the bride's natal household lost one member, and the

[17] See n. 10 above.

groom's gained one. Sometimes adult sons left the father's house upon marriage, or as soon as they had the economic means to do so. Thus the five sons of Bouselus each established an *oikos*.[18] In another pattern, married sons continued to live together with their wives in their father's house. This was the case in Pericles' family (Plut. *Per.* 16. 4). Both patterns seem to have been popular. That Pericles' family lived together suggests that the choice did not depend only upon having the means to afford separate accommodations.

Political events also affected household composition. During the Peloponnesian War (431–404), Athenians sought refuge with relatives who lived in safe locations. For example, a large number of kinswomen moved in with a certain Aristarchus, and a certain Chrysilla with her two sons seem to have moved in with her married daughter and son-in-law.[19]

Architecture and the allocation of household space by gender, age, and status both defined and affected family relationships. Primary sources for private dwellings at Athens are both archaeological and literary.[20] In the *Oeconomicus* Xenophon gives a full description of the domestic arrangements of a wealthy Athenian couple in the context of a conversation between husband and wife that was reported to Socrates:

I said to my wife: '. . . We have large storerooms in the house so that we can keep things separately in them, and the house rests on a firm foundation. Wouldn't it be sheer stupidity on our part if we don't find some good place where each thing can be easily found? I have already told you that it is good for equipment to be arranged in order and that it is easy to find a place in the house that is suitable for each piece of it. How beautiful it looks, when shoes are arranged in rows, each kind in its own proper place, how beautiful to see all kinds of clothing properly sorted out, each kind in its own proper place: how beautiful bed linens, bronze pots, table-ware. . . .

'I thought it was best to show her the possibilities of our house first. It is not elaborately decorated, Socrates, but the rooms are constructed in such a way that they will serve as the most convenient places to contain the things that will be kept in them. So the rooms themselves invited what was suitable for each of them. Thus the bedroom (*thalamos*), because it was in the safest

[18] Dem. 47. 34–6, 53, and see Ch. 5.

[19] Xen. *Mem.* 2. 7. 2–12, Andoc. 1. 124–7, and see further Pomeroy, *Xenophon Oeconomicus*, 261–2. In the case of Chrysilla the daughter failed to serve as her mother's chaperone.

[20] For domestic architecture see further Pomeroy, *Xenophon Oeconomicus*, esp. 285–301.

possible place, invited the most valuable bedding and furniture. The dry store rooms called for grain, the cool ones for wine, and the bright ones for those products and utensils which need light. I continued by showing her living rooms for the occupants, decorated so as to be cool in summer and warm in winter. I pointed out to her that the entire house has its façade facing south, so that it was obviously sunny in winter and shady in summer. I also showed her the women's quarters (*gynaikonitis*), separated from the men's quarters by a bolted door, so that nothing might be removed from them that should not be, and so that the slaves would not breed without our permission. For, generally, honest slaves become more loyal when they have produced children, but when bad ones mate, they become more troublesome. After we had gone through these rooms', he said, 'we sorted the contents by type. We began', he said, 'first by putting together the things that we use for sacrifices. After that we separated the fancy clothing that women wear at festivals, the men's clothing for festivals and for war, bedding for the women's quarters, bedding for the men's quarters, women's shoes, and men's shoes. Another type consisted of weapons, another of spinning implements, another of bread-making implements, another of implements used for other food, another of bathing implements, another of kneading implements, another of dining implements. And we divided all this equipment into two sets, those that are used daily and those used only for feasts. We set aside the things that are consumed within a month, and stored separately what we calculated would last a year. That way we will be less likely to make a mistake about how it will turn out at the end of the year. When we divided all the contents by types, we carried each thing to its proper place. After this, we showed the slaves where they should keep the utensils they use every day—for example, those needed for baking, cooking, spinning, and so forth, and we handed these over to them and told them to keep them safe. Whatever we use for festivals or entertaining guests or at rare intervals we handed over to the housekeeper; and when we had shown her where they belong, and had counted and made an inventory of each thing, we told her to give every member of the household what they required, but to remember what she had given to each of them and when she got them back, to return them to the place from which she had taken each of them.'[21]

As in other aspects of Athenian life, the fundamental division of private space was between male and female. Even in a small house such as the one referred to by the speaker who murdered his wife's seducer (Lys. 1, see above) with only two rooms, one upstairs and one on the ground floor, the upper room was normally the women's

[21] 8. 17–19. 10, trans. Pomeroy, *Xenophon Oeconomicus*, 153–7.

quarters ('*gynaikonitis*'), and the lower room the men's. The women in the household, both free and slave, slept in the women's quarters. They also produced textiles there, though in warm weather they might move their looms into the courtyard and work outdoors, protected by the surrounding walls.

The *andron*, as the name indicates, was a room for men. Here the men in the family dined and entertained male guests at symposia ('drinking parties'). The visitor to the Greek house would meet only male members of the family; when strangers were in the house, female members would withdraw to the secluded parts of the house, and not even be mentioned by name. The *andron* was the most elaborately decorated and expensively furnished of all the rooms in the house. Men dined reclining on couches. No respectable woman would be found in such a position. Thus, one wonders if that icon of modern bourgeois life, the family dinner, had an analogue in classical Athens, and, if so, where in the house, and how frequently, it took place. The sources are remarkably reticent on this point; perhaps such an event was too banal to report, or perhaps it rarely occurred. Vase-paintings do not depict Greek couples eating together, though contemporaneous Etruscan paintings do.[22] On the one hand, Herodotus (1. 146. 2–3, 4. 186) reports that at Miletus the wives of Athenian settlers refused to eat with their husbands, and that at Cyrene the wives would not eat cow's meat, suggesting that the norm was for a married couple to eat together.[23] The context indicates that these wives' behaviour was unusual. On the other hand, in the *Oeconomicus* (11. 12–13, 17; cf. 4. 24) Xenophon describes the eating pattern of a healthy, wealthy Athenian gentleman who comes home for lunch, and depicts a married couple who communicate well with one another; but he does not indicate that they dine together, although he describes their daily routines.

The house was often the site not only of the domestic production of food and clothing for use at home (though potentially for sale in financial exigencies), but also of commercial production strictly for the cash economy. Sections of the house that faced the street could be

[22] Theopomp. 115 = *FGrH* F 204 = Ath. 12. 517d reports that not only do Etruscan women dine with men, but they share couches with men other than their husband.

[23] The title of Menander's *Synaristosai* (fr. 385, 'Women Eating Together') alludes to single-sex dining; whether this play depicted a normal or unusual occasion cannot be determined.

used for shops, factories, and other business establishments (see Plate 2[24]). Thus, as was probably true in the days of Demosthenes' father, slaves manufactured swords and furniture in workrooms adjacent to the domestic quarters, and funds used for banking and other commercial transactions would be permanently deposited in the house (Dem. 49. 22, 52. 8, 14, Aeschin. 1. 124, and see Ch. 5).

The existence of the *andron* and shops draws attention to the fact that the *oikos* was not totally private space reserved for members of the family. In the parts of the house open to men who were not kin, the family would be represented as totally male. The *gynaikonitis* appears at the other end of the spectrum. In terms of occupants, however, the *gynaikonitis* was not the exact opposite of the *andron*, for the husband and young boys in the family could enter it.[25] The other parts of the house were available to both men and women, but since women spent most of their time in the women's quarters, the occupants of these must have been principally, though not exclusively, male. Thus it would appear that the members of the family were conscious of the male and female distribution in the public and private manifestations of the family and constantly reaffirmed this trichotomy in their use of space in their daily lives at home.

A substantial area of household space was devoted to storage. If the house was also the site of manufacture, raw materials such as ivory, wood, metals, leather, or other items would need to be stored. The prudent household manager would be certain to store provisions

[24] After Wolfram Hoepfner, and Ernst-Ludwig Schwandner, *Haus und Stadt im Klassischen Griechenland*, Wohnen in der klassischen Polis, 1 (Munich, 1986), 171.

[25] For women's quarters at Athens see e.g. Xen. *Oec.* 9. 5; Ar. *Thesm.* 414–17, *Eccl.* 693, 961; Lys. 1. 9, 3. 6; and Eur. *Phoen.* 89–100. In Dem. 47. 56 female slaves live in a tower. Scholarly opinion is not unanimous on the subject of the *gynaikonitis* at Athens. Gareth Morgan, 'Euphiletos' House: Lysias I', *TAPhA* 112 (1982), 115–23, suggests that women spent most of their time upstairs in the women's quarters. Susan Walker, 'Women and Housing in Classical Greece: The Archaeological Evidence', in Averil Cameron and Amélie Kuhrt (eds.), *Images of Women in Antiquity* (London and Canberra, 1983), 81–91, assumes that women's quarters in Athens existed, and that these were isolated from areas frequented by men. In direct contrast to Walker, Michael Jameson, 'Private Space and the Greek City', in Oswyn Murray and Simon Price (eds.), *The Greek City: From Homer to Alexander* (Oxford, 1990), 172, 186–92, maintains that Greek domestic architecture does not reveal a distinction between genders, but that the use of space by men and women was flexible, though prescribed by custom. In agreement with Jameson is Lisa Nevett, 'Separation or Seclusion? Towards an Archaeological Approach to Investigating Women in the Greek Household in the Fifth to Third Centuries BC', in Michael Parker Pearson and Colin Richards (eds.), *Architecture and Order. Approaches to Social Space* (London and New York, 1994), 98–112. See further Pomeroy, *Xenophon Oeconomicus*, 295.

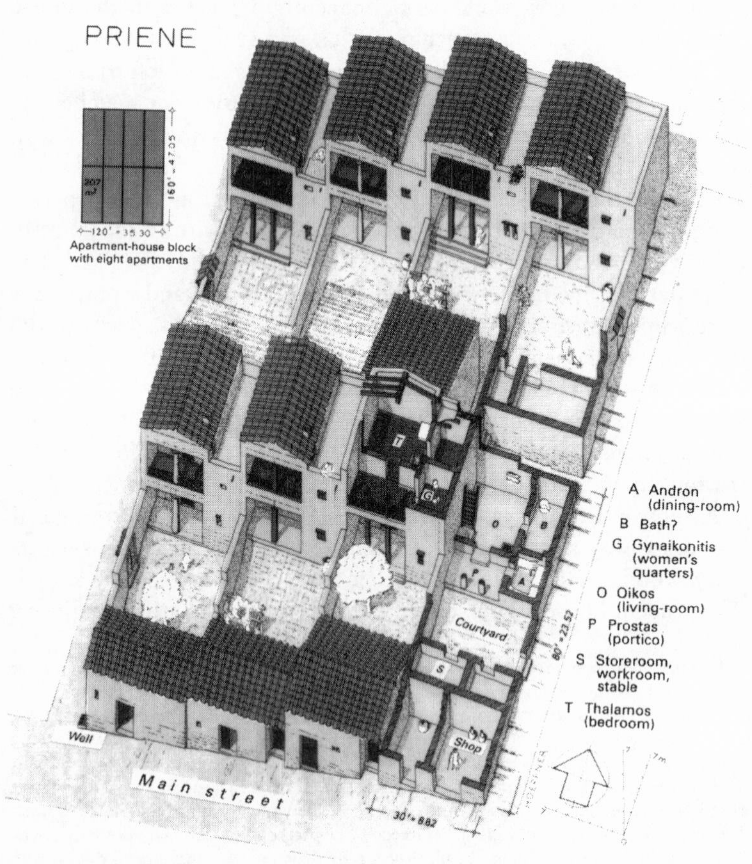

PLATE 2. Reconstruction of houses at Priene, showing women's quarters and thalamos upstairs

sufficient to feed all the human beings and domestic animals for at least a year, and preferably for several years in case of emergencies such as drought or siege. Supplies might be depleted by theft or by natural causes, including mildew, rodents, and flood. These supplies often constituted a family's principal wealth, and in fact ensured the family's survival. Consequently, the two most important aspects of a wife's job were producing children, and guarding the household (Ps.-Demos. 59. 122; cf. Xen. *Oec.* 7. 25).

Family Formation

Marriage was the foundation of the *oikos*.[26] The express purpose of marriage was reproduction. A passage in New Comedy sets forth the brief formula that was used:

FATHER. I give you my daughter to sow for the purpose of producing legitimate children.
GROOM. I take her.
FATHER. I also give you a dowry of three talents.
GROOM. I take it, too, gladly.[27]

The manner of selecting a spouse changed over time from the archaic to the classical period. This change appears most vividly among the upper class, who had more choices. The archaic period is marked by the exogamy of aristocrats and of tyrants who used international marriages to secure political alliances. For example, around 575 the Athenian aristocrat Megacles wooed Agariste, daughter of Cleisthenes, tyrant of Sicyon;[28] and the mothers of Themistocles and Cimon were not Athenians.[29] Around 514 Miltiades IV married a daughter of Olorus, the king of Thrace.[30] With the end of tyranny and the increase in democratic reforms in the fifth century, men of the upper class eschewed foreign brides in favour of Athenian women from powerful families. For example, around 480 Cimon, son of Miltiades IV, married Isodice, a descendant of Megacles, and his sister Elpinice married the wealthy Callias.[31] Thus Pericles' citizenship law (see

[26] See further Cynthia Patterson, 'Marriage and the Married Woman in Athenian Law', in Sarah B. Pomeroy (ed.), *Women's History and Ancient History* (Chapel Hill, NC, 1991), 48–72.

[27] Men. *Pk.* 1012–15, similarly *Sam.* 897–900, *Dysc.* 842–5.

[28] Hdt. 6. 130.

[29] Davies, *APF* 6669 and 8429X.

[30] Ibid. 8429X.

[31] Ibid. 7826V–VI and 8429XI, and n. 39 below.

below) was anticipated by actual practice. In the first half of the fifth century, endogamy among kinsmen can be traced in the Athenian upper class.[32] For example, Pericles' first wife was a relative.[33] In the classical period wealthy families also engaged in economic endogamy, sometimes as a means of affording liturgies (Dem. 40. 25, and see Ch. 5). Of course, heiresses always married very close relatives. There is little information about marriage in the lower classes, but doubtless their choices were limited by their experiences. Accordingly, Hesiod (*Op.* 700) advises the would-be bridegroom to choose a bride from the neighbourhood, so that he knows what he is getting. This too, along with familial endogamy, must have been a fairly common norm.[34]

Athens had no systematic corpus of civil law, but there were some rules about marriage which never changed. Marriage was monogamous,[35] and there were incest taboos. Marriage between parents and children, full siblings, and between uterine half-siblings was unlawful.[36] Adoption, however, provided for a pragmatic exception. The father of an *epikleros* might adopt his daughter's husband, transforming him, in effect, into her brother. The Greeks, who were an agricultural people and familiar with animals, may have observed some ill effects from inbreeding. Xenophon (*Mem.* 4. 4. 20–3) argues that children born of incest are badly begotten, because one parent is past his or her prime and the other has not yet reached it. Moreover, anthropologists have suggested several reasons for incest taboos before modern knowledge of genetics led to concern about the biological consequences of incest. According to a structuralist interpretation, taboos derive from the ubiquity of family organizations in human society and from the fact that some of the social relationships which such organizations imply are incompatible with the presence of sexual relations.[37] The relationship which is appropriate between

[32] See further Wesley E. Thompson, 'The Marriage of First Cousins in Athenian Society', *Phoenix*, 21 (1967), 273–82, and Cheryl Ann Cox, 'Incest, Inheritance and the Political Forum in Fifth-Century Athens', *CJ* 85 (1989), 34–46.

[33] Davies, *APF* 118III.

[34] On the deme, or location, as a factor in the choice of a wife, see Robin Osborne, *Demos: The Discovery of Classical Attika* (Cambridge, 1985), 127–38.

[35] But see p. 39 below.

[36] Dem. 57. 20, Plut. *Them.* 32. 2. The rule was just the reverse in Sparta, where marriage between homopatric half-siblings was outlawed (Philo, *De spec. leg.* 3. 22). No one has yet supplied an adequate explanation for this difference.

[37] Claude Lévi-Strauss, *The Elementary Structures of Kinship* (London, 1969), 12–25, *et passim*, trans. J. H. Bell and J. R. von Sturmer from *Les Structures élémentaires de la parenté*, 2nd edn. (Paris, 1967).

parents and children is totally different from, and incompatible with, the relationship between spouses. Thus there is no known society in which the father–daughter relationship could be assimilated to the husband–wife one. They serve entirely different social ends, and in every society they are regarded completely differently. Incest erodes the most basic definitions: for example, the distinction between parent and child. Thus Tiresias told Oedipus that the truth would put him on the same level as his children (Soph. *OT* 457–60). Most societies also find that the relationship between siblings, half-siblings, or step-siblings should not be assimilated to the husband–wife relationship. The Greeks, however, were not strict about considering sibling marriage as taboo.[38] Plutarch's discussion of Roman exogamy raises issues about endogamy that are relevant to a discussion of marriage patterns in the Greek family (*Quaest. Rom.* 108 = *Mor.* 289d–e):

Q. Why do they [i.e. Romans] not marry women who are their close relatives?

A. Do they wish to increase by marriage the size of their families and acquire additional relatives by giving wives to and taking them from other families? Or do they fear the quarrels which take place in marriages between close relatives, in case these should destroy even natural rights? Or because they saw that the weakness of women causes them to need many protectors, they did not wish to let near kinsfolk marry, in order that if the husbands wrong their wives, their relatives may help them?

The Roman upper class in the late Republic exploited fully the political value of exogamous family alliances. Similarly, the marriages of aristocrats in fifth-century Athens—for example, the unions of Cimon, Isodice, Elpinice, and Callias—linked the most powerful families of the time, the Alcmaeonids, Philaids, and Ceryxes.[39] At the same time, two counter forces to such dynastic marriages operated to keep marital arrangements separate from politics: the anti-aristocratic emphasis that increasingly developed in classical Athens and the familial endogamy of the powerful. The exchange of women, whether with another lineage or with relatives within a lineage,

[38] But see Ch. 6.

[39] See n. 31 above. For an attempt to view Periclean politics in terms of familial alliances see R. Sealey, 'The Entry of Pericles into History', *Hermes*, 84 (1956), 234–47; repr. in *Essays in Greek Politics* (New York, 1967), 59–74, esp. 64–5.

creates or reinforces reciprocal relationships between men. These links between families weave a complex social web. Therefore, a father obtains more profit from a daughter by exchanging her for a daughter-in-law. Through marriage, a man and his family gain the wife's entire family as allies, and the family is still able to exploit the productive and reproductive capacity of a woman. Wives produce legitimate children, and serve as faithful guardians of the household, but daughters can perform only the latter job. In the Hellenistic period, the taboo preventing marriage between parents and children was retained, but the Ptolemies practised brother–sister marriage with some frequency and bigamy occasionally (see Ch. 6). In Roman Egypt some commoners began to follow the example of their former rulers who had assimilated the sibling relationship to the marital one.

The actual process of marrying consisted of three essential steps. First was the betrothal, or pledging, of the bride (*engue*) and the transfer of the dowry. This transaction took place preferably in front of other men, who served as witnesses. The bride's father or guardian and the bridegroom or his father made the contract. The bride was not present, nor, as we see in quotations of the betrothal formula from Menander, was she named.[40] Second was the wedding celebration (*gamos*), consisting of sacrifices and a procession from the house of the bride's parents to the groom's house. This public event created many witnesses who could testify to the fact that a marriage had actually taken place. Vase-paintings depicting brides in a wedding procession show the bride's head and hair covered by a veil which shadows her face. If she is riding in a chariot, she is at some distance from public view, or if she is walking, her face is modestly downcast. The procession took place at night by torchlight. Therefore it is likely that the casual spectator would know that the daughter of some man whose name was announced was marrying a man whose name was also announced, but not the bride's name or appearance. Third was sexual union and cohabitation (*sunoikein*, literally 'living together').

Family and Polis

According to Aristotle (*Eth. Nic.* 1162a17–19), who uses the word *oikia*, the family is earlier and more fundamental than the *polis*. A

[40] See n. 27 above, and further Oakley and Sinos, *Wedding in Ancient Athens*, *passim*.

foundation of strong *oikoi* was essential to a strong *polis*. In Athens, however, before the reforms of Solon in the first quarter of the sixth century BC, the free poor did not have a stable, permanent *oikos* of their own.[41] A poor man had scarcely any economic basis on which to construct and preserve a permanent *oikos*. A man who was in debt could be forced to sell members of his family, including himself, into slavery; the consequence was the dissolution of his *oikos*. Solon was chosen to serve as sole archon in 594/3, with a mandate to solve the economic and political problems that plagued Athens in the archaic period. The history of his legislation is far from clear. His reforms may actually have been promulgated twenty years after he held office. Moreover, some legislation was falsely attributed to Solon in order to endow it with an aura of eternity and inviolability (see below). Solon's laws were posted in the *agora* at the end of the fifth century, and were often referred to by speakers in private lawsuits. They were held in such high regard that they were not to be changed, although the sovereign demos freely altered non-Solonian laws. Solon brought hitherto private matters into a public forum. Among his many achievements, Solon gave permanence and strength to the Athenian *oikoi*, and increased their number. He brought back Athenians who had been sold into slavery abroad, and invited foreigners to settle permanently as metics ('resident aliens') in Athens. Metic *oikoi* seem to have functioned according to principles similar to those governing citizen *oikoi*.[42] Solon divided the Athenians into four property classes, based on annual agricultural productivity: *pentakosiomedimni* (500 bushels), *hippeis* (horse owners), *zeugitai* (owners of an ox team), and *thetes* (hired labourers). His legislation prevented individual *oikoi* from becoming extinct, and protected their independence. For example, orphans and pregnant widows were placed under the protection of the magistrate titled *archon basileus* ('king archon'). Rules were spelled out concerning the guardianship and marriage of an *epikleros*, a fatherless, brotherless woman whose son would perpetuate the *oikos* of his maternal grandfather (Dem. 46. 19). Kinsmen of an impoverished heiress (*epikleros thessa*) were required to marry her, following the order of the *anchisteia*, or to provide a dowry and

[41] On Solon see further Ch. 3 n. 2; on his dates Ch. 6 n. 23.

[42] Like much else with respect to legislation attributed to Solon (see Ch. 3 n. 5 below), whether metic status was actually part of his reforms is disputed. On metics see Harrison, *Law of Athens*, i. 148, 151, and in general David Whitehead, *The Ideology of the Athenian Metic* (Cambridge, 1977).

give her in marriage (Dem. 43. 54). The integrity of a patrilineage was protected by legislation concerned with women's virginity, rape, and adultery. The permanence of the *oikos* was also assured by regulations intended to preserve an economic foundation. Until well into the classical period, land was considered inalienable, whether by custom or by law.[43] A son automatically inherited his father's farm. A father was required to teach his sons a means of making a livelihood, and sons, in turn, were required to maintain their elderly parents (see Ch. 4). A son could not be disinherited except for a cause such as mistreating his parents. Wills were to be employed only in order to adopt an heir or to arrange for marriages of women, not to bestow legacies outside the family. A jury would tend to overturn such a will in favour of the next of kin.[44]

Although Cleisthenes' legislation was not concerned primarily with private matters, his democratic reforms (508/7) also had repercussions for the Athenian family. The pseudo kin groups can be traced back to Cleisthenes' legislation (see above and Ch. 2). The phratry served as one of the chief mechanisms by which citizens produced by the *oikoi* were validated as members of the *polis*. Cleisthenes also divided the citizens into demes. According to Aristotle (*Ath. Pol.* 21. 4), thenceforth men were to be identified by demotic rather than by patronymic. This regulation is probably a fourth-century invention to account for the increased use of the demotic in that century rather than a law which fell out of use. At any rate, it was not regularly observed. In the classical period a man was identified by both his patronymic and his deme, but sometimes only one was used.[45]

[43] On the market in land in the late fifth and early fourth centuries, see Pomeroy, *Xenophon Oeconomicus*, 54, 339–40. How common sale of land was before this period, and whether there was a law against such sale, or whether custom discouraged it, is controversial; for an overview see David Asheri, 'Laws of Inheritance, Distribution of Land and Political Constitutions in Ancient Greece', *Historia*, 12 (1963), 1–21, esp. 2–4, and *idem*, 'Supplementi coloniari e condizione giuridica della terra nel mondo greco', *RSA* 1 (1971), 77–91.

[44] Arist. *Pr.* 29. 3; Isae. 9, 11; Ps.-Dem. 43, and see further Harrison, *Law of Athens*, i. 149–50, 152.

[45] See Ch. 3 n. 89. Although it has been argued that a member of the upper class with aristocratic sympathies was often identified by his patronymic, while a common citizen with democratic tendencies would usually be known by his demotic, this hypothesis has not yet been corroborated by statistical evidence. See further P. J. Rhodes, *A Commentary on the Aristotelian Athenaion Politeia* (Oxford, 1981), 254, and David Whitehead, *The Demes of Attica 508/7–ca. 250* BC (Princeton, 1986), 69–72. T. F. Winters, 'Kleisthenes and Athenian Nomenclature', *JHS* 113 (1993), 162–5, has shown

The final major, and long-lasting, piece of legislation affecting the Athenian family was the citizenship law of Pericles (451/50). According to this law, descent from a father and mother who were both citizens was a prerequisite for citizenship (Arist. *Ath. Pol.* 26. 4; cf. *Pol.* 1275b21–2, etc.). Except during the last years of the Peloponnesian War, this rule was enforced, affecting the membership of the Athenian *oikos* and consequently that of the *polis*. According to Aristotle (*Ath. Pol.* 26. 4), the reason for the law was the large number of citizens. A direct result was a curb in population growth, because the supply of citizen brides was finite.[46] Pericles himself witnessed the demographic consequences of his legislation. In the funeral oration he delivered over the soldiers who had fallen in the first year of the Peloponnesian War, he exhorted women of child-bearing years to produce more children (Thuc. 2. 44. 3). We also hear that in the second half of this lengthy war, after the population in general had been depleted by the plague and the number of marriageable men had also been reduced by the ongoing war and the defeat in Sicily, the Athenians passed a law permitting a man to take an additional woman in order to produce children. It seems likely that these women were widows who were still fertile; at least, this is true in the case of Socrates and Myrto that is cited.[47]

SPARTA

Almost all the major primary sources on the Spartan family are the work of authors who were not Spartans. Moreover, most of these authors lived much later than the times they discuss. There are few inscriptions concerning family matters in pre-Hellenistic Sparta, for, in addition to the kings, only men who died in battle or women who

that the use of the demotic increased just after Cleisthenes' legislation, but because it does not appear consistently thereafter on dedications and ostraca, its use must have been voluntary; and Stefan Brenne, 'Cleisthenes' Name System and Names on Ostraka', in *Abstracts of the 95th Annual Meeting of the Archaeological Institute of America* (Washington, DC, 1993), 3, found that on *c.*10,000 ostraca from the Cerameicus, identification by patronymic rather than by demotic predominates.

[46] It does not appear likely that before Pericles' law foreign men could, or did, gain Athenian citizenship by marrying Athenian brides: see Pomeroy, *Goddesses, Whores, Wives, and Slaves* (New York, 1975), 66–70; Cynthia Patterson, *Pericles' Citizenship Law of 451–50* BC (Salem, NH, 1981), 125 n. 73; and Rhodes, *Commentary*, 332.

[47] Diog. Laert. 2. 26; Plut. *Aristides*, 27. 2, and Ch. 6 n. 36 below.

died in childbirth were permitted to have inscribed epitaphs.[48] Archaeological evidence for private life is almost nil. Most important, in Sparta there were no counterparts to the private orations and visual arts that supply so much information about the Athenian family. Our knowledge of the Spartan family depends chiefly on a few crucial texts. So that the reader may become aware of contradictions and other problems in these texts, excerpts are printed below. For clues about Spartan law, including regulations on marriage, reproduction, inheritance, and heiresses, some scholars have turned to the law code of Gortyn in Crete, which was, like Sparta, a Dorian city.[49] The extant version of the code was published *c.*450 BC, but it incorporates earlier legislation. There is no proof, however, that the laws of Sparta and Gortyn were similar.

Although the chronological parameters of this volume are classical and Hellenistic, the following discussion of the Spartan family will include the archaic period, inasmuch as most of our information about the earlier period, as well as the inspiration for writing about it, comes from the classical and Hellenistic periods, when much of Spartan 'history' was invented and exploited as propaganda for social reform (see below). It is also essential to alert the reader to the fact that often the primary sources do not distinguish between prescriptive and descriptive writing. Scholars, as well, differ in their assessment of what constitutes historical reality, on the one hand, and what was part of the 'Spartan mirage' on the other.[50]

Xenophon is the only authority who wrote extensively about the Spartan family from the perspective of a direct eyewitness.[51] In 399 BC, after their return to Greece, Xenophon and other remnants of the Ten Thousand who had taken up service with Cyrus the Younger, joined the Spartans in an attempt to free the Ionian cities from Persia (Xen. *Hell.* 3. 1. 11–28). In 396 Xenophon met the Spartan king

[48] Plut. *Lyc.* 27. 3, *Mor.* 238C; Paus. 3. 12. 8, 3. 14. 1, 3. 16. 6, 6. 1. 9. The reference to childbirth depends upon Latte's emendation of Plut. *Lyc.* 27. 3.

[49] For this approach see most recently Claudine Leduc, 'Marriage in Ancient Greece', in Pauline Schmitt Pantel (ed.), *A History of Women in the West*, vol. 1 (Cambridge, Mass., 1992), 235–94, and in general see Douglas M. Macdowell, *Spartan Law* (Edinburgh, 1986).

[50] Below, and see further F. Ollier, *Le Mirage Spartiate* (2 vols., Paris, 1933, 1943).

[51] That Xenophon was the author of the *Spartan Constitution* is no longer doubted. See most recently Macdowell, *Spartan Law*, 8–14, and P. A. Cartledge, *Agesilaos and the Crisis of Sparta* (London, 1987), 56–7.

Agesilaus, and returned to Greece with him in 395. Agesilaus was victorious against Athens and her allies at Coronea in Boeotia.

Probably soon after the battle of Coronea, Xenophon was sentenced to exile by the Athenians for having supported the Spartans. Because of Xenophon's friendship with Agesilaus and other Spartans, he was granted an estate at Scillus in Triphylia, south of Olympia (Xen. *An.* 5. 3; Diog. Laert. 2. 52; Paus. 5. 6. 5). His two sons were educated according to the Spartan system.[52] After the Spartans were defeated at Leuctra in 371 BC and Scillus was attacked by the Eleans, Xenophon moved to Corinth. Although the Spartans were notoriously hostile to strangers, Xenophon had lived in Sparta for more than twenty years, and had associated with Spartans even longer. His *Spartan Constitution* (*Lac. Pol.*) is thus our most valuable testimony on the Spartan family.

Xenophon states that he does not know whether the laws of Lycurgus were still unchanged in his day, because they were often disobeyed (*Lac. Pol.* 14. 1). Nevertheless, he describes them:

> For it was not by imitating other states, but by devising a system utterly different from that of most others, that he [i.e. Lycurgus] made his country pre-eminently prosperous.
>
> First, to begin at the beginning, I will take the begetting of children. In other states the girls who are destined to become mothers and are brought up in the approved fashion, live on the very plainest fare, with a most meagre allowance of delicacies. Wine is either withheld altogether, or, if allowed them, is diluted with water. The rest of the Greeks expect their girls to imitate the sedentary life that is typical of handicraftsmen—to keep quiet and do wool-work. How, then, is it to be expected that women so brought up will bear fine children?
>
> But Lycurgus thought the labour of slave women sufficient to supply clothing. He believed motherhood to be the most important function of freeborn women. Therefore, in the first place, he insisted on physical training for the female no less than for the male sex: moreover, he instituted races and trials of strength for women competitors as for men, believing that if both parents are strong they produce more vigorous offspring.
>
> He noticed, too, that, during the time immediately succeeding marriage, it was usual elsewhere for the husband to have unlimited intercourse with his wife. The rule that he adopted was the opposite of this: for he laid it down that the husband should be ashamed to be seen entering his wife's room or leaving it. With this restriction on intercourse the desire of the one for the

[52] Diog. Laert. 54; Plut. *Ages.* 20. 2; and on education see below.

other must necessarily be increased, and their offspring was bound to be more vigourous than if they were surfeited with one another. In addition to this, he withdrew from men the right to take a wife whenever they chose, and insisted on their marrying in the prime of their manhood, believing that this too promoted the production of fine children. It might happen, however, that an old man had a young wife; and he observed that old men keep a very jealous watch over their young wives. To meet these cases he instituted an entirely different system by requiring the elderly husband to introduce into his house some man whose physical and moral qualities he admired, in order to beget children. On the other hand, in case a man did not want to cohabit with his wife and nevertheless desired children of whom he could be proud, he made it lawful for him to choose a woman who was the mother of a fine family and of high birth, and if he obtained her husband's consent, to make her the mother of his children. He gave his sanction to many similar arrangements. For the wives want to take charge of two households (*oikoi*), and the husbands want to get brothers for their sons, brothers who are members of the family and share in its influence, but claim no part of the money.

Thus his regulations with regard to the begetting of children were in sharp contrast with those of other states.[53]

In other states each man exercises control over his own children and slaves and property. Lycurgus wanted to find a way that the citizens would profit from one another without doing harm. He therefore gave each man authority over his own children and over the children of others as well.[54]

Aristotle viewed Sparta as a *gynaikokratia* (i.e. a state ruled by women), and, as such, contrary to the natural hierarchy in which men were to rule women (see above). In Athens and some other Greek states women were not permitted to own land or to manage substantial amounts of wealth.[55] Aristotle criticized the Spartan system of land tenure, which permitted women to own land, to manage their own property, and to exercise authority in the family:

Again, the license of the Spartan women hinders the attainment of the aims of the constitution and the realization of the good of the people. For just as a husband and a wife are each a part of every family, so may the city be regarded as about equally divided between men and women; consequently in all cities where the condition of women is bad, one half of the city must be regarded as not having proper legislation. And this is exactly what happened

[53] *Lac. Pol.* 1. 2–10, reprinted by permission of the publishers and the Loeb Classical Library from *Xenophon in Seven Volumes*, VII: *Scripta Minora*, trans. E. C. Marchant (Cambridge, Mass.: Harvard University Press, 1971), 137–41.

[54] *Lac. Pol.* 6. 1.

[55] See further Ch. 5 n. 98.

in Sparta. There, the lawgiver who had intended to make the entire population strong in character has accomplished his aims with regard to the men, but has neglected the women, who indulge in every kind of luxury and intemperance. A natural consequence of this lifestyle is that wealth is highly valued, particularly in societies where men come to be dominated by their wives, as is the case with many military and warlike peoples, if we except the Celts and a few other races who openly approve of male lovers. In fact, there seems to be some rational justification for the myth of the union of Ares with Aphrodite, since all military peoples are prone to sexual activities with either men or women. This was evident among the Spartans in the days of their supremacy, when much was managed by women. But what is the difference between women ruling, or rulers being ruled by women? The result is the same. . . . It is not surprising, however, that the license of the women was characteristic of Spartan society from the earliest times, for the men of Sparta were away from home for long periods of time as they fought first against the Argives and then against the Arcadians and Messenians. When they returned to a peaceful life, having grown accustomed to obedience by military discipline, which has its virtue, they were prepared to submit themselves to the legislation of Lycurgus. But when Lycurgus attempted to subject women to his laws they resisted and he gave up, as tradition says. These, then, are the causes of what happened and thus it is clear that the constitutional shortcoming under discussion must be assigned to them. Our task, however, is not to praise or blame, but to discover what is right or wrong, and the position of women in Sparta, as we have already noted, not only contravenes the spirit of the constitution but contributes greatly to the existing avarice. This problem of greed naturally invites an attack on the lack of equality among the Spartans with regard to the ownership of property, for we see that some of them have very small properties while others have very large ones, and that as a result a few people possess most of the land. Here again is another shortcoming in their constitution; for although the lawgiver rightly disapproved of the selling and buying of estates, he permitted anyone who so desired to transfer land through gifts or bequests, with the same result. And nearly two-fifths of all the land is in the possession of women, because heiresses are numerous and the customary dowries are large. The regulation of dowries by the state would have been a better measure, abolishing them entirely or making them, at any rate, small or moderate.[56]

Although Plutarch was the latest of all the authors who wrote extensively about the family in archaic Sparta, he has been our most influential source. Plutarch lived AD *c.*46–120 in Boeotia, which

[56] Arist. *Pol.* 1269b12–1270a6, adapted from Spyridakis and Nystrom, *Ancient Greece: Documentary Perspectives*, 183–4. Copyright 1988 by Kendall/Hunt Publishing Company. Used with permission.

was then part of the Roman province of Achaea. He travelled widely throughout the Roman Empire and his perspective is often one of comparison between Greece and Rome. In many of his works, Plutarch displays a special interest in the family, marriage, and education. Information about the Spartan family appears particularly in the biographies of Lycurgus, Agis IV (ruled *c.* 244–241), and Cleomenes III (ruled *c.* 235–222), and in *The Sayings of Spartan Women,* which is included in the work of Plutarch, but probably not written by him. Plutarch wrote biographical, ethical, and philosophical works, not history, and he was well aware of the hazards of his enterprise. He begins the *Life of Lycurgus*: 'There is so much uncertainty in the accounts which historians have left us of Lycurgus, the lawgiver of Sparta, that scarcely anything is asserted by one of them which is not called into question or contradicted by the rest.' Plutarch criticizes Aristotle's comments on Sparta in the *Politics* (see below), and probably read Aristotle's *Constitution of the Spartans,* which is no longer extant.[57] A principal source for the lives of *Agis* and *Cleomenes* was Phylarchus of Athens, who wrote moralizing history in the third century BC. Plutarch also read Thucydides, Xenophon, and Plato, and consulted the works of many other historians which are no longer extant. An indirect source could have been Plato's *Laws* and *Republic*, which are to some extent based on an idealized picture of archaic Sparta. Plutarch's presentation of archaic Sparta was influenced by the allegations of Agis IV and Cleomenes III, activist Spartan kings of the third century BC, who in order to win support for their reforms, claimed that they were restoring neglected laws first promulgated by Lycurgus. The law code, or Great Rhetra ('Saying'), was said to have been given to Lycurgus by the Delphic oracle. The Lycurgan Constitution was in existence by the sixth century and perhaps even earlier. It touched on almost every aspect of life, including the choice of whether and when to marry, the conditions of conjugal intercourse, and the decision as to whether to rear a child. Thus the Spartan system may be called 'totalitarian', for it was designed to regulate the life of its citizens totally.

Lycurgus persuaded the citizens to pool all the land and then redistribute it afresh. Then they would all live on equal terms with one another, with the same amount of property to support each. . . . Each person's lot was suffi-

[57] On Plutarch's historical methods see *inter alia* Philip A. Stadter (ed.), *Plutarch and the Historical Tradition* (London and New York, 1992).

cient to provide a rent of 70 medimni of barley for a man, and 12 for his wife, along with proportionate quantities of fresh produce. . . . There is a story that at some later date when on return from abroad he was passing through the country just after the reaping, and saw the heaps of grain side by side and all equal in size, he smiled and remarked to the bystanders that the whole of Laconia had the look of a property which many brothers had recently divided between themselves.[58]

He attempted to divide up their movable property too, in order to remove inequalities and contrasts altogether. But when he saw their adverse reaction to outright expropriation, he went about this in a different way and devised constitutional measures against their greed. . . . Those who had great possessions won no advantage because there was no public outlet for their wealth, but it had to be kept unused in storage at home.[59]

Aristotle claims wrongly that he [i.e. Lycurgus] tried to discipline the women but gave up when he could not control the considerable degree of licence and power attained by women because of their husbands' frequent campaigning. At these times the men were forced to leave them in full charge, and consequently they used to dance attendance on them to an improper extent and call them their 'Ladyships'. Lycurgus, rather, showed all possible concern for them too. First he toughened the girls physically by making them run and wrestle and throw the discus and javelin. Thereby their children in embryo would make a strong start in strong bodies and would develop better, while the women themselves would also bear their pregnancies with vigour and would meet the challenge of childbirth in a successful, relaxed way. He did away with prudery, sheltered upbringing, and effeminacy of any kind. He made young girls no less than young men grow used to walking nude in processions, as well as to dancing and singing at certain festivals with the young men present and looking on. . . . There was nothing disreputable about the girls' nudity. It was altogether modest, and there was no hint of immorality. Instead it encouraged simple habits and an enthusiasm for physical fitness, as well as giving the female sex a taste of masculine gallantry, since it too was granted equal participation in both excellence and ambition. As a result the women came to talk as well as to think in the way that Leonidas' wife Gorgo[60] is said to have done. For when some woman, evidently a foreigner, said to her: 'You Laconian women are the only ones who can rule men,' she replied: 'That is because we are the only ones who give birth to men.'

There were then also these inducements to marry. I mean the processions of girls, and the nudity, and the competitions which the young men watched,

[58] Plut. *Lyc.* 8, trans. Richard J. A. Talbert, *Plutarch on Sparta* (London: Penguin, 1988), 16–17. Reproduced by permission of Penguin Books Ltd.

[59] Plut. *Lyc.* 9, trans. Talbert, *Plutarch on Sparta*, 17–18.

[60] Born in 506 BC.

attracted by a compulsion not of an intellectual type, but (as Plato says) a sexual one. In addition Lycurgus placed a certain civil disability on those who did not marry, for they were excluded from the spectacle of the Gymnopaediae.[61] . . .

The custom was to capture women for marriage—not when they were slight or immature, but when they were in their prime and ripe for it. The so-called 'bridesmaid' took charge of the captured girl. She first shaved her hair to the scalp, then dressed her in a man's cloak and sandals, and laid her down alone on a mattress in the dark. The bridegroom—who was not drunk and thus not impotent, but was sober as always—first had dinner in the messes, then would slip in, undo her belt, lift her and carry her to the bed. After spending only a short time with her, he would depart discreetly so as to sleep wherever he usually did along with the other young men. And this continued to be his practice thereafter: while spending the days with his contemporaries, and going to sleep with them, he would warily visit his bride in secret, ashamed and apprehensive in case someone in the house might notice him. His bride at the same time devised schemes and helped plan how they might meet each other unobserved at suitable moments. It was not just for a short period that young men would do this, but for long enough that some might even have children before they saw their own wives in daylight. Such intercourse was not only an exercise in self-control and moderation, but also meant that partners were fertile physically, always fresh for love, and ready for intercourse rather than being sated and pale from unrestricted sexual activity. Moreover some lingering glow of desire and affection was always left in both. . . .

What was thus practised in the interests of breeding and of the state was at that time so far removed from the laxity for which the women later became notorious, that there was absolutely no notion of adultery among them.[62]

The father of a newborn child was not entitled to make his own decision about whether to rear it, but brought it in his arms to a particular spot termed a 'lesche' where the eldest men of his tribe sat. If after examination the baby proved well-built and sturdy they instructed the father to bring it up, and assigned it one of the 9,000 lots of land. But if it was puny and deformed, they dispatched it to what was called 'the place of rejection' (*Apothetae*), a precipitous spot by Mount Taygetus, considering it better both for itself and the state that the child should die if right from its birth it was poorly endowed for health or strength.[63]

[61] The festival of naked boys, or boys without armour.
[62] Plut. *Lyc.* 14–15, trans. Talbert, *Plutarch on Sparta*, 24–6.
[63] Plut. *Lyc.* 16. 1–2, trans. Talbert, *Plutarch on Sparta*, 27.

Neither was it permissible for each father to bring up and educate his son in the way he chose. Instead, as soon as boys reached the age of seven, Lycurgus took charge of them all himself and distributed them into Troops (*agelai*).[64]

He said about government to a man who demanded establishing democracy in the polis: "First establish a democracy in your own household (*oikia*)."[65]

After hearing that her son was a coward and unworthy of her, Damatria killed him when he made his appearance. This is the epigram about her:

Damatrius who broke the laws was killed by his mother,
She a Spartan lady, he a Spartan youth.

A woman, when she saw her son approaching, asked how their country was doing. When he said: 'All the men are dead', she picked up a tile, threw it at him and killed him, saying: 'Then did they send you to bring us the bad news?'

As a woman was burying her son, a worthless old crone came up to her and said, 'You poor woman, what a misfortune!' 'No, by the two gods, a piece of good fortune', she replied, 'because I bore him so that he might die for Sparta, and that is what has happened, as I wished.'[66]

When an Ionian woman was priding herself on one of the tapestries she had made (which was indeed of great value), a Spartan woman showed off her four most dutiful sons and said they were the kind of thing a noble and good woman ought to produce and should boast of them and take pride in them.[67]

Another woman, as she was handing her son his shield and giving him some encouragement, said, 'Son, either with this or on this'.[68]

The sources provide information about upper-class and royal Spartiates. For some topics relevant to family history, including bigamy, adultery, and the rearing of a lame male infant, the only examples we have are in the royal family, and it is dangerous to generalize from these. We have little information about the families of the lower classes: the *perioikoi* (free, non-Spartiates) or helots (subject population). Following the rebellion of neighbouring Messenia against Spartan domination and the subsequent Second

[64] Plut. *Lyc.* 16. 4–5, trans. Talbert, *Plutarch on Sparta*, 28. [65] Plut. *Lyc.* 19. 3.

[66] Ps.-Plut. *Sayings of Spartan Women* = *Mor.* 240. f. 2, trans. Talbert, *Plutarch on Sparta*, 159.

[67] Ps.-Plut. *Sayings of Spartan Women* = *Mor.* 241. d. 9, trans. Talbert, *Plutarch on Sparta*, 160.

[68] Ps.-Plut. *Sayings of Spartan Women* = *Mor.* 241. f. 16, trans. Talbert, *Plutarch on Sparta*, 161.

Messenian War, Sparta evolved into a militaristic society continually working to preserve its domination over the subject population. This hierarchical society had become entrenched by the sixth century. Because the Spartiates constituted, at most, only one-twentieth of the population of Laconia and Messenia, it is obvious why so much attention was paid to reproduction.[69]

Public and Private

In defining the Spartan family, as in defining the Athenian one, the chief variables are public/private orientation. Just as there were several versions of the Athenian family, so there were two versions of the Spartan family, one artificial, the other consisting of people actually related by blood or marriage. At Sparta the public version was shaped by legislation attributed to Lycurgus, a legendary figure who was said to have created the social institutions that are distinctively Spartan. Because of its uniqueness, this society has attracted much attention from antiquity to the present.

The Spartan lawgiver emphasized communal responsibilities, and usurped family terminology and imagery with the purpose of strengthening bonds among members of the larger group.[70] In this respect, the legislation of Cleisthenes at Athens followed the Lycurgan model. Lycurgus organized the Spartans into one artificial family. Because all Spartan men received equal shares of land from the state,[71] as Plutarch (*Lyc.* 8) reports, they were like brothers who had shared a patrimony. In this pseudo-family, marriage and parenthood existed primarily for the purpose of reproducing healthy warriors for the good of the state. The decision whether to raise babies was in the hands of the state immediately. The vitality of male newborns and their potential as soldiers determined whether they would

[69] On the population problem see Thomas J. Figueira, 'Population Patterns in Late Archaic and Classical Sparta', *TAPhA* 116 (1986), 165–213.

[70] Following the precedent of classical authors, I will refer here to Lycurgus, but do not imply thereby a belief that this individual necessarily existed.

[71] This distribution of inalienable lots in the conquered territory of Messenia was similar to the allocation of *kleroi* in archaic colonies, and rules governing inalienability of land were also found elsewhere in archaic Greece: see Asheri, 'Laws of Inheritance', esp. 2–3. S. J. Hodkinson, '"Blind Ploutos"? Contemporary Images of the Role of Wealth in Classical Sparta', in A. Powell and S. Hodkinson (eds.). *The Shadow of Sparta* (London, 1994), 183–222, esp. 199–200, 204, rejects the report of an equal distribution of land, and categorizes the tradition as part of the Spartan 'mirage'.

be raised or exposed.[72] (Female babies, apparently, were not subjected to such scrutiny.) Fathers did not decide how to raise their sons. Rather, all boys received the same education under state supervision. Every father treated all the children as though they were his own. The boys were invited to eat their meals in the *syssitia*. These were army mess groups consisting of approximately fifteen adult men who regularly took their meals together. These groups would function as all-male, pseudo-family units, and would assume some responsibility for the education of the youths who joined them. For example, they would teach the young to drink in moderation by bringing helots into the *syssitia* who were forced to consume wine that had not been mixed with water and to perform vulgar and ridiculous songs and dances. Young Spartans, who were invited to the *syssitia*, saw and laughed at the spectacle of the drunken helots.[73]

Because Lycurgus recognized the importance of maternal health, women were part of the community-focused programme, but only as far as reproduction was concerned. They were well nourished, exercised out of doors, and married later than women in other parts of the Greek world. Hence, despite Lycurgus's intention, late marriage reduced the fertility of Spartan women; for, in the several years between puberty and marriage they could have produced one or two children. Spartans were not obliged to perform enervating housework, though, as the passage from Pausanias quoted above indicates, like all Greek women they knew how to weave.[74] Thus they enjoyed a more pleasurable life-style than other Greek women, and they never gave it up. Nevertheless, they did reject the burden of continuous child production that was the long-range goal of their physical education. According to Cicero, the women refused to bear children (*Tusc.* 2. 36).[75]

[72] Plut. *Lyc.* 16. 1–2; Xen. *Lac. Pol.* 6. 1–2. Perhaps exceptions were made in order to assure the continuity of the royal lineages. One Spartan king went to war, but the second was able to stay home, and therefore did not need to be in perfect physical condition. According to Cartledge, *Agesilaos*, 20, 22, Agesilaus II was born lame. Apparently his infirmity did not limit his activities. It certainly did not keep him home in Sparta.

[73] Plut. *Lyc.* 28. 8; *Dem.* 1. 4; *Mor.* 239a(30).

[74] Paus. 5. 16. 2.

[75] Cicero was probably evaluating Spartan women by the standard of Roman women, and his judgement here was shrewd. Both Spartans and Romans enjoyed wealth, high status, and access (through formal medical care or word of mouth) to contraceptive methods that, though primitive, were not ineffective. See further Pomeroy, *Goddesses, Whores*, 166–8, and John M. Riddle, *Contraception and Abortion from the Ancient World to the Renaissance* (Cambridge, Mass., 1992), 17–19, 23–4, *et passim.*

The private version of the Spartan family, or *oikos*, more closely resembles the *oikos* found in Athens and other Greek states. Not only were Spartan women fully integrated members of the *oikos*, but, as Xenophon (*Lac. Pol.* 1. 9) observed, women ruled the *oikoi*. Aristotle reasons that this situation developed because Spartan men were away on military campaign for long periods of time.

Our definition in terms of public and private does not rest on the same sort of gender distinction as it does at Athens, however, for the role and status of Spartan and Athenian women were different. Unlike Athenian women, Spartans were not secluded. Although the Spartan marriage had elements of stealth and secrecy, there was no attempt to conceal female members of the family from men who were not their relatives. There is no doubt that the women followed the part of the Lycurgan curriculum which required that they exercise out of doors.[76] Yet, Aristotle (*Pol.* 1269b19–23, 1270a6–8) observes that women were outside the communal ideal, and that they rejected the Lycurgan programme from the start.[77] As at Athens, the pseudo kinship group was basically male.

Legal and Linguistic

The Spartan ideal of austerity was more severe than that imposed by Solon's sumptuary laws (see Ch. 3). Extravagant burials were prohibited. As we have noted, only Spartans who died in battle or in childbirth received inscribed tombstones in recognition of their services to the community. No offerings were to be placed in the grave except a chaplet of olive leaves and a red cloak, and the period of mourning was limited to eleven days.[78] Xenophon (*Lac. Pol.* 10. 11. 3) states that the red cloak was chosen as a uniform for the Spartan soldier precisely because it was not feminine attire. The olive wreath is usually associated with males. We do not know of any legislation specifying female grave-goods. Thus, the limitation on grave-goods reflects the ideal of equality of wealth among men. Furthermore, in death, as in life, the most basic ties among blood-relations were de-emphasized. In fact, as the pithy remarks which Pseudo-Plutarch attributes to Spartan mothers indicate, women were not to mourn,

[76] Xen. *Lac. Pol.* 1. 3; Plut. *Lyc.* 14; Ar. *Lys.* 78–84.

[77] As the reader for Oxford University Press stated (in a personal communication), there were no female Spartiates.

[78] Plut. *Lyc.* 27. 2–4, likewise *Mor.* 238d; Ael. *VH* 6. 6.

but rather to celebrate the death of their sons in battle, and several women were said to have killed their sons for being cowards (see above). When a king died, however, public mourning was imposed, as though he had been the father of the communal family. The report on royal funerals in Herodotus (6. 58), however, alludes to individual families: one man and one woman from each family (*oikia*) were ordered to lament.

Sparta differed from Athens not only in regulations concerning death, but in its systems of property ownership and inheritance.[79] The utopianism and confusion of some of the sources (especially Plutarch), as well as change over time, have given us a picture which is difficult to understand. Lycurgus's attempt to equalize the possession of movables was unsuccessful (Plut. *Lyc.* 8–9). Yet the Spartan style connoted simplicity and an absence of public display of wealth. Spartan soldiers all had the same military equipment.[80] They did, however, continue to keep some items of luxury in private at home. For this reason, no doubt, Aristotle associated women with greed and luxury, for these were features of private life. The single item of conspicuous consumption that Spartans were permitted were racehorses. It is no accident that Spartans were the first women whose horses were victorious at pan-Hellenic games, for these triumphs provided women with an approved avenue for the display of their wealth.

The following discussion of property will focus on land, for land was the most valuable commodity in the ancient world. Furthermore, little is known about the tenure of other property at Sparta. Two systems of land tenure, a public one and a private one, prevailed in classical and Hellenistic Sparta. In comparison with the regime at Athens, the private system at Sparta was unregulated, and was notorious for excesses. The regime governing the tenure of public land was attributed to Lycurgus. He was said to have divided up into equal parcels (*kleroi*) the publicly owned land, acquired from the Spartan conquest of Messenia. The conquered people, called 'helots', worked

[79] On these much disputed topics see most recently S. J. Hodkinson, 'Inheritance, Marriage and Demography: Perspectives upon the Success and Decline of Classical Sparta', in A. Powell (ed.), *Classical Sparta: Techniques behind her Success* (Norman, Okla., and London, 1988), 79–121, and *idem*, 'Land Tenure and Inheritance in Classical Sparta', *CQ* n.s. 36 (1986), 378–406.

[80] See further P. A. Cartledge, 'Hoplites and Heroes: Sparta's Contribution to the Technique of Ancient Warfare', *JHS* 97 (1977), 11–27, esp. 13, 15, and 27.

this land as serfs,[81] and were required to send a portion of the produce to the current holder of the *kleros*. At birth each Spartan was allocated a *kleros*. Possession of the *kleros* meant that the Spartan did not need to attend to farming in order to acquire sustenance, but was free to devote himself to military service. Whether a *kleros* was allocated to each girl is unclear, but it seems unlikely. Just as girls were exempt from state scrutiny at birth, so they were also excluded from the distribution of public property. Plutarch (*Lyc.* 8. 7) reports that each *kleros* was able to produce seventy medimni (bushels) of barley for a man and twelve for his wife, as well as comparable portions of liquid produce.[82] The Spartan man contributed some of his food to his mess group (*syssition*), where the menu was notoriously unrefined and monotonous. Thus possession of a *kleros* fostered a separation and inequality between men and women, who regularly not only ate different food, but ate it in different locations. One man was supposedly equal to another, and one woman to another, but a woman was not equal to a man. When a man died, his *kleros* was to revert to the state, and then be distributed to another Spartan baby, who was not necessarily related to the previous owner.[83] By the fourth century, however, a man could give his *kleros* and his house to anyone he wished, or bequeath them by testament (Plut. *Agis* 5. 1, 3–4).[84]

By the classical period (if not earlier), in addition to the land designated for distribution as *kleroi*, some land was held as private property. Though, as we have seen, women were probably excluded from the distribution of *kleroi*, being allocated a small fraction of the produce from their husband's *kleros*, they were very prominent as

[81] Macdowell, *Spartan Law*, 21, refers to helots as 'public slaves'.

[82] Arist. *Pol.* 1271a6–37; Plut. *Lyc.* 10. 1, 12. 3–4. Plutarch, *Lyc.* 12. 2, however, does not give sufficient data to enable us to calculate the Spartan diet. See further below and Lin Foxhall and H. A. Forbes, '*Σιτομετρεία*: The Role of Grain as a Staple Food in Classical Antiquity', *Chiron*, 12 (1982), 41–90, esp. 59.

[83] Plutarch's report (*Agis* 5. 1) that the father left his inheritance to his son is accepted by Macdowell, *Spartan Law*, 94, who hypothesizes that the son needed to wait for his father's death to succeed to the *kleros*. Not every father, however, would have a son, and some would have more than one. Therefore I prefer to accept Plutarch's statement (*Lyc.* 16. 1) that the new-born was allocated a *kleros*.

[84] Similarly in the Hellenistic period, cleruchic land ('allotments'), designed to attract soldiers to Ptolemaic Egypt, was at first heritable only by males, but after 200 years daughters began to inherit it too. See further Sarah B. Pomeroy, *Women in Hellenistic Egypt from Alexander to Cleopatra*, rev. with a new foreword and addenda (Detroit, 1989), 151.

owners of private land, and must have received the bulk of their sustenance from such property. If Plutarch's report that a wife received twelve medimni of barley is true, a Spartan woman would have had more than 1½ choinixes daily, an adequate diet of staples even for an athletic or pregnant or nursing woman.[85] If, however, the twelve medimni were intended to feed the entire household, including children and domestics, it would have been insufficient. Mothers, in fact, saw to it that their daughters were well nourished: Xenophon points out that only in Sparta were girls fed as well as boys (*Lac. Pol.* 14).

Land came into women's hands as dowry and inheritance. The remark attributed to Lycurgus after the distribution of *kleroi* indicates that inheritance among men was partible in equal shares (Plut. *Lyc.* 8). (Primogeniture appears only in determining succession to the throne, where priority is given to the eldest son born after a king's accession.) If the inheritance rules at Sparta before the free bequest of land was introduced were the same as those at Gortyn, then daughters inherited half as much as sons.[86] Thus the inheritance regime for Spartan males was the same as for Athenian males, but the system was more favourable for Spartan women than for Athenian women. The rules governing heiresses[87] also contributed to women's accumulation of land. Heiresses were numerous (Arist. *Pol.* 1270a23–9). Sparta was always plagued by what Aristotle called *oliganthropia*.[88] This word seems to connote lack of men, for men were continually lost in battle, or left Sparta for mercenary service (especially after the Peloponnesian War), or failed to meet the census requirements for full citizenship. Moreover, though male infanticide was practised, it seems unlikely that female babies were eliminated (see below). The kings had jurisdiction over adoptions and over the marriages of heiresses who had not been betrothed by their fathers for adoptions (Hdt. 6. 57. 4–5). Though heiresses were numerous, apparently adoptions were rare—perhaps because there were few excess sons available. If the law at Sparta was the same as at Gortyn, then an heiress was permitted to keep part of the patrimony and marry outside her father's lineage. A woman could inherit all her father's land, as did

[85] See n. 58 above.

[86] *Lex Gort.* = *Inscr. Creticae*, 4. 72 IV. 40–6.

[87] i.e. fatherless, brotherless women. Hdt. (6. 57. 4) refers to the heiress as *patrouchos*; Arist. (*Pol.* 1270a24, 27) as *epikleros*; the Code of Gortyn uses *patroiokos*.

[88] 'Sparse population'. Arist. (*Pol.* 1270a33–4) gives *oliganthropia* as a reason for the Spartan decline.

Agiatis, who inherited all the land of Gylippus (Plut. *Cleom.* 1. 2). As we have seen, the kings were supposed to approve the marriages of heiresses. Yet, since the royal family itself profited from the accumulation of property in few hands, the kings did not prevent this development. Thus Aristotle's statement (*Pol.* 1270a) that in his day women owned two-fifths of the land of Sparta is credible.

Oikos

Sparta served as 'The other' *vis-à-vis* Athens, and differences between the two societies were often exaggerated. Sparta was also idealized as a utopia, and used as a means of criticizing other city-states. Thus many features of the constitution attributed to Lycurgus reappear in Plato's vision of the life of the guardians in the *Republic*.[89] Central to both social systems are communality and totalitarian control. The private family, with its emphasis on women's monogamy and the transmission of property to legitimate male heirs, is eliminated. Guided by eugenic considerations, the state controls sexual intercourse. Women and men are trained to defend and govern the state. In the *Republic* women do not need to perform domestic labour: the only task that they must perform, according to the sexual division of labour, is giving birth to children. A stable marriage is not needed to assure that children are reared, for the state educates all children. Private property and money are outlawed. Hence, there can be no *oikos*, and indeed there is no need for one.

In actuality, however, there was a private version of the Spartan family that was based on the *oikos* system. The references to heirs, heiresses, dowries, adoption, and private property are understandable only in the context of an *oikos*. Xenophon's report emphasizes economic motivation within the Spartan *oikos*. Both the Athenian and the Spartan *oikos* were social units for reproduction and production; but it is more difficult to determine the productive element at Sparta. As we have seen, Spartan women could weave; but, like aristocratic women in Athens, they were not required to work.[90] They did, however, supervise the household and the work of the domestic staff.[91] Spartan men were trained only for military service,

[89] See further Pomeroy, *Xenophon Oeconomicus*, 37–9.

[90] See further Xen. *Oec.* 7. 6, and Pomeroy, *Xenophon Oeconomicus*, *ad loc.*

[91] Whether the Spartans used slaves or helots as domestic staff, and whether this changed over time, is unclear.

and though they might supervise the cultivation of their estates, they were strangers to most of the means other Greek men mormally employed for gaining sustenance and making money (Xen. *Hell.* 3.3.5, and see Ch. 4). At Sparta, because both women and men owned property, both sexes practised heirship strategies. As at Athens, where, according to Plutarch (*Sol.*, 20. 8), Solon had limited the size of dowries, the dowry system nevertheless prevailed without apparent limits. Moralists claimed that Lycurgus had also forbidden dowries, but certainly by the fourth century (if not earlier), they were common and sizeable, and were a means of concentrating property.[92] Many families had only daughters and no surviving sons. As we have seen, there is no evidence for female infanticide at Sparta. Perhaps the system of land tenure was linked to the lack of female infanticide, despite the dowry regime which might have fostered it. Unlike Athenian women, Spartan women could own land. Hence land-owning parents would always be able to find a dowry, even if they were 'land-poor' and unable to furnish other property.

In the classical period, and perhaps earlier, an effort was apparently made to try to assure that individual families did not die out. Children are not the property of the state, nor are they held in common. Rather, each child belongs to a specific father (Xen. *Lac. Pol.* 6. 1–2). When two brothers disagreed with one other, the Spartans punished the father for permitting his sons to quarrel (Plut. *Mor.* 233. 32). There was some concern for the continuity of individual lineages. For his suicide mission at Thermopylae, Leonidas selected men who had children (Her. 7. 205. 2, 5. 41. 3). Furthermore, the practice of wife lending for the purpose of reproduction was based on the premiss of the monogamous individual *oikos*: the husband's consent was required, though the wives wish to take control of two *oikoi*.[93]

At Sparta, as at Athens, it is clear that the legal regulations governing property ownership reflect gender relationships within the family. The perpetual absence of men on military duty created a *de facto* division of labour in which women managed domestic affairs. Aristotle no doubt exaggerates when he complains that Sparta was ruled by women, for they had no share in the government; but clearly

[92] Plut. *Mor.* 227f–228a, *Lys.* 30. 5–6; Ael. *VH* 6. 6; Ath. 13. 555c; Justin 3. 3. 8.

[93] Xen. *Lac. Pol.* 1. 7–9; cf. Polyb. 12. 6b. 8; Plut. *Lyc.* 15. 8–9, *Comp. Lyc. and Numa*, 3. 1–2, *Mor.* 242b(23).

their ownership and control of property gave Spartan women far more authority than their Athenian counterparts.

Household

The state regulated the composition of the Spartan population and consequently of the household, starting with the decision to raise or expose male infants. The double standard concerning adultery and extramarital sexual relationships seems to have prevailed at Sparta. Childbirth outside marriage (or without the approval of a woman's father or husband) was not countenanced. Thus Pseudo-Plutarch (*Mor.* 242) praises the bravery of a Spartan girl who procured a secret abortion after she became pregnant without telling her father. This story implies a view of premarital female chastity similar to that which prevailed elsewhere in Greece. We also hear that there was no rape or adultery in Sparta (Plut. *Lyc.* 15. 9–10). Perhaps this means that there were no laws concerning rape and adultery. The only adultery that we know of in Sparta occurred in the royal family. The queen Timaea bore a son fathered by Alcibiades (Plut. *Alc.* 23. 7–8, *Ages.* 3. 1–2), and Anaxandridas resorted to bigamy rather than adultery because he had not produced any children with his first wife (Hdt. 5. 39–41). Of course, royal families are subject to different constraints than those that apply to commoners, because of the need to produce an heir, and because that heir had to be a blood heir for the kingship to be justified. The lack of concern about the potential for adultery among non-royal women may have been because so few non-Spartans were admitted to Sparta that it could be assumed that all babies born to Spartan women were the product of intercourse—even if forced or extramarital—with a Spartan man.[94] A questionable

[94] By comparison with the Romans, the Greeks do not seem to have been obsessed by the possibility of respectable women having extramarital sexual relationships with lower-class men. Though there are plenty of jokes about such liaisons in Athenian comedy, there is no serious evidence that they occurred. In Sparta, the *perioikoi* lived in their own villages, and thus, we presume, were not available for scenarios of seduction. The helots probably performed domestic services in Sparta itself, and were thus in closer proximity to the women. But at the *syssitia* helots (presumably male) were regularly forced to become drunk, to perform lewd dances, and to wear ridiculous costume. We may speculate that such grotesque dehumanized creatures were unlikely to appear attractive to Spartan women, and that death would have been the penalty for any helot involved in such a relationship. See p. 46 above, and see further Ephraim David, 'Laughter in Spartan Society', in A. Powell (ed.), *Classical Sparta: Techniques behind her Success* (Norman, Okla., and London, 1988), 1–25.

story recounts a single exception to this pattern, purportedly occurring during the archaic period, when the army was in the field for many years, and when it was uncertain whether the men would ever return safely.[95] The Ephors directed that the women have intercourse with helots in order to produce a new crop of children who could replace the men in case they did not ever return from war. The women themselves did not initiate these adulterous sexual relationships; they merely obeyed the magistrates' command. It is reasonable to suppose that the women readily concurred, for without men to defend them, their fate would have been slavery or death. When the army did return to Sparta, the children born of miscegenation were sent off to found the colony that became known as Tarentum. This episode—if it actually occurred—was exceptional, and clearly an emergency measure. Even more so than the Athenians, the Spartans were ethnically endogamous throughout their history, and did not regularly recruit large numbers of new citizens of non-Spartan or mixed parentage.[96] Certainly we do not hear of challenges to citizenship or inheritance at Sparta (as we frequently do at Athens) on the grounds of foreign descent or illegitimacy. Like Greeks elsewhere, Spartan men did not restrict their access to sexual partners. There was a special category of bastard sons born from helot mothers, who were reared along with pure-bred Spartans.[97] For a male adult, acceptance into the *agoge* ('educational system') and subsequently into a *syssition* constituted verification of his citizenship (Plut. *Lyc.* 12. 5–6). We know of no analogous testing of women.

Because from the age of 7, boys spent most of their time outdoors training for a military life, and men ate their meals with other members of their army groups, women must usually have

[95] Polyb. 12. 6b5; Strab. 6. 3. 3 [279–80], etc. The veracity of this anecdote is questionable. The probable source was Ephorus. Irad Malkin, *Myth and Territory in the Spartan Mediterranean* (Cambridge, 1994), esp. 139–42, understands it as aetiological: derived from the fact that the colonists were called *Partheniai* (children of unwed women).

[96] According to Plut. *Cleom.* 10. 6, a large number of new citizens was created by Cleomenes' revolutionary programme.

[97] Xen. *Hell.* 5. 3. 9 refers to them as *nothoi ton Spartiaton*; *mothakes*, a term which probably includes sons of foreigners, helots, and former Spartan citizens, refers to non-citizens who were educated along with the Spartiates in the *agoge*. On this controversial subject, see most recently Daniel Ogden, *Greek Bastardy in the Classical and Hellenistic Periods* (Oxford, 1996), 217–24, 250–1.

outnumbered men in the household. Consequently, the Spartan household would consist of adult women, girls, boys up to the age of 7, and helots who performed domestic labour. Before the age of 30 the husband would visit the house only occasionally. Older men, however, slept at home. In fact, Xenophon's report (*Lac. Pol.* 5. 7) that after the *syssitia* all the men go home makes the Spartans' attendance at the *syssitia* resemble the Athenians' at symposia.

We have no information about domestic architecture at Sparta, but it seems likely that physical arrangements were less complex than those at Athens. We do not hear of separate quarters for men and for women at Sparta. The division of labour did not dictate that women spend their lives working at home, as was the case at Athens. Unlike the Athenian slaves described by Xenophon in the *Oeconomicus* (see above), helots lived on farms with their families, though we know little about them. In any case, there appears to have been no need to furnish separate dormitories to prevent the males from gaining access to the females; indeed, Sparta needed to have helots breed. As we have mentioned, the *syssitia* were the Spartan version of the symposia and dinner parties of men elsewhere in Greece. Therefore there was no need for the two most definitively gendered spaces found in Athenian houses: the *gynaikonitis* and the *andron*. Domestic production must have been much more limited than at Athens, for Spartan clothing was simple, and there was no need to produce a surplus for the market. Nor would any domestic space be devoted to commercial activities, since the *perioikoi*, not Spartiates, were concerned with the cash economy. Because helots were obliged to supply a fixed amount of food annually, Spartans did not need to store at home more supplies than would be consumed in a year. Even a year's supply of food would have been less than its equivalent at Athens, for Spartan men ate their main meal outside the home. Since Spartans were not permitted to use gold or silver money, and did not invite other men to their homes for symposia, they must not have owned cups and platters made of precious metals, as wealthy Greeks did elsewhere, though certainly as time went on, some did possess valuables (Hdt. 6. 62, Xen. *Hell.* 6. 5. 27, 30). Thus it seems likely that the Spartan home did not require extensive storage space or the security of a *thalamos*, unless the occupants were concealing illicit treasure.

Family Formation

In both the public and the private versions of the family the purpose of marriage was reproduction.[98] The Lycurgan regime included eugenic goals. The purpose of women's physical training was to create healthy mothers. Spartan girls married when they were fully mature, so that they would be in prime physical condition at their first pregnancy.[99] Men married before the age of 30. Hence the Spartan husband and wife were closer in age than their counterparts at Athens, where it was common for a 14-year-old girl to marry a 30-year-old man. In the private version of the Spartan family, wife lending was permitted for the purpose of reproduction, and in the public version the trial marriage helped to assure that a union was fertile.

Plutarch mentions men's reluctance to marry and the efforts of the state to provide incentives for marriage and the production of children.[100] Homosexual ties among Spartans were common.[101] Although Aristophanes (*Lys.* 78–85) depicts Spartan husbands as just as sex-starved in wartime as the rest of the Greeks and cowed by their wives' refusal to have intercourse, the poet also makes some jokes about the Spartan male's homosexual activities and interest in anal intercourse (*Lys.* 1105, 1148, 1162, 1173–4).

The Spartan incest taboo was the mirror image of the Athenian: marriage between paternal half-siblings was not permitted.[102] Because of Spartan xenophobia and the lack of trade and colonization, there are no parallels to the exogamous alliances sometimes found in other states. The Spartans practised aristocratic endogamy.

Plutarch describes some quaint wedding customs, including marriage by capture,[103] the random selection of spouses by cohorts of potential brides and bridegrooms groping in a dark room, the secret marriage, and transvestism of the bride. The transvestism has been

[98] For regulation of reproduction by the state see Plut. *Lyc.* 16. 1–2; cf. Plato, *Laws* 631D–E, 720E–721D, 842D–E.

[99] Perhaps because of their athletic curriculum, Spartan girls experienced menarche later than other Greeks.

[100] The mandatory examination of new-born males may in some cases have prevented the elimination of babies who would have been exposed if the decision had been left to the biological father.

[101] See now F. D. Harvey, 'Laconica: Aristophanes and the Spartans', in A. Powell and S. Hodkinson (eds.), *The Shadow of Sparta* (London, 1994), 35–58, esp. 41–2.

[102] See n. 36 above.

[103] *Lyc.* 15. 3, likewise Ath. 13. 555C, citing Hermippus (*fl.* late third century).

interpreted as a stage in a rite of passage marked by unusual behaviour, or as a means of averting the evil eye or of easing the bridegroom's transition from homosexual to heterosexual intercourse.[104] These customs belong to the publicly oriented family. In a system of aristocratic endogamy the haphazard selection of spouses is a symptom of equality. One spouse is as good as the next. Since the sole purpose of marriage is reproduction, the secret marriage permits the couple to find other spouses if their union is infertile.

If these customs were ever practised, they apparently had died out by the classical period.[105] The random selection of spouses runs counter to the economic motivations for marriage reported by Xenophon and Aristotle. These motives are nowhere more apparent than in royal families. For example, in the 270s the elderly Agiad Cleonymus married Chilonis, a young Eurypontid heiress, and Agiatis, who had inherited the great wealth of her father Gylippus, was married first to Agis IV and then, when widowed, to Cleomenes III (Plut. *Cleom.* 1. 2). Eudamidas II, a Eurypontid, married his paternal aunt Agesistrata (Plut. *Agis* 3. 2). Such marriages fostered the accumulation of wealth in the hands of the few at the expense of the ideal of equality.[106] According to Xenophon, the role of the bride is, in fact, the reverse of that in the peculiar rituals described by Plutarch. Rather than serving as a passive victim of a rape-marriage, the Spartan woman is reported to have selected her partner or multiple partners on the basis of her own self-interest.

Family and Polis

It is obvious that the historian must not use law as the sole basis whereby to construct a picture of lived reality. For example, there is no evidence that the Code of Hammurabi was ever enacted as law or obeyed. There are no witnesses to the full operation of the Spartan commune as described by Plutarch. Therefore, in the case of Sparta we must admit the possibility that much of the legislation concerning the 'communal family' was observed only briefly or not at all. Readers in the twentieth century will be able to supply modern parallels

[104] On these customs see Barton Lee Kunstler, 'Women and the Development of the Spartan Polis' (Ph.D. diss., Boston University, 1983), 436–7.

[105] Herodotus mentioned betrothals in the royal family (6. 65; but cf. 57. 4).

[106] Hence the utopian proposals of e.g. Phaleas (Arist. *Pol.* 1270a25–6) that the wealthy could not receive dowries, and the abolition of dowries in Plato, *Laws* 742C.

for the failure of similar totalitarian utopias or dystopias. The failure of these modern experiments may be attributed in part to legislation which, in giving priority to public rather than private concerns, imposed patterns and ideals of behaviour that human beings were unwilling or unable to practise.

Did Sparta change over time from a communal society to the one described first by Herodotus and Xenophon, based, like that of Athens, on the *oikos*, with dowry, private property, inheritance? The shadowy appearance of the *oikos* at Sparta has often been viewed as a symptom of the degeneration of the Lycurgan polity. Yet there are no trustworthy accounts of a Sparta without these features. Nevertheless, most historians today follow the general model traced by Aristotle of drastic change over time in Spartan society, with Sparta having lost its distinctive way of life by the end of the fifth century.[107] Such a change may be observed in the public behaviour of male Spartiates, but it is not at all clear that private life had been altered. In fact, it would be surprising to find a thorough change in the most conservative of Greek cities.[108]

It seems more likely that the publicly oriented family and the privately oriented family existed simultaneously, and that both changed differently over time, and changed relative to one another. The *oikos* existed even before the programme of Lycurgus, and certainly outlived it. Nevertheless, although he is portrayed as recognizing the existence of the *oikos*, he made little attempt to regulate it, for in a remark attributed to him in response to a request to turn Sparta into a democracy, he said: 'make your own household (*oikia*) a democracy first' (Plut. *Lyc.* 19. 3). Furthermore, Aristotle's comment that the women rejected the Lycurgan Code suggests that it was merely a blueprint for a society that was never fully constructed according to plan. Indeed, the *oikos* system remained intact despite political

[107] Thus Figueira, 'Population Patterns', 194. Claude Mossé, 'Women in the Spartan Revolutions of the Third Century', in Sarah B. Pomeroy (ed.), *Women's History and Ancient History* (Chapel Hill, NC, 1991), 138–53, esp. 143, suggests that the bigamous arrangements described by Xenophon were a temporary solution to increase the population at the end of the Peloponnesian War. In P. A. Cartledge and Antony Spawforth, *Hellenistic and Roman Sparta. A Tale of Two Cities* (London and New York, 1989), 110, Cartledge dates the 'normalization' to the later fifth century; likewise Macdowell, *Spartan Law*, 14, and Hodkinson, 'Inheritance, Marriage and Demography', 79, 94–5.

[108] Though it is always possible that stolid cautiousness was part of the Spartan 'mirage', Thucydides certainly accepted it as a characteristic that contrasted with the mercurial volatility of the Athenians: 1. 84–5, 2. 40–1, 4. 5, 5. 107, 8. 96. 5.

efforts to superimpose a communal family structure. The *oikos* at Sparta, as at Athens, preceded the *polis*, and served as a model for it. Thus, for example, partible inheritance by brothers in equal shares preceded the equal distribution of *kleroi* to males.

Opinions have varied concerning sameness or difference between family structures in different Greek cities. Previous historians followed their ancient texts in pointing to major differences between Athens and Sparta. This dualism resulted from the tendency of Greek writers to organize their concepts in polarities, and it is difficult for scholars to reconceptualize these sources. Analogy with Athens, rather than polarity, is the key to understanding Spartan families.

'Family Values': The Uses of the Past

The Peloponnesian War transformed the Greek world. In the fourth century and the Hellenistic period at both Sparta and Athens nostalgia for a so-called ancestral constitution was patent.[109] As far as the family was concerned, such nostalgia was expressed in a reverence for legislation attributed to Lycurgus and Solon. Athenian orators invoked the spectre of Solon as a rhetorical artifice with some frequency. Xenophon's *Spartan Constitution* shows a recognition that the Lycurgan Constitution was no longer enforced, though whether this attitude should be attributed to Xenophon personally, or whether he is reflecting the beliefs of his Spartan hosts is unclear. New laws were also promulgated and purported to be revivals of archaic legislation. Thus the record of the past was revised as was expedient for current purposes, and the historical testimony to change over time was blurred.[110]

The Peripatetics were especially active in this conservative movement, for they specialized in antiquarian research. Aristotle and his followers collected the constitutions of various Greek cities. Bookworms that they were, they put more trust in the written word than most practising politicians would have. They failed to consider that some laws could have been promulgated and published, but never, or only briefly, put into effect. Perhaps such considerations were irrelevant to Demetrius of Phaleron when he seized the opportunity to

[109] See further A. Fuks, *The Ancestral Constitution* (London, 1953), and most recently M. H. Hansen, *The Athenian Democracy in the Age of Demosthenes* (Oxford and Cambridge, Mass., 1991), 296–9.

[110] See pp. 101–2 below.

govern Athens (317). Demetrius had studied with Theophrastus.[111] Demetrius was a historian; thus it was natural for him to look to the past. He was also a politician who exploited the past as propaganda for his reforms. Instituting measures affecting the conduct of private life, Demetrius attempted to make them more acceptable by claiming that he was reviving Solonian legislation. According to Cicero, Demetrius outlawed the use of large decorated gravestones which drew attention to the burials of the wealthy. Such tombstones had been used in the archaic period, but had gone out of fashion during the first three-quarters of the fifth century when democracy flourished. The precise date in the fifth century when large marble grave stelae were reintroduced into Attica is debatable.[112] At the end of the fifth century and in the fourth, the wealthy often favoured burials in *periboloi*, or family enclosures that included several large expensive grave monuments and inscriptions. In the fourth century, as well, classical funerary monuments were reused by later generations of Athenians who were not descended from the families named on the monuments, perhaps in an attempt to fabricate family networks.[113] Whether these changes in commemoration were the result of legislation, artistic fashion, or personal inclination is uncertain. Changing funerary monuments certainly reconfigure the public image of the family, but reusing old ones is at least a symptom of nostalgia, if not an exhortation to return to the family values of the past. In any case, though the older stelae remained, the sumptuary legislation of Demetrius of Phaleron put an end to the production of new monuments that advertised invidious distinctions between very wealthy Athenians

[111] Diog. Laert. 5. 75; Strab. 9. 398; Cic. *Leg.* 3. 14, *de Off.* 1. 1, *de Fin.* 5. 54; *Suda* s.v. Demetrius.

[112] See recently W. K. Kovacsovics, *Kerameikos XIV: Die Eckterrasse an der Gräberstrasse des Kerameikos* (Berlin, 1990), 73–87. J. D. Mikalson, 'Religion and the Plague in Athens, 431–423 BC', in K. J. Rigsby (ed.), *Studies Presented to Sterling Dow*, Greek, Roman, and Byzantine Studies Monograph, 10 (Durham, NC, 1984), 217–25, esp. 223–4, argues that the production of grave stelae was resumed *c.*425/4, as compensation for prior maltreatment of the dead during the plague years. Elizabeth G. Pemberton, 'The *Dexiosis* on Attic Gravestones', *Mediterranean Archaeology*, 2 (1989), 45–50, suggests that the *dexiosis* motif was introduced at this time and indicates reconciliation. See further Ch. 3.

[113] On the reuse of classical stelae in Hellenistic Athens, see most recently Sanne Houby-Nielsen, 'Gender Roles and Conventional Values in Hellenistic Athens', paper delivered at conference on 'Conventional Values of the Hellenistic Greeks', sponsored by Danish Research Council for the Humanities, Copenhagen, 26 Jan., 1995.

and their less fortunate countrymen.[114] Although we know of no specific legislation curbing the use of such monuments until the enactments of Demetrius, and we have only Cicero's testimony that he was reviving earlier laws, the legislation is consistent with the sumptuary intention of laws attributed to Solon.

Demetrius also created a board of *gynaikonomoi* ('regulators of women'). Aristotle (*Pol.* 1322b37–1323a3) had approved of such magistrates. At Athens their duties included control over women's participation in funerals and festivals.[115] Some fragments of New Comedy constitute the earliest evidence for *gynaikonomoi* at Athens, though they appear earlier in inscriptions at other Greek cities such as Thasos and Gambreum.

These retrogressive social notions were not confined to the old Greek cities. Peripatetic philosophers, including Demetrius of Phaleron, advised Ptolemy I concerning the design of the administrative structures of his new state.[116] The Ptolemies were faced with an unfamiliar family structure in Egypt. Herodotus (2. 35) had, in fact, described the sexual division of labour in Egypt as exactly the opposite to that in Greece, with men working indoors and women outdoors. Nevertheless, the design of the census reflects traditional Greek priorities and values. A papyrus of 280–250 mentions a *gynaikonomos*. Perhaps this refers to a magistrate in Alexandria, and constitutes another example of Demetrius's influence.[117] What other advice could one have expected from a historian? Like Demetrius and Ptolemy I, historians tend to look back, not forward, or forward only in the expectation that history will repeat itself.

At Sparta, as well, old values were exploited in an attempt to solve new problems. The revolutionary kings Agis IV and Cleomenes III claimed to be restoring the Lycurgan polity. They were faced with vast inequalities in the distribution of wealth among Spartans, where women, especially members of the royal family, owned two-fifths of the public land and the major portion of private land (Arist. *Pol.* 1270a23–4; Plut. *Agis* 7. 3–4). They had gained this property through

[114] Demetrius of Phaleron, fr. 135 (Wehrli) = Cic. *Leg.* 2. 64–6 = Jacoby, *FGrH* ii. B 228 F 9, and Ch. 3 n. 2 below.

[115] Philochorus, *FGrH* iii. 328 F 65, Timocles fr. 34 (Kassel-Austin) = Ath. 7. 245b–c, Plaut. *Aul.* 498–502.

[116] Ael. *VH* 3. 17 = Dem. Phal. fr. 65 (Wehrli), and see Ch. 6.

[117] *PHib.* II 196 = *SB* VI 9559: see further J. Bingen, 'Le Papyrus du gynéconome', *CE* 32 (1957), 337–9.

dowry and inheritance. Heiresses and wealthy widows were sought in marriage. For example, Agis's mother Agesistrata and grandmother Archidamia, both widows, were the richest of all Spartans, both men and women. As we have seen, Agiatis, who had inherited the great wealth of her father, Gylippus, was married first to Agis IV, and then to Cleomenes III (Plut. *Cleom.* 1. 2). The programs of Agis and Cleomenes were multi-faceted, but the *sine qua non* was a redistribution of land. Women agreed to contribute property for redistribution, but, as in the past, they do not seem to have been affected by other reforms. Agis and Cleomenes also succeeded for a time in reviving the male educational system known as the *agoge.*[118] Agis himself set an example by wearing the old-fashioned short cloak and living a life of austerity (Plut. *Agis* 4, 14) and Cleomenes followed suit (Plut. *Cleom.* 13). The *syssitia* were revived. The Hellenistic period was a time when dining clubs were popular;[119] thus the communal messes were not anachronistic. In another tribute to the past, Plutarch (*Cleom.* 18. 4) ascribed Cleomenes' military successes to the revival of the ancient virtues of courage and obedience.

Stoic influence was a factor in the Spartan revolution.[120] Sphaerus, a follower of Cleanthes, went to Sparta and lectured the youths and ephebes (Plut. *Cleom.* 2). He wrote 'Peri Basileias' (On Kingship) for Agis or Cleomenes, and also wrote two other treatises dealing with Sparta: 'Peri Lakonikes Politeias' (On the Spartan Constitution) and 'Peri Lukourgou kai Sokratous' (On Lycurgus and Socrates).[121] Although Zeno's *Politeia* had included the sharing of women (Diog. Laert. 7. 33, 131), there is no evidence that the Hellenistic revolutionaries attempted to create a 'communal family' that would include women. The ultimate goal of the land redistribution was to increase

118 Plut. *Cleom.* 11, 18. See further A. Fuks, 'Agis, Cleomenes and Equality', *CPh* 57 (1962), 161–6, repr. in M. Stern and M. Amit (eds.), *Social Conflict in Ancient Greece*, (Jerusalem and Leiden, 1984), 250–5; *idem*, 'Patterns and Types of Social-Economic Revolution in Greece from the Fourth to the Second Century BC', *Anc. Soc.* 5 (1962), 51–81, repr. in *Social Conflict in Ancient Greece*, 9–39.

119 See Ch. 3 n. 36 below.

120 The extent of this influence is debatable. For the view that it was minimal see most recently Peter Green, 'Philosophers, Kings, and Democracy, or How Political Was the Stoa?', *Ancient Philosophy*, 14 (1994), 147–56; for the opposite view see Andrew Erskine, *The Hellenistic Stoa* (Ithaca, NY, 1990).

121 Diog. Laert. 7. 177, for the fragments Von Arnim *SVF* 1. 620–30, pp. 139–42. See further Jacoby, *FGrH* 585, and most recently, Erskine, *Hellenistic Stoa*, esp. 123–49, who, however, does not indicate whether women are included in his discussion of Spartan 'citizens'.

the number of citizen soldiers and create an army equal to the Spartan force of the past. Once again, women were not to receive *kleroi*. As far as the details of the revolution are known, the laws concerning women's ownership of property, inheritance, and dowry remained intact. Thus, in attempting to revive 'the good old days', they recreated the same problems that, according to Aristotle, had allowed women to be 'ungoverned' (*anesis*), and had ultimately been responsible for the degeneration of the original Lycurgan polity. The failure of the Spartan revolutionaries to take account of women after they had contributed their property is perhaps attributable, at least in part, to the general failure of the hegemonic Stoic doctrine to transform women's role and to educate them in conformity with the new social order.[122]

The picture of the development of families in the Greek world that emerges is not that of a simple linear progression, but is complicated by nostalgia, by the influence of reformers and intellectuals who are politically conservative, and by the idealization and exploitation of the past as propaganda. Problems have resulted from scholars' attempts to simplify this picture by imposing a synchronic interpretive model on Greek family history. Problems have also arisen from the imposition of an explanatory model that merely polarizes public and private. A more nuanced interpretation that takes account of gender in the definition of public and private is more appropriate to the study of the Greek family.

[122] See further Pomeroy, *Goddesses, Whores*, 131–2. Stoicism did have an effect on a few women as, presumably, in the case of Cleomenes' mother Cratesicleia, who courageously met her death in Egypt, exhorting her son not to be fearful on her account (Plut. *Cleom.* 22. 6–7).

2

Heredity and Personal Identity

> The destiny of birth is decisive in every deed
>
> Pind. *Nem.* 5. 40–41

Family membership was a critical factor in shaping a person's identity.[1] Those of us who live anonymously in vast cosmopolitan cities of the Western world and who cherish our individuality and our freedom to create our own identity may consider such a situation stifling, but, as the following discussion will show, family membership could serve not only as an unfailing source of security and welfare, but also as a font of honour, achievement, and social and political privilege, or, conversely, might confer an inescapable burden of debt, dishonour, or physical imperfection. In Athens a man became a citizen only by being acknowledged first as a member of a citizen family. Women's identity was more hazy than men's, and because of this ambiguity, family membership could be challenged on the basis of female descent. As we shall see, however, women's invisibility varied geographically, chronologically (even within their own life cycle), and according to social class.

How much of a person's identity accrues to him or her merely by being born and acknowledged as a member of a particular family? In what ways does this ascribed identity vary according to whether the baby is a boy, who, unless he is adopted, will remain a member of the same family for his entire life, or a girl, who will upon marriage inevitably add an attachment to a second family to her identity? How do changes in the political structure affect familial identity, and in what ways do these changes vary according to gender? In this chapter,

[1] The material in the first half of this chapter was presented in 'Women and the Family in the Classical Polis', at the Berkshire Conference on the History of Women, Vassar College, June 1993; at the University of Amsterdam, 31 Aug., 1993; at the International Conference on Women in Antiquity, St Hilda's College, Oxford, 4 Sept., 1993; and published in 'Women's Identity and the Family in the Classical Polis', in R. Hawley and B. Levick (eds.), *Women in Antiquity: New Assessments* (London, 1995), 111–21.

evidence from poetry, prose, law, archaeology, and biological theory will be mustered to show how ideas about heredity function in a wide variety of areas as a consistent symbolic system, creating and reproducing, in turn, the identity of a family and its successive members.

RITES OF INCORPORATION

Membership in the family group preceded the identity conferred by an individual name, but gender identity came first of all. When a boy was born, the door of the house was wreathed with olive branches. Garlands of spun wool announced the birth of a girl (Hsch., s.v. *stephanon ekpherein*). Next, the baby was admitted to the cult of the hearth, for this act signified acceptance into the family. The head of the household was the chief priest for his family, and he determined who was to be admitted to its cults. If the father decided to raise the infant and it appeared capable of surviving, it was carried around the hearth at a ceremony called the Amphidromia (see below).[2] Contemporary sources doubtless considered the ceremony too banal to describe, and late lexicographers do not concur in their descriptions. According to various sources, the ceremony took place five or seven days after the baby's birth.[3] There is also disagreement about the identity of the person or persons who carried the baby around, and as to whether the baby's name was bestowed at the Amphidromia or whether the naming occurred ten days after birth.[4] The *Suda* (s.v. *amphidromia* [Adler] p. 153) reports that on the fifth day the women

[2] The 'trial period', or delay, in incorporation into the family probably affected the relationship between parents and child. The best evidence comes from later historical periods. Sarah Blaffer Hrdy, 'Fitness Tradeoffs in the History and Evolution of Delegated Mothering with Special Reference to Wet-Nursing, Abandonment, and Infanticide', *Ethology and Sociobiology*, 13 (1992), 409–42, esp. 436–7, discusses the connection between infanticide and customs encouraging emotional distancing between mother and neonate. A study of nineteenth-century French mothers showed that post-partum mothers who did not bond immediately with the new-born—for example, by breast feeding—were more likely to give up the baby for adoption than those who spent more than eight days in close association with the baby.

[3] The period of ten days mentioned in schol. *Lys.* 758 (Dindorf) is probably the result of confusion with the timing of the naming day.

[4] Arist. *HA* 588a8–9 refers to the seventh day. Schol. *ad* Plat. *Tht.* 160E states that on the fifth day they run around the hearth and give the baby a name. *Etym. Magn.*, s.v. *amphidromia*, and Harp., s.v. *amphidromia* (Keaney), do not specify the day. Ath. 9. 370c–d refers to the feast eaten at the Amphidromia. See further R. Hamilton, 'Sources for the Athenian Amphidromia', *GRBS* 25 (1984), 243–51.

who had been present at the delivery purified their hands and ran around, and on the tenth day they gave the baby a name. Yet Hesychius (s.v. *dromiamphion hemar*) states that seven days after the birth they ran naked around the altar. (The gender of the runners is not specified, but because they are said to be naked, they are probably men, not the women who had attended the delivery.) Hesychius also notes that friends and relatives sent gifts. These people became witnesses to the existence of the baby and to its membership in the family.

Inclusion in their father's cult established that infants were members of the family group. Participation in a cult that excludes others confirms such affiliation. Family cults included those of Hestia, Apollo Patrous, Zeus Ctesius, and Zeus Herceius.[5] At the *oikos* level, these cults were exclusive. These divinities were, of course, also major figures in the Greek pantheon, and *oikos* religion was thus linked to *polis* religion through the figure of the father acting as domestic priest.

RELIGIOUS AFFILIATION

The obligations caused by a death automatically befell men and women who were closely related to the deceased (see Ch. 3). These family commitments were not optional, but were enforced both by custom and by religious and secular law. Inclusion in family cults or presence in a family group at public festivals created a presumption of family membership. For example, at the Feast of the Choes (Wine Jugs) that was part of the Anthesteria which were celebrated in honour of Dionysus in early spring, 3-year-old children came along with their family, and joined the rest of the community in tasting the new wine.[6] Inclusion in private, domestic ceremonies could also be cited as evidence for family membership. A man who argued that his mother was born of a legitimate marriage and that he and his brother consequently were their maternal grandfather's heirs told the court that his grandfather had always included them when he made

[5] Arist. *Ath. Pol.* 55. 3; Harp., s.v. *Herkeios Zeus* (Keaney); Lycurg. *Leocr.* 25, p. 71, below, and see further, Christiane Sourvinou-Inwood, 'Further Aspects of Polis Religion', *AION (archeol.)*, 10 (1988), 259–74, esp. 271–2.

[6] See further Ch. 3 and Richard Hamilton, *Choes and Anthesteria. Athenian Iconography and Ritual* (Ann Arbor, 1992).

sacrifices and had taken them along when he attended the rural Dionysia. The grandfather had even invited them to join him when he sacrificed to Zeus Ctesius, a rite which he considered especially private (Isae. 8. 15–16).

SHARING A HEARTH

Plato (*Laws* 729C) refers to kinsmen as those who share the worship of the family gods and who have the same natural blood. It is important to keep Plato's second point in mind when considering the family affiliation of a married woman.

The various words for 'baby' that appear in the sources do not differentiate between girls and boys. Therefore we assume that the Amphidromia was the same for a daughter as for a son. Even upon marriage, the daughter did not renounce her father's cults. Unless they were adopted, the children of the head of the household were lifelong members of their family's cults. Fustel de Coulanges wrote erroneously of the bride: 'She must abandon the paternal fire, and henceforth invoke that of the husband. She must abandon her religion, practise other rites, and pronounce other prayers. She must give up the god of her infancy, and put herself under the protection of a god whom she knows not. Let her not hope to remain faithful to the one while honouring the other; for in this religion it is an immutable principle that the same person cannot invoke two sacred fires or two series of ancestors.'[7] Fustel was probably influenced by the Roman law of marriage with *manus*, and the Roman family's cultivation of the genius and iuno of the paterfamilias and materfamilias respectively. Yet the Romans of the late Republic differed so markedly from the Athenians of the classical period in terms of the status of women and the laws and practise of marriage that to conflate the two

[7] Fustel de Coulanges, *Ancient City*, bk. 2, ch. 2, sect. 35. H. J. Rose, 'The Religion of a Greek Household', *Euphrosyne*, 1 (1957), 95–116, also conflates Greeks with Romans. He bases his generalization (p. 98) that 'in the household . . . [women] are the conspicuous worshippers' on a few bits of evidence, the most important of which are Cicero's letter to Terentia (*Fam*. 14. 4. 1) and Prudent. *Symm*. 1. 207–8. W. Burkert, *Greek Religion* (Oxford, 1984); originally published as *Griechische Religion der archaischen und klassischen Epoche* (Stuttgart, 1977), 255, goes further than the evidence he cites from Phot. *Bibl*., s.v. *zeugos hemionikon*, and Iambl. *Vit. Pyth*. 84 in stating that 'The bride is led from the hearth of her father's house to the new hearth which she will have to tend as mistress of the house,' and see n. 43 below.

societies (as the scholar is tempted to do when faced with the small amount of evidence available for either individually) creates a fiction. Moreover, the idea that an Athenian could have ties to only one family is based on the male model. The married woman's situation is both more complex and more difficult to interpret.[8] Aristotle does not deal with it at all in his discussions of Greek family structure. In the *Oeconomicus* Xenophon describes the steps by which a young bride gradually becomes a full-fledged member of her husband's family. Wife and husband worship his household gods together, but the wife's relationship to her father's domestic cults is not mentioned, because it is not relevant to the treatise. Law, custom, and myth-based literature[9] reflect the ambivalence of the married woman's placement in society, and this ambivalence is one of the themes of this book.

Inasmuch as the sojourn of brides and slaves was more tentative than that of a child born to the head of the household and they did not share the same blood, the ceremonies of incorporation were less elaborate and definitive than those that concerned infants, and we know less about them. Although in scholia and lexica, antiquarians record many diverse customs, no complete description of a classical Greek wedding is extant.[10]

It is often asserted that when they entered a new household, brides and slaves were introduced to the family cults;[11] but I have not found any evidence for this. A shower of dates, cakes, sweets, dried figs, and nuts marked the entrance of the bridegroom and bride when they arrived home after the wedding procession.[12] Such a shower also marked the admission of a new slave. The nature of the objects showered suggests that by their work both bride and slave were expected to bring prosperity and fruitfulness to their new household. The inclusion of the bridegroom indicates that the shower marked a

[8] On the married woman's obligations to the dead see Ch. 3.

[9] e.g. Soph. *Ant.* See recently Maitland, 'Dynasty and Family'.

[10] See further Sarah B. Pomeroy, 'Marriage: Greece', in Michael Grant and Rachel Kitzinger (eds.), *Civilization of the Ancient Mediterranean* (New York, 1988), 1333–42.

[11] e.g. n. 7 above.

[12] Schol. Aristoph. *Plut.* 768; Theopompus, frg. 15 (Kassel-Austin); Harp., s.v. *katachysmata*, Demos. 45. 74 (in Steph. 1); Hsch., s.v. *katachysmata*, etc. Robert F. Sutton, Jr.,'On the Classical Athenian Wedding: Two Red-Figure Loutrophoroi in Boston', in Robert F. Sutton, Jr. (ed.), *Daidalikon. Studies in Memory of Raymond V. Schoder, S.J.* (Wauconda, Ill., 1989), 331–59, esp. 351, argues that the *katachysmata* is depicted on a *loutrophoros hydria*, Boston Museum of Fine Arts, 10. 223, James Fund and Special Contribution; *ARV*^{2} 1277. 23. See also Oakley and Sinos, *Wedding in Ancient Athens*, esp. 34–5.

rite of passage, an introduction to a new role, for usually he was not being introduced to a new home.

As I have mentioned, the hearth and the family cults, like the rest of the household, belonged to the husband, but he might invite his wife or slaves or other persons to participate (Isae. 8. 15–16). For example, in Xenophon's *Oeconomicus* (7. 8) a husband and wife offer sacrifices together at home; but he initiates these, though she is often the leader in other activities. The Pseudo-Aristotelian *Oeconomica* notes that the Pythagoreans stated, and common custom directed, that the husband was not to harm his wife, but to treat her as if she were a suppliant raised from the hearth.[13] Literary references to the hearth are found, as in descriptions of the Amphidromia, but archaeological evidence for a fixed hearth in private homes is virtually nil. Practical considerations, however, make it likely that it was situated on the ground floor or even in the courtyard (see Ch. 1). Despite symbolic associations of women with the hearth,[14] in Athens it certainly was not upstairs in the women's quarters. (Hestia, goddess of the hearth, was not married.)

NAMING

Names were an indication of family membership. Children were identified by their own name and patronymic. Matronymics were not normally used, except in derogatory contexts such as accusations and curses. One would expect to find matronymics in the identification of slaves and illegitimate children, but there is little evidence for such nomenclature in the classical period. We do note, however, some use of matronymics without opprobrium in Ptolemaic Egypt (see Ch. 6).

The names of boys tied them securely to their ancestors, both paternal and, to a lesser extent, maternal.[15] It was usual to name

[13] Ps.-Arist. *Oec.* 1344a10–12; Iambl. *Vit. Pyth.* 84; likewise Phot., *Bib.*, s.v. *zeugos hemionikon e boeikon.*

[14] For these see Jean-Pierre Vernant, 'Hestia-Hermès. Sur l'espression religieuse de l'espace et du mouvement chez les Grecs', in *Mythe et pensée chez les Grecs*, rev. edn. (Paris, 1985), 155–201.

[15] e.g. Dem. 39. 27: a man named for his paternal grandfather; Isae. 2. 36. 3–4; Plato, *Rep.* 330B: a man named for his maternal grandfather; and Plato, *Lach.* 179A: a man named for his father, etc. For the adoption of names establishing fictitious affiliations see Ch. 4.

the first son after his paternal grandfather, and the second after his maternal grandfather.[16] A certain Sositheus relates that he named his sons after various male relatives in his wife's family and his own:

When I had claimed the mother of this boy in marriage and I had four sons and one daughter, I gave them names. The eldest I called Sosias after my own father, as was proper; the son born after him I named Eubulides, which was the name of the father of this boy's mother; the next one I named Menestheus, for Menestheus was related to my wife; and the youngest I named Callistratus which was the name of my maternal grandfather. (Ps.-Dem. 43. 74)

We note that Sositheus does not reveal either the name of his daughter or whether he named her after some relative.

Because rules of etiquette required the suppression of respectable women's names, at least while they were living, the quantity of evidence available for the study of their names is far less than that for men of the same social class. Moreover, because a married woman not only spent the major portion of her life with her husband's family, but also was often buried alone or with her husband's family or even anonymously, it is difficult to detect links between her name and those in her natal family.[17] The scanty evidence that is available indicates that, like a boy, a girl was given a name that was derived from those in the patriline, skipping a generation. Thus the first daughter would be named after her paternal grandmother (Isae. 3. 30). Very few families about whom we have evidence raised more than one daughter,[18] and even if more than one existed, rarely are the names of more than one known. Yet, as far as we can tell, for both women and men the same names, or names constructed on the same stem, are repeated in families through generations. Thus we have just noted that Sositheus, son of Sosias, named his first son Sosias. Some funerary stelae list two

[16] This practice continued into the Hellenistic period; e.g., according to Angeliki Petropoulou, *Beiträge zur Wirtschafts-und Gesellschaftsgeschichte Kretas in hellenistischer Zeit, Europäische Hochschulschriften,* Reihe. 3, Gesch. und ihre Hilfswissenschaften, vol. 240 (Frankfurt, 1985), esp. 180–1, among Cretans, the name of the paternal grandfather was used more than twice as often as the name of the maternal grandfather. See below for the repetition of names, or related names, in successive (rather than alternate) generations.

[17] On women's burials see Ch. 3.

[18] See p. 118. For a family with two daughters see Introduction, n. 33 above, perhaps a display of wealth and pride, and n. 62 below, a curse on (probably a non-citizen) family with two daughters.

homonymous women who must be relatives.[19] Some names, such as those built on the stem 'Demos', were common throughout the citizenry, but others were associated with particular families. Women in the family that supplied priestesses of Athena Polias sometimes bore a name beginning with 'Lys' (see Fig. 4). Agariste was a common name for an Alcmaeonid woman, and the name Coisyra was also used. Nevertheless, because there is so little evidence for women's history, the historian is stymied when trying to connect a specific Agariste with a particular historical event, or even in trying to determine whether there were three Alcmaeonids named Coisyra or only one.[20]

A daughter might be less securely incorporated into her natal family than a son, for some fifteen years after birth she would need to become part of her husband's family as well. Naming patterns appear to reflect the more tentative quality of girls' ties to their natal family. This conclusion may be drawn from a study of inscriptions recording the names of two generations of members of various families. Because they name only two generations, these inscriptions do not provide information for the pattern of repeating names in alternate generations mentioned above. A cursory examination of some 448 Athenian epitaphs from the *agora* yielded eighty-one in which the name of a father and his daughter were clearly identifiable.[21] In only eleven of these, or 14 per cent, was there any correlation[22]: for example, Cleo, daughter of Cleon;[23] Chairestrate, daughter of Chairephanes;[24] and Aristagora, daughter of Aristoteles.[25] These epitaphs, however, do not record the mother's name, so it is not possible to determine how often a woman's name reflected

[19] e.g., for two women named Phainarete on the stela of Euphranor, see Basileios X. Petrakos, *Ἀνασκαφὴ Ῥαμνοῦντος*, *Πρακτικά* (1975), 5–35, esp. 9.

[20] According to T. Leslie Shear, Jr., 'Koisyra. Three Women of Athens', *Phoenix*, 17 (1963), 99–112, there were three Almaeonid women named Coisyra, but see Davies, *APF* 9888X.

[21] Donald W. Bradeen, *The Athenian Agora*, 17. *Inscriptions: The Funerary Monuments* (Princeton, 1974), 35–90, nos. 31, 36, 54, 56, 59, 79, 80, 82, 88, 103, 112, 120, 121, 128, 132, 139, 141, 142, 145, 150, 153, 155, 157, 158, 162, 164, 166, 168, 172, 186, 192, 200, 213, 224, 231, 243, 258, 285, 304, 320, 329, 332, 333, 342; M. J. Osborne, 'Attic Epitaphs—A Supplement', *Anc. Soc.* 19 (1988), 5–60, nos. 4, 6, 7, 8, 11, 25, 26, 30, 32, 37, 38, 39, 41, 44, 46, 51, 56, 57, 60, 62, 66, 67, 69, 79, 82, and see n. 22 below.

[22] Bradeen, *Athenian Agora*, 17, nos. 69, 81, 135, 140, 151, 191, 194(?), 346, 357, and Osborne, 'Attic Epitaphs', nos. 35, 59.

[23] Osborne, 'Attic Epitaphs', 13, no. 35.

[24] Bradeen, *Athenian Agora*, 17, no. 81; for the family see also Davies, *APF* 11221.

[25] Bradeen, *Athenian Agora*, 17, no. 140.

her matrilineage. In the same group of epitaphs there were 153 in which the name of a father and son could be identified. In this sample the names of forty men, or 26 per cent, correlated with that of their father[26]: for example, Eubius, son of Eubius,[27] and Euxithius, son of Euxithius.[28] In short, naming patterns linked 26 per cent of men and 14 per cent of women with their fathers. Another study showed a rise in the number of men's names connected to the patrilineage at the end of the sixth century and from 466 to 401.[29] Gender difference in naming patterns continued through the Hellenistic period, where we find it at its most obvious in Ptolemaic Egypt: every royal male was named Ptolemy after the founder of the dynasty, even when there was more than one in a single generation. By contrast, the princesses were given a variety of names, including Arsinoë, Berenice, and Cleopatra.

GROUP MEMBERSHIPS: PHRATRY AND DEME

Family and kin groupings were fundamental to the political structure of the Greeks. Until the Hellenistic period, when states were not reluctant to grant citizenship to individuals whose parents had not also been citizens, the family regularly mediated between the individual and the political group. Citizens became members of a classical *polis* not as individuals, as they are in most modern states; rather, they first had to be accepted as members of a family. Thus, although ancient historians have traditionally given priority to political rather than social history, the public sphere cannot be divorced from the private.

[26] Bradeen, *Athenian Agora*, 17, 35–90, correlation: nos. 28, 35, 48, 51, 53, 65, 138, 147, 152, 159, 170, 179, 188, 189, 216, 218, 237, 252, 264, 289, 312, 324, 350, and see nn. 27, 28 below; no correlation: nos. 27, 29, 30, 34, 46, 52, 55, 59, 66, 72, 77, 81, 83, 84, 89, 91, 96, 101, 106, 113, 114, 125, 129, 133, 136, 148, 149, 160, 163–5, 167, 178, 183, 185, 187, 188, 197–9, 202, 205, 212, 225, 231, 233, 240, 241, 259–61, 263, 275, 277, 279, 284, 290–6, 298, 302, 303, 306–9, 314, 321, 323, 327, 341, 344, 345, 347, 353–5, 363, 364. Osborne, 'Attic Epitaphs', correlation: nos. 2, 9, 10, 15–17, 19, 23, 47, 59, 63, 68, 70, 80, 85; no correlation: nos. 1, 3, 12, 14, 20–2, 24, 27, 29, 33, 42, 45, 48, 49, 52–4, 58, 65, 71–9, 86.

[27] Third to second century: Bradeen, *Athenian Agora*, 17, no. 47.

[28] Fourth century: ibid. no. 174. Naming for the father became more common in the Roman period, in imitation of the Roman practice.

[29] Mark Golden, 'Names and Naming at Athens: Three Studies', *EMC* 30 (1986), 245–69, esp. 262–4, explains the first increase as a reaction against Cleisthenes' imposition of the use of demotics, and the second as an assertion of familial solidarity in the face of fragmentation owing to the stress of war.

After a baby was accepted as a member of his father's family, he needed to be accepted by his father's quasi- or pseudo-family. Membership in phratry ('brotherhood') and deme ('local ward') was inherited from the father. Members of the phratry were all considered descendants of the same legendary male ancestor; no female ancestor was cited. Enrolment in the father's phratry was certainly a desirable, if not absolutely essential, step towards becoming a full-fledged Athenian citizen.

The father introduced and enrolled his baby in his phratry as being legitimate and his own (see Isae. 6. 64, 8. 19), and presented him at the festival of the Apaturia held annually by his phratry.[30] Some Byzantine lexicons mention the introduction and enrolment of both boys and girls; perhaps this occurred in the Hellenistic period or in cities other than Athens. Classical sources, which must be considered more reliable, inasmuch as they are contemporaneous, refer to the enrolment of males.[31] The name 'phratry' implies that women were peripheral.[32] Only one text indicates that a father had the option of letting his phratry know that he had a daughter, but even she was not enrolled.[33] The speaker in Isae. 3. 73 alludes to the possibility of introducing (*eisagonti*) a daughter to a phratry if she was destined to be her father's *epikleros* and eventually to produce a son who was to be enrolled in the phratry as the adopted son of his grandfather. The speaker in Isaeus 3 is describing an event which did not occur, contentiously asking why a certain father did not introduce his daughter into his phratry, and the case is special inasmuch as the girl was potentially an *epikleros*.[34] The decree of the Demotionid phratry, the only extant complete decree describing admission, men-

[30] See further S. D. Lambert, *The Phratries of Attica* (Ann Arbor, 1993), 143–61.

[31] Poll. 8. 107, s.v. *phratores*, and the *Suda*, s.v. *Apatouria*, pp. 265–6 (Adler) mention both boys and girls. Sadao Ito, 'The Enrolment of Athenian Phratries', *Legal History Review*, 31 (1981), 35–60, with English summary, 7–8, rejects Pollux's statement that the *gamelia* was sacrificed by *phrateres* when girls reached puberty. In the English summary Ito does not cite any evidence to substantiate his suggestion that girls were introduced to *phrateres* at the first Apatouria after they were born. See also n. 37 below.

[32] Although the Greeks used the word *phrater* for phratry member, cognates in other Indo-European languages mean 'brother': see further Lambert, *Phratries of Attica*, 269.

[33] The Byzantine scholars were probably influenced by this text: see ibid. 179.

[34] The girl's adoptive father had no sons; therefore, upon his death she would become an *epikleros*. On Isae. 3, see A. Ledl, 'Das attische Burgerrecht und die Frauen, I', *WS* 29 (1907), 173–227, esp. 173–96. Ledl argues that women were not registered. Susan G. Cole, 'The Social Function of Rituals of Maturation', *ZPE* 55 (1985), 233–44, esp. 237 n. 26, follows Ledl.

tions the introduction of a son, but does not refer to daughters.[35] Rules, and whether they were observed, varied from phratry to phratry (cf. Isae. 7. 30, 8. 15). In his edition of the scholia to Aristophanes, *Acharnenses*, 146, Dindorf[36] cited the *Suda* (s.v. *meiagogein*), and expanded the Greek text so as to give the impression that both girls and boys were inscribed in the phratry lists. This emendation, which became a crucial piece of evidence for the registration of girls, is now properly omitted in Wilson's edition.[37] In *Laws* (785A) Plato mentions the enrolment of women in phratries. He is not describing Athens, however, but rather an idealized state in which women do participate to a limited extent in politics. Inasmuch as a phratry was a 'brotherhood' with such political responsibilities as reviewing the qualifications of prospective citizens, it is difficult to conceptualize why a girl would be admitted or even how membership might be exercised. For boys, by contrast, admission to the phratry, along with deme membership, was the principal route to full membership in the *polis*. Age, birth, and sex criteria for membership in the phratry were the same as those for deme membership.[38] Adopted sons were also admitted to citizenship after scrutiny by the adoptive father's phratry.[39]

Yet, according to a new historical model, the phratries of classical Athens were not a survival from a tribal society; nor were they groups of blood-relations. Rather, they were pseudo kinship groups of men only (see Ch. 1).[40] Indeed, if the *phrateres* were actually kinsmen related by blood or marriage, why would it be necessary to introduce them formally to one another at festivals under state authority?[41]

[35] *IG* II[2] 1237 = *SIG*[3] 921 = *LSCG* 19, l. 110. On this document see further below and Charles W. Hedrick, Jr., *The Decrees of the Demotionidai*, American Classical Studies, 22 (Atlanta, 1990). Women are not named in other extant phratry lists: *IG* II–III. 2. 2, 2344–5.

[36] P. 346, ll. 5–7.

[37] Nigel G. Wilson, *Prolegomena de Comoedia Scholia in Acharnenses, Equites, Nubes*, 1B: *Scholia in Aristophanis Acharnenses* (Groningen, 1975), p. 29, 146b *ad loc.* Lambert, *Phratries of Attica* (414), uses Dübner's edition of the scholia, but nevertheless (20, 37, 178–88, etc.) comes to the same conclusion as I have, that women were not phratry members.

[38] On women's lack of demotics, or deme name, i.e. evidence of citizenship, see pp. 81, 127. See further Sadao Ito, 'Phrateres as Athenian Citizens', *JCS* 31 (1983), 1–18, with English summary, 149–50, who argues that legitimacy, as well as descent from Athenian citizens on both sides, were necessary, and Ch. 1 n. 46 above.

[39] See further Rubinstein, *Adoption in iv. Century Athens*, 19.

[40] See e.g. J. K. Davies, 'Religion and the State', in *Cambridge Ancient History*, 2nd edn., vol. 4 (Cambridge, 1988), 368–88, esp. 380.

[41] For similar arguments distinguishing the clan from the family, see Wesley E. Thompson, 'Harpokration on γεννῆται', *Hermes*, 11 (1983), 118–21.

Family members who live in the same city generally know one another, and even distant kinsmen have occasional contact in person or through hearsay. Like demes, phratries were part of the political structure of the mature *polis* traceable back to the Cleisthenic reorganization.[42] This view makes the pre-Cleisthenic period more antipathetic to historical analysis, and consequently it is even more difficult to detect change over time from the earlier period. Nevertheless, I prefer the new historical model, not only because it provides a better explanation of the development of the Athenian *polis*, but because I have found it to be more consistent with what is known about women's function as citizens and with their separation from men who were not their close relatives.

Using the old evolutionary framework based on actual family relationships, scholars had been obliged to carve out a niche for women (see Ch. 3). Nevertheless, the only way this framework was able to accommodate women was by importing ideas about early Roman history. Roman historians have now discarded most of these notions, but the Greek versions persist (see above). The revisionist view of the phratry has important implications for the placement of women in the family and the city. It is clear that Athenian women had

[42] See Denis Roussel, *Tribu et Cité*, Annales Littéraires de l'Université de Besançon, 23 (Paris, 1976), esp. 144; F. Bourriot, *Recherches sur la nature du genos*. Étude d'histoire sociale athénienne. Périodes archaïque et classique (Thèse de Lille; Paris, 1976), esp. 518–20, 622–62, *et passim*. Adopting Roussel's and Bourriot's interpretations, or giving them serious consideration are: M. I. Finley, *Ancient History, Evidence and Models* (New York, 1987), 90–3; C. Meier, *Die Entstehung des Politischen bei den Griechen* (Frankfurt, 1980), 96–9, and Richard C. Smith, 'The Clans of Athens and the Historiography of the Archaic Period', *EMC* 29 (1985), 51–61. Anthony Andrewes, 'Philochoros and Phratries', *JHS* 81 (1961), 1–15, had argued that phratries were not a survival from pre-Mycenaean times, but had been created in the aristocratic world of the Homeric period. The Greeks did not use the term *phrater* to refer to a blood-brother, and members of phratries were not kinsmen. In this context Aristotle's report in *Ath. Pol.* 21. 6 that Cleisthenes left phratries untouched is so brief that we can only speculate that he meant either that phratries were not abolished because they were not loci of aristocratic or anti-democratic sentiment but merely administrative structures, or, as concerns the present argument, that women were not enrolled even before Cleisthenes. On the apparent conflict between *Ath. Pol.* 21. 6 and *Pol.* 1319b19–27, see Rhodes, *Commentary,* 258. Emily Kearns, 'Change and Continuity in Religious Structures after Cleisthenes', in P. A. Cartledge and F. D. Harvey (eds.), *Crux* (London, 1985), 189–207, argues that the phratries continued to be constituted as they had been before Cleisthenes. Kearns, however, bases her view that women were members of phratries on schol. Ar. *Ach.* 146 (Dindorf): on the current status of this testimony see n. 37 above. On the revised history of the *genos* see Ch. 3. Lambert, *Phratries of Attica*, 268, argues that the phratry dates from Mycenaean times.

no place in purely political institutions. Like Spartan girls, Athenians were not subjected to public scrutiny. The father alone vouched for his daughter's citizenship. Thus in Pseudo-Demosthenes 59.122 the speaker distinguishes between male and female progeny: 'This is what marriage is: when a man engenders children and presents his sons to the *phrateres* and demesmen and gives his daughters as being his own in marriage to husbands.'

As a corollary of the discussion about a married woman's family membership, some scholars have assumed, without justification, that a girl belonged to her father's phratry, and have then debated whether she remained in it throughout her lifetime, as a boy did, or whether she was transferred to her husband's upon marriage.[43] Yet if the father did not introduce his baby daughter to his phratry, it is even less likely that the bridegroom introduced his wife. The notion that a wife was introduced to her husband's phratry at the *gamelia* ('marriage feast') is not supported by the most trustworthy ancient sources.[44] The source problems are similar to those encountered in the description of the Amphidromia (see above). Ancient scholia and lexicons disagree among themselves. Harpocration (s.v. *gamelia* [Keaney]) reports that Didymus stated that Phanedemus's definition of *gamelia* was erroneous (*FGrH* 325 F 17). Although Didymus reported that Phanedemus had said that wives were introduced to the phratry at the *gamelia*, he had said no such thing. Furthermore, Didymus had not been able to cite any evidence from the orators. In fact, Isaeus (3. 76, 79, 8. 18) and Demosthenes (57. 43, 69) speak of presenting the marriage feast to the phratry (*gamelia*) on behalf of (*huper*) a wife.[45] In other words, the *gamelia* served as an occasion at which

[43] On the debate see Max Collignon, 'Matrimonium 1. Grèce', *Dar.-Sag.* (Paris, 1877–1919), ii, pt. 2, 1639–54, esp. 1642, 1644. Collignon decides that the wife remains in her original phratry.

[44] J. D. Mikalson, *Athenian Popular Religion* (Chapel Hill, NC, and London, 1983), 85; Burkert, *Greek Religion*, 255; and Mark Golden, '"Donatus" and Athenian Phratries', *CQ* 35 (1985), 9–13, retain the notion that the bridegroom introduced the bride to his phratry, *contra* Collignon, 'Matrimonium 1. Grèce', 1642, 1644–5; John Gould, 'Law, Custom, and Myth: Aspects of the Social Position of Women in Classical Athens', *JHS* 100 (1980), 38–59, esp. 40–2; R. Sealey, *The Athenian Republic. Democracy or the Rule of Law?* (University Park, Pa., 1987), 16–19; and Davies, 'Religion and the State', 380. P. Stengel, 'Γαμηλία', *RE* vii. 1 (Stuttgart, 1910), cols. 691–2, asserts incorrectly that the *gamelia* was an offering at the Apaturia when a son was introduced to his phratry. The latter notion is based on *Anecd.* Gr. (Bekk.) 1. 228. 5 and *Etym. Magn.* (s.v.), among the least reliable of all the sources on the *gamelia*. See also n. 46 below.

[45] Sim. Poll. 8. 107, s.v. *phratores.*

a marriage was made public and created witnesses to the legitimacy of the children born as a result of it. In view of the obscurity of respectable women that I have mentioned briefly above, it is extremely unlikely that a bride was introduced at the *gamelia* which was apparently a festive party of the 'brotherhood'.[46] The Athenian bride, at the age of 14, had ideally spent her previous years under careful supervision, so that she might see and hear and speak as little as possible (cf. Xen. *Oec.* 7. 5). According to the most reasonable estimates, the average phratry consisted of several hundred members.[47] If an entire phratry knew a woman, such familiarity would be prima-facie evidence of her lack of respectability, and if she were introduced to a series of phratries (her father's, each husband's at subsequent marriages),[48] she would be quite notorious. It is more likely that in the classical period the bridegroom announced that he was marrying the daughter of so-and-so, and did not specify the woman's name but gave the name and demotic (deme name) of his bride's father, as in the decree of the Demotionid phratry concerning the introduction of sons (*IG* II^2 1237, ll. 119–20): 'let a deposition be made to the phratriarch . . . of his name, patronymic, demotic, and the name and demotic of his mother's father.'[49] Moreover, the consequence of the revisionist view that the *phrateres* were not relatives at all, but only pseudo-kin is that it is even more unlikely that a

[46] According to Poll. 3. 42 the *gamelia* was a sacrifice; according to Hsch., s.v., a banquet; according to Harp. (s.v.) (Keaney) and *Suda* (s.v.), p. 507 (Adler) a donation (probably for a banquet).

[47] Roussel, *Tribu et Cité*, 143, suggests that the size varied from several dozen to several hundred. M. A. Flower, '*IG* II^2 2344 and the Size of Phratries in Classical Athens', *CQ* 35 (1985), 232–5, esp. 234, gives an average of 133, and Lambert, *Phratries of Attica*, 19–20, estimates between 140 and 1,000. The statement of Aristotle, *Ath. Pol.* fr. 3, that there were 12 phratries would indicate far larger memberships, but Aristotle must be incorrect: see Rhodes, 69.

[48] So Golden, '"Donatus"', 13 n. 26. Lambert, *Phratries of Attica*, 237, also believes that a bride was presented to her husband's phratry at the *gamelia*.

[49] Cf. a similar reference to the mother's father in the scrutiny of archons mentioned by Arist. *Ath. Pol.* 55. 3 in describing a procedure that also includes naming the mother. Despite the importance of descent from two citizens after the passage of Pericles' citizenship law, in other texts such as private orations there does not seem to be any less reluctance to give the actual name of a respectable woman in public in the classical period while she was still alive. Certainly there was a change in the treatment of respectable women in the Hellenistic period, and their names were revealed while they were alive: see Pomeroy, *Women in Hellenistic Egypt*, 42–4. This change is perhaps reflected in Arist. *Ath. Pol.* 55. 3. In any case, in view of the normal female life span, the mother of an archon (who was apparently at least 30) would have died before her son was old enough to hold office.

husband would introduce his bride to them. In two speeches where it would have been useful to call as witnesses a woman's *phrateres* (had such existed), this step is not taken. A man whose citizen status had been challenged partially on the allegation that his mother was not a citizen did not call his mother's *phrateres* as witnesses, but he did call *phrateres* of his mother's male kin.[50] Another man who had to verify the identity of his mother and prove that she was married to his father argued that his father had offered the *gamelia* to his phratry upon the marriage, and had subsequently introduced the speaker and his brother as his sons to his phratry (Isae. 8. 18–20).

It seems likely that females were even more marginal to the classificatory system of phratries than they were to deme identification, for the latter at least had some implications for women (see Ch. 3). Before the Peloponnesian War most demesmen had residences in their demes, and many continued to do so in the fourth century.[51] Thus wives of the members of a deme knew each other well enough to be able to select one of their number to be in charge of the Thesmophoria, an annual festival of Demeter. The Thesmophoria were celebrated by respectable women only, and acceptance of a woman by other women in the neighbourhood was better verification of her respectability than the testimony of men would have been. Isaeus (8. 19–20) refers to these women as the wives of demesmen, not as members of the deme in their own right. In her epitaph a woman is often identified by her father's name and his demotic. By contrast, a woman is not referred to simply as a wife or daughter of a man who belongs to a particular phratry.

A final consideration in discussing women's relationship to the deme and phratry system is the extent to which these institutions were based, at least in the time of Cleisthenes, on residence and property ownership in a particular territory.[52] Because women did not own land in Attica, and marriages potentially could involve

[50] Ps.-Dem. 57. 67–9. After Pericles' citizenship law of 451/50 it was necessary to prove descent from parents who were both citizens: see Ch. 1. The speaker would be able to prove that his mother was descended from two citizens by showing that the *phrateres* of his mother's male kinsmen had accepted her father as one of their number and been present at the *gamelia* when his marriage to her mother was announced.

[51] Dem. 57. 10 for demesmen of Halimous residing in their deme, and see further Whitehead, *Demes of Attica*, 353–8, and Rosivach, 'Distribution of Population'.

[52] Recently Charles W. Hedrick, Jr., 'Phratry Shrines of Attica and Athens', *Hesperia*, 60 (1990), 241–68, argued that there was a geographic relationship between demes and phratry shrines.

drastic changes in residence for them,[53] they could not be intrinsic to a classificatory system based on geography.

The girl's membership in her natal family was declared only at the Amphidromia in the presence of close friends and relatives, whereas a series of ceremonies at the phratry level made the boy's family membership indelible in the minds of a large group of men. We have also observed that naming patterns are more likely to tie boys than girls to their ancestors. Indeed, it is precisely the lack of explicit identity in her natal family that permits a bride to leave it and join another. Nevertheless, she is not incorporated as a permanent member of her husband's family, for if she is divorced or widowed, she may join the family of another husband or return to her family of birth.

The fact that women were not members of phratry or deme not only contributed to their mobility, but also has important implications for historiography, inasmuch as it contributes to women's obscurity. Two of the most useful books on the Greek family published in the second half of the twentieth century are J. K. Davies's *Athenian Propertied Families* and J. K. Lacey's *The Family in Classical Greece*.[54] Recognizing that women are hidden in the family context Lacey wrote a separate chapter entitled 'Women in Democratic Athens'. Davies's work includes elaborate genealogical charts frequently showing descent directly through males (e.g. Fig. 7). Sometimes male kin on the mother's side are known; the mother, however, is not identifiable by name, but only as a daughter, wife, and mother. Davies includes such a woman on his charts as *hede* ('this female'). The charts also reflect the Athenian practice of regarding the married woman as an invisible link between two families of men. Of course, we know more about the élite than about less fortunate members of Greek society, but upper-class women were those who could best afford to avoid the public eye.

[53] The deme relationship was a less significant factor than others in the choice of spouses: see Osborne, *Demos*, 127–37.

[54] See Introduction, nn. 3 and 37 above.

HEREDITARY SHAME AND HONOUR

Curses

In the popular view, the pollution of guilt and the obligation to take revenge was not confined to an individual, but rather spread to his or her social group. Collective curses on particular families appear not only in myth-based literature, but in historical texts. Some curses are public in origin, others private. Curses on a malefactor and his descendants served as a common civic sanction. For example, Andocides (1. 31) reminded the jurors at his trial that if they broke the oath they had sworn to decide fairly, a mighty curse would fall on them and their children. The curse on the Alcmaeonids is the best-known public curse. It lasted over two centuries, affected thousands of family members, and is well documented.[55] The saga of the Alcmaeonids (like the allusions to maternal kin in Pindar described below) demonstrates that, at least in the case of an aristocratic and illustrious family, matrilineage as well as patrilineage had far-reaching implications in politics and society. The curse originated *c.*632 with the conspiracy of Cylon, who wanted to establish a tyranny in Athens. Cylon and his supporters secured asylum on the Acropolis. Magistrates referred to as the 'presidents of the naukraroi' (Hdt 5. 71. 2) or archons (Thuc. 1. 126. 8) promised the suppliants that they would not be killed, but they broke their promise. Megacles, an Alcmaeonid, was an archon, and his family was subsequently blamed for the sacrilege. Four generations after the killing of the Cylonians, seven hundred *oikiai* ('families') had inherited the responsibility.[56] Considering the demographic and reproductive regimes postulated for Athens,[57] so large a number is inconceivable unless female as well as male descendants were included. Even if husbands of Alcmaeonid women were technically free from the curse, political rivals or ordinary folk associated them with it, and would assert that they were contaminated. It is likely that Peisistratus chose not to engage in procreational sex with the daughter of Megacles (Hdt. 1. 61) not only because he already had heirs, but also because he wanted to avoid

[55] On the tradition see, most recently, the sophisticated analysis in Rosalind Thomas, *Oral Tradition and Written Record in Classical Athens* (Cambridge, 1989), esp. 144–54, 272–81.

[56] Arist. *Ath. Pol.* 20. 3; the term 'epistia' in Her. 5. 72. 1 has a similar connotation.

[57] Intro. nn. 20–1 above, and Ch. 3 nn. 66–7 below.

having children who would inherit the curse. Xanthippus married Agariste, a niece of Cleisthenes sometime before 490. On an ostracon that has been associated with his ostracism in 484 he is called 'accursed'.[58] For a politician, one of the most dire consequences of a curse would be expulsion from the city. The tragedy of Oedipus the King, produced soon after 430, demonstrates that a curse on a leader pollutes his city (Soph. *OT* 25–30). Political rivals certainly identified Pericles, the 'first citizen' of that time, as an Alcmaeonid, for his mother was a member of that lineage (Thuc. 1.127).

Curses were not only large-scale and public. Often enough private individuals cursed their enemies.[59] Such imprecations included not only their target, but also the accursed person's entire household and descendants, so the suffering of the principal victim might be increased by witnessing the fate of his or her kin.[60] For example, Diocles laid a curse on a group of people: 'All of these I consign (inscribed) in lead and in wax and in water (?) and to unemployment and to destruction and to bad reputation and to defeat and in tombs—both these and all the children and wives who belong to them.'[61] The following imprecation was directed against a woman, and secondarily against her male relatives. The principal victim is identified by a matronymic: 'I am sending a letter to the daimons and to Persephone, and deliver (to them) Tibitis (daughter of) Choirine, who wronged me, (and her) daughter, husband, and three children, two female and one male.'[62]

[58] 'This ostracon states that Xanthippus, son of Arriphon and a curse of the prytaneis, has been especially harmful.' See further A. Raubitschek, 'The Ostracism of Xanthippos', *AJP* 51 (1947), 257–62. A. Wilhelm, 'Zum Ostrakismos des Xanthippos, des Vaters des Perikles', *AAWW* 86 (1949), 237–44, suggests that *aleitron* is genitive plural: 'This ostracon states that Xanthippus, son of Arriphon, is the most guilty of the accursed prytaneis.'

[59] See further Christopher A. Faraone and Dirk Obbink (eds.), *Magika Hiera* (New York, 1991).

[60] Like the victim of curses, the breaker of oaths brings his or her family, even those yet unborn, into peril: Lys. 12. 10, 32. 13; Dem. 19, 23. 67, 24. 151, 29. 26, 33, 54, 54. 40; Ps.-Dem. 59. 10; Andoc. 1. 31, 98, 126, etc.

[61] *DTA* 55, Attica, original location not known, late fourth century: see further John Gager, *Curse Tablets and Binding Spells from the Ancient World* (New York, 1992), 158–9, no. 64.

[62] *DTA* 102, Athens, original location not known, fourth century: see further Gager, *Curse Tablets*, 201–2, no. 104.

Atimia

The penalty for a heinous crime against the state could be not only a hereditary curse, as in the case of the Alcmaeonids, but also disenfranchisement. In Athens the punishment imposed on any man found guilty of treason, or of attempting to subvert the democracy, or to establish a tyranny, or to abolish certain laws was *kathapax atimia* ('immediate loss of civic rights') for himself and his descendants.[63] They could no longer be active citizens, for they lost their rights to participate and speak in the assembly, to initiate decrees, to serve as a juror or prosecutor, to hold a magistracy, to give legal evidence, to enter sanctuaries, and to enter the *agora*. All women were barred from most of these activities anyway; the last three restrictions, however, would seem to pertain to female descendants as well as to males. Though there is no evidence that the restrictions were enforced against specific women, as we have seen in the case of the Alcmaeonids, women might transmit liabilities to their spouses and descendants. Men who were convicted of bribery and theft (probably in connection with public duties) were also punished with hereditary *atimia*.[64] *Atimia* was imposed upon persons who owed money to the state, and devolved upon their descendants when the original debtor died.[65] Only in the case of debtors to the state could the heirs avoid the penalty by paying the debt, or by being adopted out of the family. The consequence of the latter dodge was the extinction of the family and its ancestral cults.[66] Such extinction would constitute the worst of all punishments, and would penalize not only the condemned man and his descendants, but his forebears as well (see Ch. 3).

Honours that Run in the Family

> Fortunate and glorious in the eyes of the wise is the man who with victorious hands or with the prowess of his feet has won

[63] Ps.-Plut. *Mor.* 834A specifies both legitimate and illegitimate descendants. See also Idomeneus *FGrH* 338, F 1; Arist. *Ath. Pol.* 16, 10; *SEG* xii. 26–7, no. 87, ll. 20–1 (337/36); Dem. 13. 62, 23. 62; *IG* I² 45. 3–4, 20–5; and see further Mogens Herman Hansen, *Apagoge, Endeixis and Ephegesis against Kakourgoi, Atimoi, and Pheugontes* (Odense, 1976), 61–3, 71–4, 81, 88–9.

[64] And. 1. 74; Dem. 21. 113; see further Hansen, *Apagoge, Endeixis*, 73.

[65] Demos. 22. 33–4, 24. 201, 43. 58, 58. 1–2, 16, 19; Lys. 20. 34; Isae. 10. 17 and fr. 129; *Suda*, s.v. *Aristogeiton*, p. 355 (Adler); cf. Hyp. fr. 139; and see Ch. 5 on Gylon.

[66] Isae. 10. 17; *Anecd. Bekk.* i. 247. 10–19; and see further Glotz, *La Solidarité*, 541–4.

> the greatest prizes by courage and strength, and who, while still living, has seen his youthful son duly win Pythian crowns
>
> Pindar, *Pyth.* 10. 22–6

Family traditions of excellence in athletics were significant in the creation and commemoration of athletes.[67] In the present discussion we will look at families which produced more than one victor in successive or alternate generations. (For hereditary professional honours such as priesthoods see Ch. 4.) The ancient sources, both textual and archaeological, indicate that families which boasted of athletic success were interested in drawing attention to themselves as a group of kinsmen with a habit of winning. In his descriptions of monuments erected at Olympia by victors, Pausanias (6. 1–18) gives the names of many families; these are especially prominent when he notes statues and monuments commemorating dyads of fathers and sons. The sequence in Pausanias's narrative indicates that the monuments of family members were grouped together within the larger space occupied by monuments erected by other members of their *polis*. For example, the statue of the famous boxer Diagoras of Rhodes stood at Olympia in the midst of statues of his three sons and two grandsons (Paus. 6. 7. 1 and see below).

Epinician *Odes* of Pindar and Bacchylides draw attention to additional victories won by the family of a champion whose recent achievement is the immediate inspiration for a poem. Pindar describes one such group as an *euathlos genea* ('a family successful in contests', *Isthm.* 6. 3). He is particularly diligent in mentioning the victorious ancestors of the athlete whose victory he is commemorating. In so doing, the poet reveals aristocratic and conservative tendencies; but he is also being practical when he not only praises the young athlete, but also commends the athlete's father who commissioned the ode.

In making birth the principal factor, Pindar gives an accurate, though incomplete description of the creation of athletes. Physical stature and innate aptitude certainly must have been factors in the manifestation of athletic prowess in more than one member of a family. Pindar mentions the gigantic size of the boxer Diagoras (*Ol.* 7. 15 and *Schol.* i. 197). Diagoras was four cubits, five fingers tall (approx. 75 inches/191 cm.), and his son Damagetus was four

[67] For honorary decrees including the eldest descendant, see the decrees for Demosthenes and Demochares: p. 181 below.

cubits (approx. 70 inches/178 cm.).[68] Blood-relations most often, though not invariably, excel in the same sort of event. Large size and heavy weight were advantageous in combat sports such as boxing, wrestling, and the pancratium (a combination of the two). Both Pindar and Pausanias draw attention to several sets of kinsmen who were notably successful in these events.[69] Furthermore, though the testimony of inscriptions is often laconic, some expend a few extra words to reveal a spark of enthusiasm for brothers who were victors in the same event (the pancratium). An inscription of *c.*370–360 from the Athenian Acropolis announces the victories of two brothers:

Diophanes, son of Empedion: victory at the Isthmus.
Two Athenians, sons of Empedion, were victorious: Diophanes in the boys' pancratium and his older brother Stephanus. They displayed the strength of their hands.[70]

Athens honoured Olympic victors by granting them the right to dine at public expense at the Prytaneion (Plato, *Apl.* 36D). In addition, the fact that an inscription like that of Diophanes and Stephanus was erected on the Acropolis indicates that the state was enhancing, if not usurping yet again, the privileges of the victors' family. The traditional focus on the family continued well into the fourth century. Epigraphical evidence from Delphi, dated to 336–332, records various victories in the pancratium and other combat events at all four major festivals of three brothers from Pharsalus: Hagias, Telemachus, and Agelaus.[71]

Sometimes it was necessary for orphaned young men to claim an athletic predecessor from the mythical past. Pindar's *Olympian* 8 celebrated the victory of Alcimedon of Aegina in the boys' wrestling

[68] According to Gallant, *Risk and Survival*, 69, the average height of men in classical Greece was 169.8 cm, and of women 156.3 cm. On Diagoras and his family see below.

[69] e.g. Alcaenetus of Lepreon had been victorious in the men's boxing. In 424 his son Hellanicus was successful in the boys' boxing, and in 420 another son, Theantus, also followed suit (Paus. 6. 7. 8). Cleander, son of Telesarchus of Aegina, was victorious in the boys' pancratium (Pind. *Isthm.* 8). Cleander's cousin Nicocles, a son of Telesarchus's brother, had been victorious as a boxer in the Isthmian games (Pind. *Isthm.* 8.62–7, and *Schol.* iii, 278 [Drachmann]). *Nemean* 11 celebrates Aristagoras of Tenedos, who was outstanding in wrestling and in the pancratium. He and his family had won sixteen victories in these events (19–21).

[70] *IG* II–III^2 3125 = L. Moretti, *Iscrizioni Agonistische Greche* (Rome, 1953), 56–7, no. 22, who observes that Stephanus, who is referred to as 'progonos', may be Diophanes' grandfather rather than his brother.

[71] *SIG*^{3} I 274 = Moretti, *Iscrizioni*, 68–75, no. 29.

(*Schol.* i. 236). His father and uncle were dead, but his grandfather was still alive. His brother Timosthenes had been victorious at Nemea (15–18), and he had asked Pindar to write the ode honouring his younger brother. This victory was the sixth for the Blepsiads, who claimed descent from the hero Ajax (75–6), who was renowned for his prowess in wrestling (Hom. *Il.* 707–37). Pindar also had to comb the remote past to create a list of predecessors for Theaeus of Argos, whose victories in wrestling he enumerated in *Nemean* 10. Two maternal ancestors of Theaeus had won chariot victories, but as ancestors who excelled in combat sports Pindar cited Castor and Polydeuces.

Specialization is apparent in one of the most illustrious and successful families. All the victories of the family of Diagoras of Rhodes were in combat events. Details about them are known through archaeological, literary, and epigraphical evidence.[72] Diagoras himself won the men's boxing in 464. His oldest son Damagetus was victorious in the pancratium in both 452 and 448; and in 448 Acusilaus, another son of Diagoras, won in boxing.[73] In 432, 428, and 424, Dorieus, the youngest son of Diagoras, was victorious as a boxer and pancratiast. Dorieus won thirty-six victories.[74] Like his father, he was a *Periodonikes* ('winner of the crown at all four major pan-Hellenic festivals in one Olympic cycle' (i.e. 'grand-slam')) at least once. In 404 two grandsons of Diagoras won victories at Olympia in the same sport in which their grandfather had excelled: Peisirodus, a son of Diagoras's daughter, appropriately named Pherenice ('Victory-Carrier'), was victorious in the boys' boxing, and Eucles, son of Diagoras's daughter Callipateira, won in boxing. Eucles' father was Callianax, but the name of Peisirodus's father is not even known, doubtless because the affiliation to the maternal grandfather was exploited as being more significant. A

[72] See Pind. *Ol.* 7; *Schol.*; Paus. 6. 7. 1–7; J. G. Frazer, *Pausanias's Description of Greece* (London, 1898; repr. New York, 1965), iv. 25–9; Cic. *Tusc.* 1. 46. 111; Dio Chrys. 31. 126; Ael. *VH* 10. 1, and nn. 73 and 74 below.

[73] An inscription recording two victories on the same day may refer to the victories of the two brothers (*SIG* III³ 1057. 5). For the story see also *Schol. Ol.* 7 (= Arist. fr. 569R); Plut. *Pel.* 34; Cic. *Tusc.* 1. 46, 111; and Paus. 6. 7. 3.

[74] Three Olympian, eight Isthmian, seven Nemean, four Pythian, four at the Panathenaia, four at the Asclepieia in Epidaurus, three at the Lycaea in Arcadia, and three at the Hecatomboea at Argos. For Dorieus see Thuc. 3. 8. 1, 8. 35. 1, 8. 84; Xen. *Hell.* 1. 1; Diod. Sic. 13. 45; *AP* 13. 11; *SIG* I³ 82 = Moretti, *Iscrizioni*, 57–60, no. 23; Arist. *Rh.* 1357a19–21; and see further M. N. Tod, 'Greek Record-Keeping and Record-Breaking', *CQ* 43 (1949), 105–12, esp. 106.

daughter of Diagoras became the first woman who was a spectator at the Olympic games. According to an anecdote, she disguised herself as a gymnastic trainer (Paus. 5. 6. 8). This ruse suggests that she thought she could get away with it, perhaps because she had a masculine physique and, like her ancestors, was taller than the average woman. When she was detected, she gained admission on the grounds that she was daughter, sister, aunt, and mother of Olympic victors.

As the sketch of Diagoras's family indicates, in their desire to boast of as many victories as possible, families also claimed maternal kinsmen, though legally they would have been members of other *oikoi*. Of course, Greek scientists had no concept of genes *per se* (see below), but they did not ignore the mother's contribution to the creation of athletic victors in so far as she transmitted her male kinsmen's talents to her son. The genetic legacy is apparent in that victors are often succesful in the same events as their maternal kinsmen. This heritage should be attributed in part to similarities in physique and aptitude. The quotation from *Nemean* 5 at the beginning of this section alludes to maternal kin. Pindar *(Nem.* 5) and Bacchylides (13) both commemorate a victory of Pytheas, son of Lampon of Aegina, in the boys' pancratium.[75] Later, Phylacidas, another son of Lampon who was probably younger than Pytheas, was victorious twice in the pancratium at the Isthmian games and once at Nemea *(Isthm.* 5, 6 and *Schol.* iii. 258). The boys' maternal uncle Euthymenes had won the same event once at the Isthmian games (*Nem.* 5. 41–2, *Isthm.* 6. 55–62, and *Schol.* iii. 258). Their maternal grandfather Themistius had been victorious in boxing and the pancratium in the games of Asclepius at Epidaurus (*Nem.* 5. 50–4; see also *Isthm.* 5. 55). Neither their father nor any other paternal ancestor had been a champion. Lampon is not mentioned except as a patronymic in *Nemean* 5, but in *Isthmian* 6. 66–73 Pindar praises him for serving as an example of the benefits of hard work to his sons, and both Bacchylides and Pindar draw attention to his virtuous character. Another wrestler, Aristomenes of Aegina, followed 'in the tracks of his mother's brothers' who had both won victories in wrestling (Pind. *Pyth.* 8. 35–7). One uncle, Theognetus, had won the boys' wrestling

[75] *Bacchylides. The Poems and Fragments*, ed. Richard C. Jebb (Cambridge, 1905; repr. Hildesheim, 1967), 212, dates the victory to 481, or probably not later than 479.

at the Olympic games (Paus. 6. 9. 1); the other, Cleitomachus, had won at the Isthmus.

Winners of the pentathlon ('five events') had to excel in a wide range of sports, but the physical traits of men who specialize in running differ from those of men who excel in combat events. Some families produced a large number of victorious runners.[76] In *Pythian* 10, Pindar described a family of successful runners. Hippocleas of Thessaly was victor in the boys' double stadium in 498 at Delphi, and later won at Olympia (Pind. *Pyth.* 10). The scholiast (ii. 244) adds that Hippocleas had also won the stadium on the same day as his other Pythian victory. His father Phricias had won the foot-race in armour twice at Olympia, and had been victorious once in the foot-race at Delphi. Pindar declares that Hippocleas's 'innate prowess trod in the footsteps of his father' (*Pyth.* 10. 20).

Although there are a few families like Diagoras's which boasted of victories in three successive generations, dyads of father and son are most common. Epinician odes, like funerary monuments (see Ch. 3), rarely refer to more than three generations, and two are most common. Furthermore, the genetic heritage would probably have been diluted in successive generations, unless the family was continually endogamous. The Greeks often married close relatives, but because the ancient sources do not usually specify women's names even when alluding to maternal kin, in most cases the mother of the athlete is not known. Female athletes were found only in Sparta, where there is little genealogical evidence (see Ch. 1). Therefore the phenomenon of skipping a generation is more likely to occur when the victorious ancestors are discovered in the maternal line, as was true of Diagor-

[76] Xenophon of the Oligaethidae of Corinth won both the stadium (short foot-race) and the pentathlon (stadium, long jump, discus, javelin, and wrestling) on a single day in 464. According to Pindar, before Xenophon, members of this family had won sixty Nemean and Isthmian victories (*Ol.* 13. 99). In 504, his father Thessalus had won a foot-race at Olympia (*Ol.* 13. 1, 35–6 and *Schol.*). Thessalus had previously been victorious at Delphi in the stadium and double stadium, at Athens in the stadium, double stadium, and foot-race in armour, and had also scored victories at the festival of Athena Hellotis and at the Isthmian games. Three other men in Xenophon's family had been Isthmian victors (*Ol.* 13. 40–2). Deinias of Aegina won the double stadium in 491. His father, Megas, who died before his son's triumph, had been victorious in the same event at Nemea (Pind. *Nem.* 8. 16, 44–50). Furthermore, Thrasydaeus of Thebes was victor in the boys' foot-race in 474, and many years later, in 454, won the double stadium (Pind. *Pyth.* 11). His father had also been victorious at Delphi (ibid. 11. 43), and other family members had won foot-races at Delphi and chariot races at Olympia (ibid. 11. 46–50 and *Schol.* ii. 261).

as's grandsons and of Pytheas and Phylacidas. Pindar points out that sometimes the talent is manifested in alternate generations. He traces four generations of one family which garnered many victories in alternate, rather than successive, generations. Alcimidas of Aegina was victorious in the boys' wrestling (Pind. *Nem.* 6). His family, the Bassidae, which traced its lineage from the Heracleidae, had won many victories, especially in boxing, but not every member of the family had been a champion. Although his father Theon was not an athlete, the victor planted 'his step in the foot-prints of his own father's father, Praxidamas' who had won one victory at Olympia, five at the Isthmian games, and three at Nemea (ibid. 6. 15–16). No other family had won more victories in boxing at the Isthmian games, and one member had been victorious at Delphi (ibid. 6. 36). The victor's grandfather, Praxidamas, three brothers of his great-grandfather, and even earlier ancestors, had won a total of twenty-five victories (ibid. 6. 17–27). Nevertheless, athletic prowess had not been distributed uniformly in earlier generations. Like Theon, Soclides, the father of Praxidamas, could bask in glory reflected from his kinsmen's victories. In *Nemean* 11 Pindar mentions both Peisander, a paternal ancestor, and Melanippus, a maternal ancestor, of Aristagoras of Tenedos. Again, as in *Nemean* 6, Pindar alludes to qualities that appear in alternate generations (ibid. 11. 38). Of course, a census of victorious athletes, as recorded in our sources, would demonstrate that the majority were the only members of their family to have triumphed. Pindar, however, does not draw attention to the uniqueness of such individuals. Yet, he does emphasize the ways in which a single triumph may signal the revival of 'family fortune' (e.g. *Isthm.* 1. 39–40, *potmos suggenes*). In *Isthmian* 1, a son's chariot victory marks the restoration of good fortune to his father, who had suffered shipwreck (either literal or metaphorical) and exile.

Pindar emphasizes heredity; but when no victorious ancestors are apparent, he remarks on nurture, praising trainers[77] and lauding fathers such as Lampon, who employed excellent trainers for their sons, and showed them by example—though in fields of endeavour other than athletics—the value of diligence and practice. No doubt,

[77] e.g. *Ol.* 8. 54: praise for Melesias who trained the fatherless Timosthenes and Alcimedon. The victor's grandfather, who was still living, had probably engaged the trainer.

in addition to employing trainers, some senior champions coached their younger kinsmen informally.[78] Their victories were the result of both nature and nurture within the family. In addition to these two factors well documented by the poets, the historian may suggest that some victories were due to psychological motives, in particular the younger generation's conscious emulation of, or wish to surpass the older, 'sibling rivalry', or the father's employment of his son in the vicarious realization of his own ambitions.

Sometimes athletes in successive generations competed in different sports, or the sources merely allude to other victories won by family members, and do not specify the events. Their talents were perhaps not so much due to genetic superiority as the result of conscious family efforts. Pausanias mentions some dyads of father and son who were victors in different events.[79]

There are fewer references to heterogeneous families of athletes, probably because the victors themselves, their families, and writers like Pindar and Pausanias were less inspired to commemorate their victories than they would have been if they could have boasted of a demonstrative family tradition.

Pindar sometimes seems more vague about the successes of predecessors when the victorious ancestors of the victor appear among the mother's kin. For example, in *Nemean* 4 he celebrates the victory of Timasarchus of Aegina in the boys' wrestling in 473. Timesarchus had also been successful at Athens and Thebes. His father, Timocritus, was dead, but his mother's brother, Callicles, had been victorious in the Olympian and Isthmian games (*Nem.* 4. 75, 80, 88). His trainer, Melesias, is also praised.[80] Pindar also wrote of Theaeus of

[78] Jan Bremmer, 'The Importance of the Maternal Uncle and Grandfather in Archaic and Classical Greece and Early Byzantium', *ZPE* 50 (1983), 173–86, assumes that uncles and grandfathers exerted an educative influence on their sisters' and daughters' sons.

[79] e.g. Lastratidas as a boy and youth won in wrestling at Olympia and Nemea. Paraballon, his father, had been victorious in the double foot-race (6. 6. 3). Aristeus of Argos won the long-race, but his father Cheimon was a victor in wrestling (Paus. 6. 9. 3). Demaretus of Heraea, his son, and his grandson each won two victories at Olympia. Demaretus was victorious twice in the race in armour. His son Theopompus won the pentathlon twice, and Demaratus's grandson, also named Theopompus, scored two victories in wrestling (Paus. 6. 10. 4–5). Pausanias mentions a Laconian, Calliteles, who was a wrestler. His son Polypeithes was victorious in the quadriga (6. 16. 6). In describing the chariot sculpture commemorating a victory of Cratisthenes, Pausanias remarks that his father Mnaseas of Cyrene was a runner, but does not mention that the father had been victorious (6. 18. 1).

[80] Melesias was important enough to have marriage connections with Cimon. His son, Thucydides, became a prominent politician: Davies, *APF* 7268I–III.

Argos, who was victorious in wrestling at the Hecatombaea in Argos, probably in 463.[81] His maternal ancestors, including Antias and Thrasyclus, had won some victories in chariot races at Nemea and elsewhere (*Nem.* 10. 37). Probably when victories had been won by maternal ancestors, Pindar had less specific information available to him about the type of event and its location. A mother may have told her daughter about the victories of members of her family in the same way that she taught her daughter how to weave or to exercise self-control (cf. Xen. *Oec.* 7. 14). Or women overheard men talking about public events, as Lysistrata recounts (Ar. *Lys.* 508–14, 517–20). Because women had not had the opportunity to witness or to participate in athletic competitions, and were doubtless less interested in them than men were, they were less certain about the specific events in which family members had triumphed. Furthermore, we assume that in the vast majority of cases, the athlete or his father or another paternal relative had paid the poet's fee, and may have related the history of his family to him. Because marriages were patrilocal, and women refrained from chatting with strangers, the poet did not enjoy similar access to the victor's female relatives.

Although Pausanias and the poets do not distinguish qualitatively between events won by athletes as individuals who had personally participated in the competitions, and those won by owners of horses, we must do so in the present discussion. Despite exceptions, such as Herodotus of Thebes (Pind. *Isthm.* 1. 14–15), in the classical period most owners of racehorses did not actually participate in the event. In such cases, the physical or genetic heredity of the owner was not a factor in the victory (although the lineage of the horse was). The most that can be safely said in general is that the victor and his family were fortunate enough to enjoy good luck or the favour of the gods, wealthy enough to own excellent animals, and astute enough to employ competent trainers and jockeys.[82] Some owners, however, were personally involved in breeding and training. The epithet '*philippon*' ('horse-loving') that Bacchylides (3. 69) applies

[81] His previous victories included another at the Hecatombaea, one at Delphi, three at the Isthmia, three at Nemea, and two at the Panathenaea (*Nem.* 10. 23–8).

[82] Of course, anyone who commissioned Pindar to celebrate his victory or who erected a noteworthy commemorative monument at a pan-Hellenic sanctuary, was wealthy. But in the present study of the influence of heredity I must confine myself to athletes whose victories were the direct result of their own efforts, without relying upon horses, chariot, and jockey.

to Hiero of Syracuse, son of Deinomenes, in his epinician commemorating a victory in the quadriga at Olympia in 468, indicates that the tyrant was interested in his horses. Pindar (*Pyth.* 2. 5) writes that Hiero drove his elegantly harnessed horses with his own hands. In 490, when the quadriga of Xenocrates of Acragas was victorious at the Pythian games, the driver was the owner's son, Thrasybulus. Pindar (*Pyth.* 6. 42–5) praises the son's achievement as evidence of filial devotion.[83] Equestrian statues—for example, that of Hiero, son of Hierocles, at Olympia—indicate that, as was normal for upper-class men, victors must have been expert at riding and driving horses, though, as we have seen, not usually in actual pan-Hellenic competitions (Paus. 6. 12. 4). Pausanias gives several examples of dyads or triads of men in the same family who bred and trained victorious horses (e.g. 6. 12. 7, 6. 13. 9–10). The Greeks, like owners of racing horses nowadays, deliberately raised victorious mares and sires.[84] Such horses would have been a significant part of the family property that was passed down from generation to generation. The Alcmaeonids bred racehorses on large tracts of land that they owned in Attica. The family's first victor was Alcmaeon, who won at Olympia in 592.[85] The Spartans also specialized in breeding horses. Among the Spartans whose statues Pausanias describes was Anaxander, who was the first of his family to win a chariot race (6. 1. 7). The inscription on his statue recorded that his paternal grandfather had been victorious in the pentathlon.[86]

In evaluating the works of poets and sculptors as evidence for popular views of heredity, it is necessary to bear in mind that these

[83] Damonon, a Spartan, dedicated an inscription recording that he won forty-three victories in his quadriga and eighteen on horseback, and that his son Enymachratidas won twenty victories in horse races and on foot. These victories were at local, rather than pan-Hellenic, competitions. The dedication has recently been dated to after 403: see further L. H. Jeffery, review of P. A. Cartledge, *Sparta and Laconia;* L. F. Fitzhardinghe, *The Spartans;* and T. A. Boring, *Literacy in Ancient Sparta, JHS* 101 (1981), 190–2, esp. 191.

[84] Damonon (n. 83 above) recorded that he had won three of his victories with horses bred from his own stallion and mares (ll. 15–17, 20–3, 27–9).

[85] Moretti, *Olympionikai*, 68, no. 81. The date in schol. Pind. *Pyth.* 7. 14 for Megacles' victory probably refers to Alcmaeon's. For the dates and distribution of the Alcmaeonid victories see further Davies, *APF*, no. 9688, pp. 370–4, 381, 384. By 486 the Alcmaeonids had won one Pythian, five Isthmian, and one Panathenaic race, and in 436 Megacles' quadriga was victorious at Olympia. Pind. *Pyth.* 7. 10–12 and schol. inscr.; Moretti, *Olympionikai*, 105, no. 320, and *IAG* 10, no. 5.

[86] Pausanias also mentions the chariot victories of Arcesilaus and his son Lichas (6. 2. 2).

works are not the product of eccentric craftsmen or of those who created 'art for art's sake'. The poets and sculptors could not merely indulge their personal whims, but were obliged to consider the preferences of their patrons and the taste of the élite and powerful international audience who read or heard their odes and visited the sanctuaries and saw the triumphal monuments. The fact that Athens offered free meals to victorious athletes indicates that pride and interest in the achievements of their fellow citizens were not confined to the upper class. Thus, social historians should not dismiss the views of the poets and artists as unpopular or esoteric. Although these poets and artists were not thinking primarily about heredity, their tacit or open acknowledgement of the contribution made by maternal relatives to the child shows more common sense than is revealed by some of the learned authors who discussed the subject at length in treatises dealing with reproduction.

MEDICAL AND PHILOSOPHICAL VIEWS OF HEREDITY

Who does the baby look like?

Scientists and physicians expressed their views in terms that appear more philosophical than scientific to the modern reader, and reveal some willingness to accept notions that contemporary readers would immediately criticize as illogical and inconsistent. Prior to the discoveries of cellular biology and the invention of modern scientific equipment such as the microscope, genetics was based on simple observation and theory. Of course, even nowadays, despite the advance of science, not only the views of lay people but also those of specialists on human reproduction and generation have been challenged as value-laden and subjective.

The Greeks, in general, believed that offspring resemble their parents in physique, personality, and character.[87] How these characteristics were transmitted, however, and the nature of the mother's contribution to the foetus was much debated. The Greek scientific, medical, and philosophical corpus dealing with human reproduction is enormous. In this section we will discuss three topics that are

[87] For bibliography see most recently Mirko D. Grmek, 'Ideas on Heredity in Greek and Roman Antiquity', *Physis*, n.s. 28 (1991), 11–34, and Ann Ellis Hanson, 'Conception, Gestation, and the Origin of Female Nature in the *Corpus Hippocraticum*', *Helios*, 19 (1992), 31–71.

particularly relevant to the issues raised earlier in the chapter: (1) heredity; (2) the maternal contribution to the child; and (3) the inheritance of acquired characteristics.

In the classical period some scientists believed in preformation. There were basically two versions of this theory. Pangenesis, one version of preformation theory, held that the embryo was formed of pre-existing parts. Preformationists believed that both father and mother produced sperm and contributed to the offspring. A child might look more like one parent than the other, but the Hippocratic author of *On Generation* (7. 480, 8. 1) states that it is impossible for a child to resemble either parent to the total exclusion of the other parent, and it is also impossible to resemble neither parent. The sex of the offspring was a crucial factor in the equation. Both parents produce both male and female sperm. The male sperm is stronger than the female. If the sperm that comes from both is strong, a male is born; if weak, a female (Hippoc. *On Seed* 6). By contrast, the homunculus theory posited the existence of a completely formed being prior to birth. The notion of the maternal and paternal sperm mingling to create offspring was incompatible with the homunculus idea.

The subject of the mother's contribution to the foetus was debated: the father's was acknowledged by all. According to Herodotus (4. 180), the intercourse of the Libyans was promiscuous. When a woman's child was grown, the men assembled and declared the child to be the offspring of the man it most resembled. This informal assessment is reminiscent of the scrutiny of a son presented by his father to his phratry (see above). In Athenian tragedy some characters maintain that the father is the true parent of the child, and that the mother supplies merely a fertile field in which the father's seed is nourished.[88] Much attention has been paid to this remarkable view. Not only does it appear in the context of tragedy, but it is stated from time to time by Aristotle, who rejects preformation theory, and instead asserts that the father's semen provides the active principle that shapes the embryo, while the mother merely provides passive matter (*Gen. An.* 738b20–6, 729a10, etc.). Aristotle, however, is inconsistent, because he must account for the obvious phenomena both of girls and of babies who resemble both parents or the mother alone. According to Aristotle, under normal circumstances a boy

[88] Aes. *Eum.* 658–61; Eur. *Or.* 551–2; Soph. *Ant.* 569; cf. Plato, *Timaeus* 91D1–2.

would be born who would resemble his father. When, abnormally, the female generative force dominates, a female is born. These products are the most common. When a son resembles his mother or maternal relatives, or a daughter resembles her father or his relatives, the female generative force has mastered the male.[89] We may speculate that in the few cases when the mother was a member of an athletic family such as those described earlier in this chapter, and the father was not, the strength of the female generative force would not be unexpected. Athenian law, however, which was often the model for the laws of other Greek states, affirmed the precedence of the father's parentage over the mother's. Children belonged to the father's *oikos*, and in cases of divorce or the father's death they remained with him or with his family. As a result of these legal arrangements and the seclusion of women, the child was seen much more frequently with his or her father and paternal relatives than with the mother and maternal relatives. Therefore the observer was more likely to perceive resemblances on the father's side.

As we have observed among the families of athletes, the inheritance of characteristics of remote ancestors was noted. Miscegenation that was concealed in immediate descendants, but revealed in later generations was a topos. Aristotle remarks that some children resemble their distant ancestors, and that these characteristics may be transmitted from one male to another through the female line. He cites the example of a woman who had intercourse with an Ethiopian. His characteristics appeared not in her daughter, but in her grandson (*Gen. An.* 722a9–11; cf. 767a36–b5). Thus, in the case of the daughter the female generative force had triumphed over the male in both gender and racial characteristics. The grandson, however, was the product of both male and female generative forces. In other words, his racial characteristics were transmitted by a woman. Plutarch (*Mor.* 563a–b) notes that a father's physical traits and personality may not appear in his children, but will emerge in later generations. He cites the example of a Greek woman who was accused of adultery after she gave birth to a black child. She then discovered that she was fourth in descent from an Ethiopian.

It was generally believed that acquired characteristics could be

[89] Arist. *Gen. An.* 737a28–34, 766b7–10, 768b15–23, and see below: See further Michael Boylan, 'The Galenic and Hippocratic Challenges to Aristotle's Conception Theory', *Journal of the History of Biology*, 17/1 (1984), 83–112.

transmitted. Aetiological myths such as those explaining how the Ethiopians became black from living in a warm region[90] or how the race of the Macrocephalics acquired long heads (first by binding, then by heredity) reveal that this belief was widespread (see e.g. Hippoc. *Airs, Waters, Places*, 14). Aristotle reports that children not only inherited their parents' characters, but some were born with scars, tattoos, and mutilations resembling those acquired by their parents or more remote ancestors.[91] Yet he also argues that children do not inevitably resemble their parents, especially when the parents are mutilated.[92] Some disabilities and diseases, including gout, dropsy, epilepsy, and consumption were considered congenital.[93] In discussions of the transmission of acquired characteristics, no distinction is made between the maternal and paternal contribution to the foetus. According to the theory of pangenesis, the healthy parts of the foetus are derived from the healthy parts of the parents, and the diseased parts similarly from the diseased parts. Since both parents are thought to contribute semen, the female legacy could not be denied.

In this chapter we have seen various manifestations of the definition of the family based on gender, ranging from totally male, to predominantly male, to both male and female. In the widely publicized acquisition of athletic honours, the family is totally male. Furthermore, inasmuch as the inheritance of dishonour most often concerns the political arena, the family members involved are predominantly, though not exclusively, male. Public ceremonies associated with incorporation into the pseudo-family were restricted to males; but the private rites of incorporation into the family group involved males and females alike. Medical theories run the gamut from regarding male ancestors as the sole source of hereditary influences, to considering males as the predominant or normal source, and finally to allocating an equal share to both male and female. We have also seen that the homunculus, bearing the same name as his grandfather or father, belonging to the same phratry and deme, and displaying the same talents, reappears generation after generation, fostering the illusion of immortality. Chapter 4 will show that he often also

[90] Hdt. 2. 22; Pliny, *NH* 2. 80. 189; cf. Strab. 15. 1, 2; and see Frank M. Snowden, Jr., *Blacks in Antiquity: Ethiopians in the Greco-Roman Experience* (Cambridge, Mass., 1970), 172–4.

[91] *Gen. An.* 721b20–36, 724a3–7, 767a35–b9.

[92] *Gen. An.* 722b30–5, *HA* 595a; likewise Hippoc. *On Gen.* 11. 1.

[93] Hippoc. *On Gen.* 11. 1, *Sacred Disease* 2. 4; Hdt. 2. 33.

practises the same trade as his forebears. Yet historical memory is usually limited to three generations. Only the aristocracy and the professional élite can cite or invent a more extensive past, sometimes reaching back to mythical heroes. Such fictions unify the family, and enhance its importance. Nevertheless, just as women did not acquire more than a small fraction of the patrimony and transmit it to their children, so they did not invariably inherit their family's names or transmit their family's identity to their descendants. Except in the case of priestesses, where the profession is inherited within a specific family (see Ch. 4), women's family identity and heredity is less well defined and less well documented than men's.

3
Death and the Family

The treatment of dead members of a family reveals much about personal relationships within the family, as well as the relationship between the family and the larger society. For the social historian of antiquity, material evidence from the dead constitutes a relatively fruitful source of information. In many cases, however, the data from individual cities span several centuries, and frequently show changes in quantity and kind over time. Local variation is marked. As usual, the best historical evidence comes from Attica, for it is abundant, and has been subjected to intensive scholarly analysis. Therefore the sources for this chapter will be principally Athenian. Yet even within the scope of one city, the various genres of evidence—legal, literary, and archaeological—often present conflicting information. This heterogeneity is the result of regional and class variation, of changes in belief, behaviour, and artistic representation over time, and perhaps of the ambivalent attitudes of families towards their dead.[1]

LEGAL RIGHTS OF THE DEAD

It was not unusual for the *polis* to dictate the parameters of funerals to be conducted by private families. The regulations of several cities are extant. Our most detailed legal information comes from Athens and from cities that adopted Athenian laws. The legislation, which was attributed to Solon and continued in effect in the classical period, included the following provisions:

the *prothesis* ('laying out of the body') must be held indoors;
the *ekphora* ('transporting the corpse to its place of burial') must be held

[1] For incongruent evidence about women's care of the dead, see Christine Havelock, 'Mourners on Greek Vases: Remarks on the Social History of Women', in N. Broude and M. D. Garrard (eds.), *Feminism and Art History* (New York, 1982), 44–61.

before sunrise on the succeeding day, with men walking in front of the cart, and women behind;

only women over the age of 60 or related to the deceased within the degree of second cousin are permitted to participate, with the latter also permitted to return to the house after the burial;

women must not wear more than three *himatia* ('cloaks'), nor must the dead be interred in more than three;

food and drink brought in the procession must not be worth more than one obol;

the offering basket must not be longer than one cubit;

mourners must not go out at night except in the funeral cart with a light;

laceration of the flesh, singing of prepared dirges, or bewailing anyone except the person whose funeral is being held is forbidden; and

visiting the tombs of non-relatives except at their funerals is forbidden.[2]

Previous discussions have emphasized the negative aspects of the legislation governing funerals.[3] One of the hypotheses behind these interpretations is that Solon's laws were designed not merely to record, publicize, or normalize existing practices, but, rather, to alter them substantially. The underlying assumption here is that the prohibitions are a negative reflection of actual behaviour. For example, adopting this line of reasoning, we might surmise that previously the *prothesis* was held out of doors, the *ekphora* took place in the daytime with women walking in front, that non-related women of all ages and women whose relationship to the deceased was more distant than that of second cousin participated, and so on. Such deductions from ancient law codes are naïve, however. Without further information, we can have little confidence about the relationship, if any, between law and prior historical reality. Burial and religious ceremonies are notoriously conservative, and not readily amenable to legislated change.[4]

[2] This list has been assembled from the testimony in Ps.-Dem. 43. 62 = E. Ruschenbusch, *Solonos Nomoi: Die Fragmente des solonischen Gestzeswerkes mit einer Text- und Überlieferungsgeschichte*, *Historia*, Einzelschr. 9 (Wiesbaden, 1966), fr. 109; Cic. *Leg.* 2. 63–4 = Ruschenbusch, fr. 72a, from Demetrius of Phaleron, fr. 135 (Wehrli) = Jacoby, *FGrH* 228 F 9; Plut. *Sol.* 21. 5 = Ruschenbusch, fr. 72c. On legislation of Solon and Demetrius see Ch. 1, and in general see Robert Garland, 'The Well-Ordered Corpse: An Investigation into the Motives behind Greek Funerary Legislation', *BICS* 36 (1989), 1–15.

[3] Thus, e.g., Margaret Alexiou, *The Ritual Lament in Greek Tradition* (Cambridge, 1974), esp. 6–7, 14–18, followed most recently by Gail Holst-Warhaft, *Dangerous Voices. Women's Laments and Greek Literature* (London, 1992), 99, 104, 114–18.

[4] Emily Vermeule, *Aspects of Death in Early Greek Art and Poetry* (Berkeley, 1979), 11–12, 15, 21, draws attention to continuities in funerary imagery from the Bronze Age through the Hellenistic period.

Moreover, the laws attributed to Solon present specific problems concerning authenticity, dating, and methods of promulgation.[5]

A second hypothesis, which emphasizes the restrictive element in the funerary legislation is that aristocratic *gene* ('clans') controlled political and religious affairs in archaic Athens, and that Solon's legislation was intended to curb their dominance. According to this interpretation, the funerary laws limited opportunities for powerful aristocratic clans to advertise their importance by parading in a huge, noisy cortège and thereby intimidating less fortunate citizens. Lavish expenditures for grave offerings by which the wealthy *gene* flaunted their superiority were proscribed. The family was defined as a smaller unit than the *genos* as far as the number of members directly affected by the death were concerned. The notion of the huge *genos* led to the hypothesis that numerous women who were distant relatives of the deceased would gather at funerals to participate in deliberations over the fate of widow, orphans, and property. Thus, in pre-Solonian Athens women who belonged to the aristocratic *gene* would have enjoyed more opportunities to get out of the house, incite vendettas, attend funerals, where they could meet kinswomen, indulge in the catharsis of lamentation, and have some influence in discussions concerning family and property. To historians of Athenian women, it seemed to be a golden age by comparison with the post-Solonian *polis*, whose restrictions are well known.[6] Unfortunately, there is at least one flaw in this line of reasoning. Clearly, since the number of male participants was not restricted, it was still possible for the bereaved to display their potential to use force in attaining objectives that may have been divisive in terms of the public good. Geometric vases depict male mourners dressed in armour. Even if male participants in funerals during later periods were unarmed, such a large group of men parading through the city had to be of more concern to the legislator than women's lamentations and conversations.

The major problem with the interpretations outlined above is that they rest on a foundation which historians are currently questioning, if not actively dismantling. The notion of huge aristocratic clans in control of political and religious life and engaged in competition and strife was imported from archaic Rome to Greece by Fustel de

[5] See Ch. 1 n. 42 above.

[6] See further Pomeroy, *Goddesses, Whores*, 43–5, 80.

Coulanges, Henry Maine, and other influential historians.[7] From this conceptual framework based on analogy with Rome followed the notion that Solon destroyed the social structure resting on the *gene*. Similar reasoning attributed to Cleisthenes a change in the composition of phratries from blood kin to pseudo-kin. Felix Bourriot has reviewed the so-called textual evidence for an Athenian social structure founded on huge archaic clans and found it unconvincing.[8] There were, of course, some large, powerful groups of kin—for example, the Alcmaeonids—and some families who controlled various cults and could stage lavish funerals, but that clans based on blood-relationship were ubiquitous and fundamental to social organization is questionable. The vast majority of the inhabitants of archaic Attica were not members of aristocratic *gene*. Bourriot found few references to any kin group larger than the *anchisteia* ('all descendants of a common great-grandfather'; see Ch. 1). Instead, in the time of Solon the *gene* were being created, not destroyed.[9] *Prothesis* and *ekphora* scenes on geometric and archaic vases show small groups of mourners, as do black-figure funerary plaques produced after the Solonian legislation. Of course, these representations may be because of artistic convention, limitations of space, or a feeling that the artist was under no obligation to represent all participants (see below). Archaeological evidence indicates that Athenians were buried in small groups or as individuals; there are no huge tumuli that might have accommodated a *genos*.

Considered together with the limitation on trousseaus attributed to Solon,[10] the funerary legislation appears to be principally sumptuary in nature and to affect women. Cicero (*Leg.* 2. 64) asserts that the laws of the Twelve Tables concerning mourning and funeral expenses were copied from Solon's laws. Plutarch understands these rules as sumptuary restrictions on women, for he discusses women's public appearances at funerals and festivals in tandem. Like the laws affecting trousseaus, those concerning funerals affected individual families, not huge clans comprised of infinitely extended families.

[7] See Introduction, n. 2, and S. C. Humphries (with A. Momigliano), *Anthropology and the Greeks* (London, 1978), 197.

[8] *Recherches sur la nature du genos*, and see Ch. 2 n. 42.

[9] Ibid. 325–6, 338–9, *et passim*. See Thomas, *Oral Tradition*, *passim*, on the deliberate fabrication of legends and traditions about heroic and archaic ancestors by aristocratic families.

[10] Ruschenbusch, fr. 71a = Plut. *Sol.* 20. 6; Ruschenbusch, fr. 71b = Poll. 1. 246.

The stipulations concerning cloaks, food and drink, and the size of the offering basket are sumptuary, and the exclusion of female mourners under the age of 60 who were not related to the deceased but who were hired for the occasion may also be so categorized. The legislation has also been viewed as an attempt to provide guide-lines for families that were uncertain about how great an expenditure was adequate and how much family participation and public display was appropriate.[11] Peer pressure and the wish to appear generous were formidable influences in Athens; under such circumstances some legal regulations may have been welcome. They were obviously effective, at least for a while. Large decorated gravestones that drew attention to the burials of the wealthy in the archaic period went out of fashion during the first three-quarters of the fifth century, when the democracy flourished. The abandonment of such monuments is consistent with the sumptuary intention of the Solonian laws (see Ch. 1). Solon's laws probably also reified appropriate behaviour for Athenian women. They were supposed to stay at home.[12] Women over the age of 60, post-menopausal and considered asexual, were safe from lustful aggression, and could not produce a spurious heir.[13] Often considered useless, at least they might earn some income as hired mourners.

The subject of regulation can also be analysed from the viewpoint of the mutual obligations of family members throughout antiquity to provide burial. Dead members of a family were entitled to burial by their descendants or heirs. Indeed, by behaving respectfully towards the dead, the living demonstrated to their heirs by example the treatment they expected when their own turn came. Sometimes, as with other laws governing family matters, the law recorded what was probably customary behaviour. Thus Pseudo-Demosthenes (43. 57–8) refers to a law stating that the demarch should instruct kinsmen of a dead person on the day of death to collect the body, bury it, and purify the deme. Most relatives would have done this anyway, without prodding by the demarch. Nevertheless, in a case where a son might

[11] For funeral expenses see, e.g. Plato, *Hipp. Mai.* 291E, *Epin.* 13, 361E, *Laws* 717D, 958D–960C; Lys. 31. 21; Ps.- Dem. 40. 52, 45. 79. See further Davies, *APF*, p. xix n. 3, and Garland, 'Well-Ordered Corpse', 15.

[12] On norms for women see further Pomeroy, *Xenophon Oeconomicus*, 276, *et passim*.

[13] See Jan N. Bremmer, 'The Old Women of Ancient Greece', in Josine Blok and Peter Mason (eds.), *Sexual Asymmetry* (Amsterdam, 1987), 191–215.

have just cause to ignore his filial obligation—for example, if his father had prostituted him—he could be prosecuted for maltreatment of parents if he failed to provide burial or to perform the customary rites (Aesch. 1. 13–14). Ignoring the family obsequies was an inexcusable mark of degeneracy (Lycurg. *Leoc.* 25). At his examination for the office of archon, a candidate was regularly asked whether he had family tombs and where they were located.[14] The candidate's response would certify not only that his family had been Athenians for many generations, but also that he himself had piously performed the usual obsequies.

RITES OF DEATH

The care of the dead consisted of observances which were so routine that they were referred to as *ta nomizomena* ('customary practices').[15] With the exception of sumptuary restrictions, details of this care were not spelled out in the law. The following discussion will be limited to death and to the relationship of the living members of the family to their dead.[16]

It is often difficult for the historian to find traces of respectable women's activities, but in the realm of death women are prominent. Much of the care of the dead was in the hands of female members of the family. Women may be the object of restrictive legislation—for example, that of Solon governing their participation in funerals and the size of their trousseaus—but they are rarely the object of positive directives affecting their activities within the home, such as the conduct of the *prothesis*. Because of the importance of women's privacy, any such directives would be unenforceable. In any event, they were probably unnecessary. Women's care of the corpse was traditional. In a demographic regime of high mortality and short life spans, and in houses that afforded little isolation, girls would become familiar with the preparation of a corpse for burial and

[14] Arist. *Ath. Pol.* 55. 3; cf. Xen. *Mem.* 2. 2. 13; Dem. 57. 54, 67; and Din. 1. 110, 2.17–18 (as emended by Valesius).

[15] e.g. Isae. 1. 10, 2. 10, 4. 19, 6. 65, 9. 4, 32; Lys. 32. 8; Aesch. 3. 77; Din. 2. 18; *ta nomima*: Thuc. 3. 58. 4; Din. 2. 8. This terminology may also be a euphemism deriving from the wish to avoid mentioning death and the dead.

[16] See further Plato, *Laws* 959A; Poll. 8. 65; Donna C. Kurtz and John Boardman, *Greek Burial Customs* (London, 1971), and Robert Garland, *The Greek Way of Death* (London, 1985).

with the rituals of lamentation. Scenes on vases used by women offered visual instruction (see below). These vases, in fact, often show children in the presence of the corpse.[17] Indeed, vases, corroborated by the scenes in tragedy, constitute substantial evidence of women's activities concerning the dead. The division of labour in the family dictated that the provision of baths and clothing, and, in general, jobs that were accomplished indoors, were women's work.[18] Women's knowledge of cosmetics and of sweet-smelling herbs and potions would have been useful in mortuary work. Because women were supposedly polluted by childbirth, evidently they were deemed more capable of coping with the pollution of death.[19] Thus women bathed and clothed the new-born as well as the dead members of the family.

The pollution of death defines the family, and sets it apart from the non-bereaved, but the boundaries of the pollution were not uniform throughout the Greek states. The legislation of fifth-century Iulis on Keos included among the polluted the mother, wife, sisters, daughters, and at most five other close female relatives.[20] As noted above, Athenian law allowed a wider circle of female kin to participate in the funerary rites and thereby share the pollution. The law is silent about the precise range of a woman's obligations after marriage, but normal practice may be deduced from other sources. A speech of Lysias supplies some unsurprising information. A married woman living with her mother-in-law in her husband's house participated in the funeral of her husband's mother, but she was also expected to mourn for members of her natal family and not wear cosmetics during the month after one of them had died (Lys. 1.14). A corpse had to be buried within three days. Because marriage was patrilocal, a married woman might live too far away, might get the news late, and thus might not manage to attend the *prothesis* and funeral. Nevertheless, she was polluted by the death of her blood-relations whether or not

[17] For children at the *prothesis*, see M. T. Charlier and G. Raepset, 'Étude d'un comportement social, les relations entre parents et enfants dans la société athénienne à l'époque classique', 40 (1971), 589–606, esp. 599–606.

[18] See further Pomeroy, *Xenophon, Oeconomicus*, 43–4, 58–61, 70, 84–5, 274, 316.

[19] So Robert Parker, *Miasma. Pollution and Purification in Early Greek Religion* (Oxford, 1983), 33.

[20] F. Sokolowski, *Lois sacrées des cités grecques* (Paris, 1969), 97, ll. 25–8, with Hoffmann's restoration: the other women are daughters' children and cousins' children. For pollution at Athens see Ps.-Dem. 43. 58, 62; in Athenian tragedy see e.g. Eur. *Hipp.* 1437–9, *Alc.* 22.

she had touched the corpse.[21] Pollution regulations are gender-specific. We do not know to what extent male relatives were polluted by the death of a kinsman, but they did show that they were in mourning by cutting their hair and wearing black cloaks (Xen. *Hell.* 1. 7. 8). Specific procedures to be followed when the corpse was female are not known, but it should not be assumed that they were the same as those for a male, inasmuch as the pollution and responsibility of living kin were directly proportionate to the status of the dead (cf. Dem. 47. 70). Furthermore, some women were so obscure even in their lifetime that it is difficult to imagine that they would command attention when dead. In lawsuits speakers were able to argue about the names, legal status, and identity of such women, and even to assert that they had never existed at all.[22] Mourning at the *prothesis* was conducted primarily by women. That the singing of dirges was customary and mourning ritualized should not lead us to conclude that members of the family did not experience genuine grief at the loss of their relatives. (For some expressions of such grief see the epigrams below.) The intensity of initial mourning probably produced a catharsis. In any case, the sharing of grief in the presence of a large family circle was surely more therapeutic than the solitary mourning that often prevails in modern Western society. We suspect that when the death was timely and there was little reason for sorrow, the funerary process provided an opportunity, especially for the women in the family, to enjoy spending time with cousins whom they saw only rarely, and cooking and eating together.

The men in the family made the arrangements for the *ekphora* ('cortège') that took place on the third day after death.[23] After the burial, both men and women in the family shared a banquet (*perideipnon*).[24] This feast ended the three days of fasting that had occurred since the death (Arr. *Anab.* 7. 14. 8; Lucian, *Luct.* 24). The family wore garlands and spoke in praise of the dead. Additional ceremonies took place at the tomb on the ninth day after burial.[25] At Athens, thirty days after the death, *triakostia* were performed: thus

[21] So Parker, *Miasma*, 39, arguing from comparative anthropological evidence in the absence of authoritative Greek sources.

[22] See further Pomeroy, *Goddesses, Whores*, 79–83, 227–9.

[23] Ant. 6. 34; Ps.-Dem. 43. 62; Plato, *Laws* 959A; cf. Isae. 3. 57.

[24] According to Artemidorus (5. 82) the deceased played the role of host. Speusippus wrote *Platonos Perideipno* ('Plato's Funeral Feast': Diog. Laert. 3. 2).

[25] *Ta enata*: Aesch. 3. 226; Isae. 2. 36, 8. 39; and William Wyse, *The Speeches of Isaeus* (Cambridge, 1904), 264–5, 619–20.

the prescribed period of mourning was terminated (Lys. 1. 14).[26] This rite included placing *kallysmata* ('sweepings') from the house floor on the grave. Annual rituals of mourning, both at home and in the cemetery, were mandatory. Women made periodic offerings at tombs, but their visits were evidently regulated by custom or personal sentiment, not law. The son and heir of the deceased was legally obliged to pay regular visits to his family's graves and to make offerings.[27] Plato (*Laws* 717B) refers to a law concerning ancestral objects. These were associated with the yearly offerings to ancestors. Because they passed down in families through the generations, their possession must have been restricted to men.

FUNERARY FOUNDATIONS

Beginning in the late fourth century, some wealthy people established foundations to institutionalize offerings to dead members of their family, attempting to ensure their own future care as well. Funds were contributed to make certain that proper attention would be paid to the memory of the dead and to support the maintenance of their tombs. As an additional bulwark against the ravages of mortality, the founders of such cults had their endowments recorded in duplicate[28] and publicized in elaborate detail on inscriptions that have endured.

Although only the wealthy could create such cults, and they were neither common nor found in all parts of the Greek world, we shall examine them briefly here, because they show both the perpetuation of traditional beliefs regarding death, the family, and society and adaptation to the new circumstances of the Hellenistic period. The evidence for the Hellenistic funerary foundations is not Athenian: the inscriptions concerned were found in the Sporades and the eastern Aegean. Whereas Athenian practices concerning the dead emphasize the involvement of close kin, these Hellenistic, non-Athenian versions were less exclusive.

The deracination characteristic of the Hellenistic period severed

[26] For regulations in other states see e.g. a law of Aeolian Gambreum, third century BC: *SIG*³ 1219 = *Michel*, no. 520. According to the law of Gambreum the period of mourning is one month longer for women than for men.

[27] e.g. Xen. *Mem.* 2. 2. 13; Isae. 1. 10, 2. 10, 6. 51, 65, 7. 30, 32, 9. 7, 36; Dem. 18. 43; Aesch. 3. 225; Arist. *Ath. Pol.* 55. 3.

[28] e.g. Epicteta, ll. 276–86: see n. 30 below.

people from both their forebears and their descendants.[29] Young men left home to seize opportunities in the new territories governed by Alexander's successors and in the older cities whose populations had been depleted and who were recruiting new citizens. An immigrant was not only separated from his blood-relations, but he could scarcely pretend to be a member of long-established artificial kinship groups like those created in Athens by Cleisthenes and in Sparta by the Lycurgan Constitution.

A micro-history of Epicteta of Thera is sufficient to demonstrate some of the changes in the Greek family in the Hellenistic period.[30] Epicteta established her foundation between 210 and 195 in honour of the Muses, her husband, her two deceased sons, and herself. The founders of Hellenistic cults could not boast of heroic ancestors like those celebrated by Pindar, whom art had immortalized. Nevertheless, Epicteta's family constructed a lineage for themselves. Four members of the family were designated as 'heroes', an example of hyperbole, euphemism, and wishful thinking.

Epicteta daughter of Grinnus, sane and in her right mind, devised by will the following . . . .

I leave [this will] according to the instruction given to me by my husband Phoinix, who had the Mouseion built for our deceased son Cratesilochus, and had the reliefs and the statues of himself and Cratesilochus and the heroic monuments brought there, and had asked me to finish the construction of the Mouseion . . . .

I leave the Mouseion and the holy precinct of the heroic monuments to my daughter Epiteleia, in order that she, having inherited the proceeds of my other estates as well, will pay every year in the month of Eleusinius 210 dr. to the association of the men's club, which I have formed from the kinsmen . . . .

My daughter's son Andragoras shall hold the priesthood of the Muses and the Heroes, but if something shall happen to him, always the eldest from the family of Epiteleia . . . .

The names of the relatives I have assembled are written below: Hypereides son of Thrasyleon; Antisthenes son of Isocles, by adoption son of Grinnus; Aristodamus son of Isocles; Timesius son of Praxiteles; Evagoras son of Procleidas; Procleidas son of Evagoras; Cartidamas son of Procleidas;

[29] See further B. Laum, *Stiftungen in der griechischen und römischen Antike. Ein Beitrag zur antiken Kulturgeschichte* (Leipzig and Berlin, 1914), i. 9, and B. Bruck, *Totenteil und Seelgerät im griechischen Recht*, Münch. Beiträge zur Papyrusforschung und ant. Rechtsgesch. 9 (Munich, 1926), 271–6.

[30] Michel 1001 = *IJG* II pp. 77–94, no. 24, and see now Andreas Wittenburg, *Il Testamento di Epikteta* (Trieste, 1990). References below will be to Wittenburg's text.

Hagnosthenes son of Cartidamas; Procleidas son of Alcimedon; Bolacrates son of Aglosthenes; Archinicus son of Gorgopas; Startophus son of Bolocrates; Gorgopas son of Archinicus; Gorgopas son of Erchestratus; Gorgopas son of Cartidamas, Agathostratus son of Cratesilochus; Mollis son of Polymedes; Cartidamas and Cratesilochus and Dion and Dorocleidas, sons of Agathostratus; Himertus son of Himerophon; Critus son of Teisanor; Polynicus and Evagoras, sons of Soteles. Also their wives, living together with them, shall be admitted and their children, the female children as long as they are under their father's guardianship, the male as well when they are of age, and their issue under the same conditions. Also the heiresses and their husbands living together with them shall be admitted and their children according to the same rules as written above. Also my namesake Epicteta shall be admitted; and my daughter Epiteleia; and the daughters of Gorgopas, Mnaso and Ainesippa; and the daughters of Thrasyleon, Basilodica and Telesippa; and Callidica, daughter of Isocles; and their husbands, living together with them. Also Aristarchus' daughter Epiteleia shall be admitted, and the children of all these.[31]

As we see, Epicteta's immediate family was small, and her natural expectation that one of her sons, at least, would look after her in her old age was unfulfilled. Her daughter, Epiteleia, was her only surviving child: she employs her son-in-law Hypereides as *kyrios* for the transaction. Like other widows who are discussed in this book, she is in charge of a substantial fortune (cf. Chs. 1, 5, and 6). She probably had become wealthy through both dowry and inheritance. The *oliganthropia* ('lack of men') that had characterized Hellenistic Sparta (cf. Ch. 1) is also evident in Epicteta's family. She had no brothers, for her father Grinnus had adopted a certain Antisthenes, son of Isocles (81–2, 108). Epicteta's own sons had died: Cratesilochus predeceased his father Phoinix, and Andragoras died two years after his father. Epiteleia, daughter of Epicteta and Phoinix, survived as her parents' sole descendant.

Perhaps because her daughter's children were legally members of another family or *oikos*, and Epicteta's had died out, she felt she needed to create inducements to secure their future ministrations. They were destined to inherit her fortune. Nevertheless, it would be natural to have been concerned lest after her death they may have wished to put the funds to other uses, although no actual grounds for such a suspicion are evident. Epiteleia's ties to her mother's family are

[31] ll. 2–107, excerpted, trans. adapted from Wittenburg, *Il Testamento di Epikteta*, 159–61.

evident, in that her son Andragoras bears the same name as her deceased brother. He was not named for a member of his father's family. As priest of the cult of the dead, Andragoras would fulfill the duty of an actual descendant, even if he had not been legally adopted. Despite the fact that only the female members of her nuclear family survive, and there is a younger eponymous woman (whose relationship to the original bearer of the name is not stated), Epicteta restricted the original beneficiaries of her foundation to males. The title is first announced as 'the association of the men's club' (22–3, etc.). This preference is understandable in the general context of Greek patriarchal tradition. The administration of the foundation is adopted from political administration, and of course only males were versed in public finance and government.[32] Furthermore, practical reasons dictated the preference for males. As a result of patrilocal marriage, Epicteta's female relatives may have lived far from the site of the cult, and may have had obligations to their husband's families that would prevent them from carrying out the duties assigned to members of the foundation. The participation of female children is limited to the period when they are under their father's guardianship (95–6). Nevertheless, Epicteta has second thoughts, more practical ones. She admits on equal terms: wives of the original members and, as we have mentioned, their daughters who are still under their father's guardianship; descendants of the original members; and *epikleroi* with their husbands and offspring. Finally she admits eight women with their husbands and children, including her own daughter, two sisters of her son-in-law, and three additional women who are daughters or sisters of other members of the group. Epicteta drafted into her family foundation people with whom she had no apparent kinship ties by either blood or marriage, at least within the degree recognized by Greek law. A large number of participants are only relatives of relatives. Thus she constructed for herself a family with as many lateral branches as any we might find in classical Athens. Even so, the entire group consists of twenty-five males and only eight females. This list of names indicates that demographic and historical forces shaped the structure and composition of both the nuclear and the extended family. The size and sex ratio of the family, in turn, affected the financial status of women such as Epicteta. Yet she attempted to create an institution where

[32] See further ibid. 100–18, 149.

mostly male kin would care for the family tomb as they had done 300 years earlier in Athens.

Such foundations would encourage and institutionalize family reunions. Participants, or beneficiaries of the foundations, were persuaded to carry out their obligations to the dead, not only because of fears about their own fate, but through palpable attractions such as elaborate banquets at the tomb. For example, Epicteta took care to specify that the annual banquet funded by her foundation should include meat, imported wine, grilled cheese, sacrificial cakes, fish, and be enhanced by crowns, music, and myrrh.[33] Were these items not merely typical ingredients of any festive meal, but, in particular, her family's favourite dishes? In any event, such periodic reunions were particularly valuable in the Hellenistic period, when the family network was likely to have been smaller than in the classical period. Some male members of the immediate family were permanently separated from their kinsmen, because they had become mercenary soldiers or had migrated, and some families who had migrated had no distant male relatives. The size and variety of the *cosmopolis* meant that migration remained an attractive option throughout the Hellenistic period, with the potential to cause fragmentation of families repeatedly. Furthermore, as may have been the case in Epicteta's family, the rate of family extinction could be accelerated by female infanticide. Thus, parenthetically, it is impossible to draw a simple conclusion concerning the status of women from the text of Epicteta's foundation alone. Female infanticide is a symptom of the low status of women (see below). On the other hand, the Hellenistic period offers plenty of evidence for the improvement of women's financial status, with women like Epicteta and her daughter Epiteleia managing a large amount of money, expecting, apparently, an obligatory nod from the male guardians whom they have selected. Specific laws governing women's guardianship in Hellenistic Thera are not known. According to the rules of the *anchisteia* in other cities, Epicteta's guardian should have been her adopted brother. In no legal system that is known was a mother-in-law part of her son-in-law's *anchisteia*; nor was there any necessity that he serve as her guardian. In other words, a widow like Epicteta who had no close male relatives was apparently free to select as her guardian any man whom she found congenial.

[33] Ibid. cols. v. 34–vi. 11.

Like Epicteta, a certain Diomedon who endowed a funerary foundation in honour of Heracles Diomedonteius in the third to second centuries BC in Cos seems to have had a dearth of kinsmen, at least in the neighbourhood.[34] The inscription is admittedly fragmentary. Though kinsmen are mentioned in general (face A, ll. 10–11), the only person named is his slave Libys (face AA, ll. 4, 11). Diomedon directs that commemorative activities be carried out by his slave, Libys, and his slave's children, all of whom he frees.[35] The arrangements for Libys and his children are made at the very beginning of the inscription, preceding and following a brief general sentence giving instructions for Diomedon's descendants. Perhaps Diomedon did not yet have children, or they had migrated elsewhere. At any rate, he shows more concern for Libys than for any relatives he may have had. Perhaps there were no laws or customs similar to those at Athens that obliged him to give preference to relatives in the disposition of his property and affections. Polybius reported that in Boeotia in 192 childless men did not bequeath their property to their relatives, as had been customary previously, but instead made it the common property of their friends to be used for feasting and drinking.[36] Even many who had relatives left the major portion of their property to their eating clubs. Polybius reports this symptom of family disintegration with disapproval. The evidence of funerary foundations is consistent with Polybius's report. Even those who have kinsmen consider them to be unreliable. Their ministrations are no longer assumed to be natural; nor are they imposed by law: rather, they must be bribed.

Families do die out or have no surviving males to perpetuate the patriline, or members move away from the site of the foundation permanently.[37] Public foundations that endowed an annual banquet for an entire citizen body were more expensive, but brought greater assurance that the memory of the dead grantor and his family and the rites that had been paid for would continue to be celebrated. Beneficiaries of such a foundation are perpetually the founder's grateful

[34] *IJG* II, 24B, pp. 94–102. Cf. Epicurus, who died in 270 leaving no direct descendants, and who directed his heirs to make an annual deduction from his estate to pay for offerings to his father, mother, brothers, and himself: Diog. Laert. 10. 16–18.

[35] *IJG* II, 24B, pp. 94–102, face A, ll. 3–6. For affective relationships with slaves in the absence of family, see Ch. 6 on the wills of Ptolemaic soldiers.

[36] 20. 6. 5–6, and see Ch. 1 n. 88.

[37] We speculate that the families of the original owners of funerary monuments that were later reused by other families were no longer in Athens: see Ch. 1 n. 113.

guests. Thus a decree honouring a certain Diogenes, son of Diogenes, also mentions the public funerary foundation established by his father.[38]

In the present context it is important to observe that although the private foundation adopts its administrative model from *polis* government,[39] the public funerary foundation is a large-scale copy of the funerary practices of the private family. Although both male and female family members participate in the private feasts, public feasts are restricted to men. Thus we have another example of the political community as a quasi-family.

BURIALS

Demography: Sex Ratios

Family foundations leave little doubt about the identity and relationships of the participants. Furthermore, most people were buried in cemeteries with marks of identification: these, however, have often become obscured over time. Nevertheless, the artefacts of cemeteries are no more ambiguous than many other primary sources available to demographers of ancient societies. Under ideal circumstances (which are, of course, rare in classical archaeology) in well-preserved, well-excavated burials, the epitaph, sculptured relief, grave-goods, and skeletal remains can provide the family historian with valuable information about the sex, age, marital status, reproductive history, and social rank of the deceased. The context should indicate whether the burial is of a single individual in a communal cemetery of unrelated people or of a person who is buried with other members of the family. Sculpted reliefs, however, frequently do not serve as accurate illustrations of family relationships recorded in an accompanying epitaph (see below). What is more surprising in a society marked by extreme gender differentiation and rites of passage between age groupings is

[38] D. M. Pippidi, 'Monumente epigrafice inedite', in E. Condurachi *et al.* (eds.), *Histria. Monografie archeologiche*, 1 (Bucharest, 1954), 473–564, esp. 477, no. 1, ll. 15–21.

[39] See p. 111, above. Pauline Schmitt-Pantel, 'Évergétisme et mémoire du mort. À propos des fondations de banquets publics dans les cités grecques à l'époque hellénistique et romaine', in G. Gnoli and J. P. Vernant (eds.), *La Mort, les morts dans les sociétés anciennes* (Cambridge and Paris, 1982), 177–88, argues that the private foundations are basically a less expensive version of civic benefactions.

that correspondence between grave-goods, sex, and age is not always exact. Nevertheless, some tendencies have been established.[40] Although a palaeontologist may mistake a mature female for a young man, skeletal remains can reveal the age of death within approximately five years.[41] The bones of the very young are fragile, but infants and small children can be readily sorted out, for they are often buried in pottery containers or in a group apart from adults. Otherwise, the deterioration of the contents of classical cemeteries over the past two and a half millennia should have been random. Often the historian wishes that earlier generations of archaeologists had been more concerned about reporting the details of burials. We may assume that even their carelessness was random, with an overemphasis on burials with valuable and artistically significant grave-goods.

In the case of individual burials, the historian can use the primary evidence with some confidence. It is the aggregate that is most difficult to analyse. The population of an ancient city's cemeteries is not a direct reflection of the total population of the city, or even of the élite citizen body. Some burial sites are likely to present a more distorted picture of some constituents of the population than are others, and the quantity and quality of the distortion may vary over time. Local variation further complicates the picture. More than one formula must be sought to reconstruct life from the artefacts of death.[42] Working in a Roman context, in which statistical evidence is certainly better than it is for Greek history, Keith Hopkins cautions

[40] Adults may be buried with child-size *choes* ('wine-jugs', see below), and a single grave may contain a variety of objects suitable for both men and women, as well as for both adults and children. See further Hamilton, *Choes and Anthesteria*, 77–81, and David M. Robinson, *Excavations at Olynthus*, 11: *Necrolynthia* (Baltimore, 1942), 181–2. J. Hall, in Marian Davis, 'Grave Goods at the Pantanello Necropolis 1982–1989: An Interim Report', (Austin, Tex., 1990), 69–70, suggests that the grave-goods reflect the sex of the donor rather than that of the deceased. For the erotic connotations of the burials of males with mirrors, and females with strigils, see Houby-Nielsen, 'Gender Roles'.

[41] See e.g. Sara C. Bisel's discussion of sixty-one skeletons in Wilfried K. Kovacsovics, *Kerameikos* XIV: *Die Eckterrasse an der Gräberstrasse des Kerameikos* (Berlin, 1990), 151–9, and Introduction, no. 20 above.

[42] B. Boyaval, 'Remarques sur les indications d'âges de l'épigraphie funéraire grecque d'Égypte', *ZPE* 21 (1976), 217–43, concluded that each of the five Egyptian sites he had studied presented a different demographic picture. Ian Morris, *Burial and Ancient Society. The Rise of the Greek City-State* (Cambridge, 1987), 100, estimated that the number of tombs excavated in fifth-century Athens represented *c.*1.7 per cent of the total population.

against the use of data from cemeteries for demographic purposes.[43] He points out that no society could have reproduced itself if it actually had a sex ratio as high as the *c.*150 males to 100 females obtained from some groups of tombstones. The Roman cemeteries that yielded such sex ratios, however, were largely military. The soldiers (who were not permitted to marry) consorted with native women, who bore them illegitimate children. In such cemeteries the historian would not expect to find women and children buried with men in the same proportions in which they encountered with them in life.

The cemeteries of Greek cities differ from those of the Romans.[44] At least, no historian has suggested a convincing reason why the burials should be severely skewed in favour of one sex or age-group and why some of the dead should be excluded. Instead, it is possible that the cemeteries approximated a cross-section of the living citizenry, albeit with several caveats. There is a class bias in the case of slaves. Although the master was required to bury his slaves, archaeologists have not detected, or at least distinguished, slave burials.[45] Either slaves were excluded from the cemeteries that have been studied, or they may have been buried anonymously in the family plot, or in death they lost their lowly status and received burial without indication that they were slaves. Furthermore, infants and small children were often buried together, apart from adults, and sometimes soldiers who died in service were buried as a group, apart

[43] 'Graveyards for Historians', in F. Hinard (ed.), *La Mort, les morts et l'au-delà dans le monde romain* (Caen, 1987), 113–26. Hopkins's discussions of mortality among the Roman élite in *Death and Renewal: Sociological Studies in Roman History,* vol. 2 (Cambridge, 1983), esp. 73–4, 98, 102–3, are not directly applicable to classical Athens, because the Romans deliberately attempted to manipulate their natural fertility. There is no evidence that the Athenians employed sophisticated legal devices such as the Julian laws to encourage childbearing as the Romans did. Nor, by contrast, did the Romans have recourse to an *epikleros* to prevent extinction of the patriline. See further Richard P. Saller, 'Roman Heirship Strategies in Principle and in Practice', in David I. Kertzer and Richard P. Saller (eds.), *The Family in Italy* (New Haven and London, 1991), 26–47.

[44] Morris, *Death-Ritual*, 81–2, uses Roman data to cast doubt on the Greek evidence for a skewed sex ratio, but in so doing he ignores not only chronological change and geographical variation, but also the difference between the status of women in the two societies. See Introduction. Furthermore, in *Burial and Ancient Society,* esp. 93, Morris correctly drew attention to the importance of rank in obtaining access to visible burial. Rank, in turn, was largely dependent upon sex and age.

[45] Ps.-Dem. 43. 58, 47. 70. See further Kurtz and Boardman, *Greek Burial Customs*, 198–9.

from their families, as happened after the Battle of Marathon and annually thereafter until the end of the first year of the Peloponnesian War.[46] In some cities—for example, Olynthus—archaeologists have been able to study the burials of both the children and adults. Thus, it might seem reasonable to assume, as a working hypothesis, that Greek cemeteries give a picture of the adult citizenry of the *polis* at least.

Because not all the burials from any one city that occurred in a limited period of time have been recovered, the data from cemeteries cannot be exploited for information about total population without correction. Unlike the tombstones of the Romans, those of the Greeks in the classical period do not record precise information about age, length of marriage, and number of progeny. Some of this information can be inferred, but the age usually can be known only in general terms, in so far as the dead person is identified as a baby, child, youth, adult, or elderly person. If we assume that the losses are random, however, the sex ratio and age structure of excavated burials should be reliable. It has recently been argued that at Athens not only the wealthy, but ordinary people as well, could afford a tombstone.[47] This view is based on the assumption that any man, no matter how low on the social and economic scale, would manage to scrape up the funds for his own sepulchral inscription. The argument is flawed, however, for it focuses on male citizens and ignores the financial, social, and legal situation of women, both those who died and their surviving female kin.[48] Athenian women were legally permitted to make contracts only for the value of one medimnus ('bushel') of barley.[49] We suppose that engaging a mason to create a custom-made monument required such a contract. Nevertheless, sometimes a married daughter assumed responsibility for burying her parents, and either provided an expensive monument herself or carried out her parents' wishes.[50] We know of one woman who was so concerned that

[46] See further Nicole Loraux, *The Invention of Athens: The Funeral Oration in the Classical City* (Cambridge, Mass., 1986), 117–24. As H. A. Shapiro, 'The Iconography of Mourning in Athenian Art', *AJA* 95 (1991), 629–56, esp. 646 n. 113, has noted, although the public burials took place annually, not every dead soldier was buried in the Demosion Sema.

[47] So Thomas Heine Nielsen *et al.*, 'Athenian Grave Monuments and Social Class', *GRBS* 30 (1989), 411–20.

[48] See also n. 50 below.

[49] Isae. 10. 10, and see further G. E. M. de Ste Croix, 'Some Observations on the Property Rights of Athenian Women', *CR* 20 (1970), 273–8.

[50] As in the case of Epiteleia of Thasos, n. 30 above, and see further below.

her son Philo would not give her proper burial that she entrusted 300 drachmas to a friend for this purpose (Lys. 31. 21, *c*.400 BC). This woman was wealthy; an average burial cost one-tenth of the price.[51] Like Ampharete's daughter (see below), she was able to act on her own initiative in the period just after the end of the Peloponnesian War when there were fewer constraints on women than were usually in force.[52] Philo's accuser asserts that the son's ignoring his obligation to bury his mother was a symptom of extreme degeneracy.[53] The argument is contentious. Moreover, the mother was expecting an extremely expensive burial. If we assume, then, for the sake of argument, that most adult female citizens received proper burial (but see below), and in addition that soldiers were often buried elsewhere, then we must account for the skewed sex ratios of the cemeteries. Almost invariably, mature women and female babies are underrepresented in enduring commemorations.[54] Sepulchral inscriptions of Athens *c*.400 BC–AD 250 give the names of 2,905 men and only 1,472 women (the sex of 142 is unknown).[55] Among the burials of wealthy families in family precincts at Rhamnous, the ratio of males to females is approximately three to two (see below). In brief, the question here is whether this skewing of the sex ratio is a reflection of female infanticide, which would deny some of them normal burial at the start of life, and of the ongoing neglect of women during their lives, which might discourage their kinsmen from giving them the kind of burial that could endure to be studied by archaeologists some two and a half millennia later.[56] In other words, we may need to reject our assumption (above) that most adult females were properly buried, as were men, with identification.

Other archaeological data attest to the devaluation of female children. Children used a small *chous* at the Anthesteria. Many

[51] Nielsen *et al.*, 'Athenian Grave Monuments', 414.

[52] See further Pomeroy, *Goddesses, Whores*, 80–1. Unfortunately there is no hard evidence about sex ratios in this period: thus Barry S. Strauss, *Athens after the Peloponnesian War* (Ithaca, NY, 1987), 70–1, discusses 'Athenian manpower'.

[53] Lys. 31. 23; cf. Aesch. 1. 99, Dem. 57. 70, Isae. 6. 64–5.

[54] Metapontum is an exception. But the men there were probably buried on the battlefield. The University of Texas at Austin. *The Pantanello Necropolis 1982–1989* (Austin, Tex., 1990), 37, 77.

[55] See Nielsen *et al.*, 'Athenian Grave Monuments', 411.

[56] For a definition of infanticide as the climax of a continuum of reduced parental investment in a child involving maltreatment and neglect that sooner or later results in death see Hrdy, 'Fitness Tradeoffs', 412.

more *choes* depict the activities of boys than of girls.[57] We may conclude that: (1) fewer girls than boys attended the Anthesteria, a festival in honour of Dionysus, because there were fewer 3-year-old girls than boys among the Athenians; or (2) the numbers of girls and boys were equal, but fathers were not enthusiastic about showing off their daughters, and did not take them to the Anthesteria; or (3) girls and boys attended in equal numbers, but because girls were less valued, they were less likely to have their own *chous* with a female design, but rather for the festival (or for their burial) would be given a hand-me-down jug with the all-purpose male image. A *chous* was sometimes included among the grave-goods at a child's burial, but many more have been found outside burial contexts.[58] These finds suggest that the *choes* were reused, and, of course, in a patriarchal society it would be humiliating for a boy to use a girl's cup, while it would be unobjectionable for a girl to use a boy's.

Social historians have devoted more study to Roman customs of commemoration than to Greek, and the number of burials available for study in the Greek world is so small as to make generalizations hazardous. In any case, it certainly appears that women's health was inferior to that of men in the same socio-economic group, and that their life span was shorter.[59] This inequity would give them less time to get into some historical records, but they should nevertheless show up in cemeteries. A woman who married at the age of 15 might well be a grandmother at 30. Yet, in an epitaph from mid-fourth-century Piraeus, a certain Chairestrate describes herself as *eudaimon* ('fortunate') to have survived to see her children's children.[60] Evidently she alludes to her longevity because it was rare for a woman to live so long. In any case, the correspondence between the demographic data of cemeteries and that of society at large was not exact, and we do not know the degree of distortion; therefore our conclusions can only be

[57] Their numbers are so overwhelming that Hamilton, *Choes and Anthesteria* 145, n. 68, observes that he has failed to consider the virtual absence of girls from his study. The depiction of clothed girls does not conform to Hamilton's formulation (p. 118): 'Naked child is to (unseen) dressed adult as grapes are to contest wine.'

[58] Hamilton, *Choes and Anthesteria*, 70–1.

[59] Introduction, n. 21, above.

[60] IG II[2] 6288, mid-fourth century or later, Piraeus. W. Peek, *Griechische Vers-Inschriften* (Berlin, 1955), p. 104, no. 421, and Clairmont, *Classical Attic Tombstones*, 1. 934. Garland, *Greek Way of Death*, 160, classifies Chairestrate among 'the elderly'. For Ampharete, a grandmother, see n. 113 below.

impressionistic. All our evidence, however, suggests that sex ratios were skewed in lifetime as in death.[61]

Until a few years ago, historians examining the demographic data from classical Athens would pronounce that the sex ratios were too unbalanced in favour of males, and did not correspond to those of any known society or demographic model. We can now cite analogies in contemporary China, India, and elsewhere. These countries display extremely high sex ratios owing to female infanticide and neglect of female children.[62] Mark Golden has argued that there was a 20 per cent rate of female infanticide at Athens, and his hypothesis is persuasive.[63] At the moment we are unable to establish a precise sex ratio for Athens. Nevertheless, I believe it is worth while to discuss the demographic data, and not simply to surrender to critics who warn that neither reliable nor statistically significant patterns can be detected. In a society with such a skewed sex ratio there are bound to be surplus males. Their number, however, was often reduced by war and migration. Because women married at a much earlier age than men, most, though not all, men managed to marry, if not a virgin, then a widow or a divorcée. Remarriage was common, and much more common for women than for men.[64]

Lasting burial with a commemorative marker is an indication of high status. Infanticide is a symptom of low status. Care in death is consistent with care in life. In other words, the skewed sex ratios of Greek cemeteries testify to the devaluation of women. That some women, however, did endeavour to provide lasting burials for kinswomen and other females who were dear to them suggests that they harboured different views about women's status (see e.g. below on Ampharete and Phanostrate). 'Statistics of commemoration'[65] reflect social status. They also reflect the prejudices of the people who controlled the funds for commemoration, who were, overwhelmingly,

[61] See further Pomeroy, *Goddesses, Whores*, 140, 227–8, and *Women in Hellenistic Egypt*, pp. xviii, 44–5, 111, 136, 172. On sex ratios in *periboloi* at Rhamnous, see below.

[62] Cf. the preference for boy babies in modern China, India, Pakistan, etc.: see e.g. Nicholas D. Kristof, 'Stark Data on Women: 100 Million Are Missing', *New York Times*, 5 Nov., 1991, C1, C12.

[63] 'The Exposure of Girls at Athens', *Phoenix*, 35 (1981), 316–31, and see Ch. 6 n. 125 below.

[64] Wesley E. Thompson, 'Athenian Marriage Patterns: Remarriage', *CSCA* 5 (1972), 211–25, esp. 218, found that in the upper class 30 women and 23 men remarried. See also Ch. 5 n. 28 *et passim*.

[65] For the phrase see Hopkins, 'Graveyards for Historians', 124.

men. Men controlled the beginning of the life cycle as well (see Ch. 2). Denial of enduring burial in a society in which care of the dead is of great significance may be situated on a continuum that extends, at its most lethal, to infanticide. To the 20 per cent rate of female infanticide postulated by Golden, we may add lack of burial with a marker of approximately another 10 per cent of women, resulting from disrespect and neglect, and then arrive at the sex ratios of the cemeteries. This generalization applies to the wealthier classes as well, for it is their commemorative monuments and other historical records that have survived out of proportion to their numbers in the population at large (see below on Rhamnous e.g.). While excavated burials may not reflect the precise age and sex ratio of the population of Greek cities, they do testify to a relationship between gender and status.

HEIRS, HEIRESSES, AND THE DEMISE OF FAMILIES

Even discounting infanticide, in ancient societies infant and juvenile mortality was high. Before the advent of modern medicine and sanitation, the early years of life were perilous. Moreover, if a mother died in childbirth the new-born was deprived of optimum, free, readily available nourishment. Ceramic baby-feeders have been excavated, but these do not seem appropriate for new-borns. Unless, by chance, the household included a nursing slave, a wet-nurse had to be obtained quickly. Thus the archaeological report that approximately 30 per cent of the burials at Olynthus were of babies seems to be a reasonable reflection of actual mortality.[66] Families were constantly threatened with extinction. Indeed, the brevity of historical memory—for the most part limited to three generations—already mentioned, as well as the information given vertically in the genealogical charts throughout this book, may reflect not only an eclipse of historical data for a particular lineage but the actual extinction of the line.[67]

A very simple demographic model will illustrate some reproductive

[66] Introduction, n. 20 above. Children constituted another 21.4 per cent of those buried: Robinson, *Excavations at Olynthus*, xi. 146–70. Children constituted 50 per cent of burials in the Cerameicus and other Attic cemeteries: Morris, *Burial and Ancient Society*, appendix A1, 218–21, and Sanne Houby-Neilsen, '"Burial Language" in Archaic and Classical Kerameikos', *Proceedings of the Danish Institute at Athens*, 1 (1995), 131–91, tables 1–2.

[67] Figs. 1–7.

possibilities. Among ten couples, two will produce two boys; two will produce two girls; four will produce one boy and one girl each; two will be infertile. Legal strategies were devised to prevent the extinction of the patriline in totally infertile families and in those that produced only girls.[68] As the demographic model above makes clear, even without the grim factor of high infant and juvenile mortality, 40 per cent of couples would need recourse to some remedy to assure the survival of the patriline. A man needed a son to perform the customary rituals of burial and tomb cult (cf. Isae. 2. 10). Adoption was an obvious solution.[69] The optimal pattern was for a family with two boys to donate one to an infertile branch of the family, or even to a wealthy unmarried kinsman. Like endogamy, intrafamilial adoption consolidated the family's property. As the demographic model described at the beginning of this paragraph indicates, however, a boy was not always available. Of the thirty-six known cases of adoption at Athens, three were of girls.[70] Even the wealthy Hagnias II adopted a girl who was his married sister's daughter and thus a member of a different *oikos*. The adoptee would become a member of the adopter's *oikos*.[71] It was expected that the sentimental relationship between a natural parent and his offspring would be found as well in the adoptive relationship: 'the lawgiver made this law because he saw that for childless men the only escape from loneliness and the only consolation in life was to be able to adopt whomever they liked' (Isae. 2. 13; but cf. Lycurg. *Leoc.* 48). Adoption of a wife's relative was not uncommon.[72] Adoption usually conferred an economic benefit upon the adoptee. The fourth-century sources on adoption focus on relatively large inheritances that were disputed, and Hellenistic

[68] The demographic analogies in Mogens Herman Hansen *et al.*, 'The Demography of Attic Demes. The Evidence of the Sepulchral Inscriptions', *Analecta Romana*, 19 (1990), 25–44, esp. 31, are too simple; for in calculating the extinction of families, they do not take account of the legal remedies.

[69] Louis Gernet, *Droit et société dans la Grèce ancienne* (Paris, 1955), 129, lists twenty-seven examples, of which two are adoptions of females. For another possible adoption see D. M. Lewis, 'Notes on Attic Inscriptions, II', *ABSA* 50 (1955), 1–36, esp. 14, and see now Rubinstein, *Adoption in iv. Century Athens.*

[70] Isae. 7. 9, 11. 8, 41–2, 45. As usual, the girls' names are not known. See further Rubinstein, *Adoption in iv. Century Athens*, 20–1, 119, cat. 9, 120, cat. 13, 121, cat. 17.

[71] e.g. Isae. 11; Ps.-Dem. 43; see further Rubinstein, *Adoption in iv. Century Athens*, 111.

[72] In addition to the adoptions in the Hagnias case, see Dem. 41. 3–5; Ps.-Plut. *Orat.* 838a; Dion. Hal. *Isoc.* 18; and Isae. 2. 3–4, 11.

inscriptions inform us of adoptions among priests and other officials.[73] It is impossible to know for certain whether adoptions occurred with any frequency in the lower echelons of society. In Greek society, where inheritance was partible (though favouring sons over daughters), adoption would ensure that siblings of the adoptee received a larger patrimony. Within Greece, some regional variation can be detected, with adoptions particularly common in Athens and Rhodes.[74]

The epiklerate served as another solution to the problem of continuity. As the simple demographic model above indicates, 20 per cent of families may produce only girls. When their father dies, these brotherless girls become *epikleroi* ('heiresses'; literally 'attached to the property'). The nearest male relative of their father is obliged to marry the *epikleros*. If either spouse is already married, he or she must divorce his or her current mate. The children of the *epikleros*, in turn, were considered descendants and heirs of their deceased grandfather, became members of his *oikos*, and were enabled to continue his patriline. Sometimes adoption was combined with the epiklerate. For example, in the case of Hagnias II (Isae. 11, Ps.-Dem. 43), the adoptee would have become an *epikleros* upon the death of her adoptive father, Hagnias, though in fact she did not survive to maturity. The father of an *epikleros* might adopt the husband of his daughter, and thus spare her the trauma of divorce and remarriage. In this way the husband of an *epikleros* would also be her brother.[75] Marriage between non-uterine half-siblings was permitted in Athenian law.

FAMILY PLOTS

As mentioned above, infants and small children were often buried as a group, in places different from those allocated to adults. Descriptions of cemeteries from the classical period indicate that the vast majority of people were not interred in family groupings, but rather as individuals or as pairs.[76] For example, at Olynthus, a site admittedly

[73] See Rubinstein *et al.*, 'Adoption in Hellenistic and Roman Athens', *C&M* 42 (1991), 139–51, esp. 146.

[74] Astrid Wentzel, 'Studien über die Adoption in Griechenland', *Hermes*, 65 (1960), 167–76. For *periboloi* only at Athens and Rhodes see n. 126 below.

[75] As in Dem. 41. 3–5.

[76] See p. 103 above and n. 79 below.

characterized by careless burials often lacking tombstones, of a total of 598 published graves from the sixth century to the middle of the fourth, only three contained family members buried together.[77] The questions put to candidates for the archonship concerning the location of their family's tombs indicates that they were not buried in one place.[78] Considering that respectable women were never independent from their families, one might have expected to find them buried predominantly in large, protective, family groups, but this is not the case. A study of the names of citizen women in family groups on gravestones found 51 per cent named together with only one other person, and 23 per cent named with two persons.[79] At Athens two family members may be buried together. Among people commemorated on the sculpted stelae discussed below we find a son buried next to his mother, a grandmother and granddaughter, and two pairs of father and son.

Family precincts are noteworthy for size and luxury. In death, as in life, the truism becomes evident: 'only the rich have families.' Such family burials may be swollen by the addition of members of other *oikoi* who were connected to the élite by marriage. Thus, for example, a man who was married to Hipparete, a granddaughter of the famous Alcibiades, was probably buried in the Ceramicus with his wife's family.[80] In a study of 100 burials in Tanagra dating from the sixth century BC to the Roman period, the presence of a few luxurious tombs in family precincts of the fourth century commands attention.[81] At Athens at the end of the fifth century and in the fourth, the wealthy sometimes favoured burials in *periboloi*, or family enclosures. In some neighbourhoods, such as Rhamnous, *periboloi* were so popular that one suspects an epidemic of 'keeping up with the Joneses'. The precise date in the fifth century when large marble

[77] Robinson, *Excavations at Olynthus*, p. 139.

[78] See n. 14 above, and further below. An exception, Cimon's family had their own plot, *ta Kimoneia mnemata*: Hdt. 6. 103; Marc. *Vit. Thuc.* 17, 55, and Plut. *Cim.* 19. 4.

[79] Vestergaard, *et al.*, 'A Typology of the Women Recorded on Gravestones from Attica', *AJAH* 10 (1985), 178–90, esp. 190 n. 10.

[80] For Hipparete: *IG* II² 7400; for her husband Phanocles: *IG* II² 6746. See further Davies, *APF*, nos. 600X and 10452. For another example see the son-in-law in the family of Demochares: Davies, *APF* 3716(B) and Ch. 5 n. 8 below.

[81] See further A. K. Andriomenou, 'La Nécropole classique de Tanagra', in *La Béotie antique, Lyon-Saint-Étienne, 16–20 mai 1983*. Coll. intern. du CNRS (Paris, 1985), 109–30.

grave stelae were reintroduced into Attica, and it became possible to use them in *periboloi*, is debatable.[82]

Sumptuary legislation of Demetrius of Phaleron put an end to these monuments that advertised invidious distinctions between very wealthy Athenians and their less fortunate countrymen.[83] Yet the vast majority of classical *periboloi* are unimpressive by comparison with the size of funerary monuments that later lined Roman roads in Italy. Attic *periboloi* rarely hold more than six burials, with two or three not uncommon.[84] They seldom encompass more than three generations.[85] Perhaps such burials would have continued, had Demetrius's legislation not intervened, or the families may actually have become extinct, or, as was not unlikely in the late fourth century, descendants moved elsewhere. Personal knowledge or oral tradition may limit family sentiment to three or four generations, less so in the paternal line because of the continuity of the household, but certainly in the case of the maternal line.[86] It may also have been thought that a huge enclosure revealing expectations of infinite descent or immortality was hubristic, and would tempt the evil eye. In a list of 192 epitaphs of persons with demotic or ethnic there is only one example of the burial of an extended family.[87] This family, which is buried as a group in the fourth century, consists of only eight persons in three generations, descended from two brothers. Six are male, two female.

The large family groups are exceptional.[88] Even they are components of a larger, communal, burial complex; most people were not buried on their private estates, but rather in public cemeteries. Within these, the vast majority of the dead are buried as individuals; or, if we assume that a cemetery was accessible to all citizens, we may consider

[82] See Ch. 1 n. 112. [83] See n. 2 above.

[84] *Periboloi* viii and xiii in Kovacsovics, *Kerameikos* XIV, 20–48, 87–130, the former with twenty, and the latter with fifty burials, are exceptional.

[85] See further Robert Garland, 'A First Catalogue of Attic Peribolos Tombs', *ABSA* 77 (1982), 125–76. Sally Humphries, 'Family Tombs and Tomb Cult in Ancient Athens—Tradition or Traditionalism?', *JHS* 100 (1980), 96–126; repr. in *The Family, Women and Death* (London, 1983), 79–130, counted four *periboloi* of four generations and seventeen of three. Since Humphries (p. 82) lamented that only one major cemetery had been properly excavated, Petrakos has been publishing the rich finds at Rhamnous almost annually. See n. 126 below.

[86] Thus Garland, *Greek Way of Death*, 106–7.

[87] For these see Osborne, 'Attic Epitaphs', esp. 12–14, no. 32.

[88] There may, however, be more than we are aware of. Publications of sepulchral inscriptions in *IG* II and II² did not record whether they were found in *periboloi*. Furthermore, many stelae are fragmentary, and it is impossible to estimate the number of missing names. See also n. 105 below.

that they are surrounded by other members of their *polis*. Although the maintenance of cults for the dead was one of the most sacred family duties, family plots comprising several generations were not the rule. Just as every citizen had to belong to an *oikos*, but was expected to put loyalty to the *polis* first, so in death the *polis* took precedence. The ideology expressed is political and male-oriented. Thus, in public the emphasis in death, as in life, is on ties to the *polis*, rather than to the family. Nevertheless, the patronymic inscribed on the tombstone continues to link every citizen to his or her father, and implies a connection to a family.[89]

EPITAPHS

Epitaphs are often banal, but they usually impart information about family relationships. Some testify to the distinction between legal and emotional family bonds. According to the legal structure of the *oikos* a widow who has produced a son may remain in her late husband's household.[90] Her son is obliged to provide maintenance and eventual burial for his mother. If she has no son, she may return to a male relative, usually a father or a brother. A married daughter's *oikos*, in turn, is different from her mother's. There is no legal obligation for the daughter to assume responsibility for her mother (see above).[91] Yet such must have been the case with Ampharete, whose gravestone shows her holding her daughter's child.[92] Because Ampharete is buried with her daughter's baby, it is likely that her daughter and son-in-law paid for the monument. The stela of Philocydis also testifies to the relationship between maternal grandparents and their motherless grandchild.[93]

Epitaphs usually provide brief, straightforward statements about

[89] See Ch. 1 n. 45. E. A. Meyer, 'Epitaphs and Citizenship in Classical Athens', *JHS* 113 (1993), 99–121, esp. 111, points out that even in the fourth century, when the use of the demotic had increased, the most common format in epitaphs is the demotic and patronymic together. Unfortunately she does not discuss women's burials or the use of demotics in connection with women's names.

[90] e.g. see widows in Ch. 5.

[91] Chrysilla was a special case. Her son-in-law was also her sons' guardian. Whether he moved in with her and her daughter and sons, or whether she moved to his house after her daughter's marriage, when her sons were still minors, is not clear. See Andoc. 1 and Pomeroy, *Xenophon, Oeconomicus*, 261–4.

[92] See n. 113 below.

[93] See n. 109 below.

the identity of the deceased, at the very least.[94] Some stelae also include sentimental and biographical remarks, often in verse, as well as sculpted and painted decorative elements (see below). For the ancient historian in general there is far less information about women than about men: an epitaph is often the only source of information about an individual woman. The reluctance to give the name of a respectable woman in public terminated when she died, and, presumably, her good reputation was assured.

Women, like men, are identified in epitaphs by name and patronymic, at the minimum. Sometimes the father's demotic ('deme name') is given, even for a married woman: this practice is additional evidence of the woman's unseverable bond to her natal family.[95] A man is identified by his own demotic, thus alluding to his role in the *polis*. Women are not identified by their own demotic until post-classical times, and even then such identification is not common. I have found only eight examples, and I interpret these as further evidence of the increase in women's social role in the Hellenistic world.[96] Because the phratry system became extinct, the women with demotics were not also members of phratries. Instead, in the classical and Hellenistic periods their family roles are recorded as essential features of their identity, but the repertoire is strictly limited. In the index of 'Significant Greek Words' in the most recent publication of funerary monuments in the Athenian *agora*, there are more entries for *gune* ('wife', i.e. 99) and *thugater* ('daughter', i.e. 88) than for any other word.[97] By contrast, no man is commemorated as a husband, and the word *huios* ('son') appears only twice. There are no citations for the actual word *pater*, for fathers are referred to by the patronymic. In light of the importance of women's reproductive role, it is interesting to find only two appearances of *meter* ('mother'). To have identified a dead woman as a mother of a daughter would have

[94] The most recently published Attic corpus is Osborne, 'Attic Epitaphs', which fills the gap in publication prior to 1976. For additional epitaphs and revisions of previously published inscriptions see *SEG*, *passim*.

[95] Or, more rarely, the deme name with the suffix *-then* ('from'). See Ch. 2 and see further Whitehead, *Demes of Attica*, 77–9. Osborne, 'Attic Epitaphs', 13, correctly rejects a restoration that would supply a demotic for a woman in the fourth century.

[96] In inscriptions that are undated or dated to the Roman period, a few women have demotics: *IG* II^2 5276, 5428, 6255, 6780, 6781, 6810, 7764; Bradeen, *Athenian Agora*, 47, no. 107.

[97] Bradeen, *Athenian Agora*, 238–4, index 11. Vestergaard *et al.*, 'A Typology', 181, found 121 examples of women named with uxorial status and almost 500 with filial status.

compromised the reputation of a daughter (if she were still living, as was likely), whereas to refer to her as the mother of a son would perhaps have suggested that she wielded authority over him. Myths of autochthony bypassed the reality of birth from mothers. The fantasy of descent from male to male found its way into a wide range of documents. (Cf. Ch. 6 for the subordination and anonymity of mothers in Ptolemaic Egypt.)

SCULPTED STELAE AND VASES

Changing funerary monuments change the public image of the family. Visual imagery depicting a death in the family, however, is among the most difficult of all the evidence from cemeteries for the modern viewer to interpret, even when the stela is well preserved and complete with image and text. The relationship between art and life is not direct. First of all, the historian must understand the conventions of sculpture, vase-painting, poetry, epitaphs, and inscriptions. Then it is necessary to determine the relationship between visual image and written text. Finally, it is essential to understand the expectations of the original audience and the ideas that are being conveyed about the dead person. For example, if the dead person is a virtuous woman who has lived a relatively obscure life, she makes her formal public début on the stela. It may nevertheless have seemed safer to depict her as a generic 'matron' rather than as an identifiable individual.[98] Furthermore, although we can obtain few certain answers, it is useful to consider who paid for the monument and how the donor wished to express his or her relationship to the dead person, to the monument, and to the passerby who glanced at it. A funerary monument translates a private relationship into a public one.

Questions arise at the most basic level. When confronting a sculpted group the modern historian asks not only: What is the relationship between the persons depicted?, but Which one died?[99] Classical sculpture masks age and emotion. Status may be shown as age: slaves may be depicted as small and thus appear to be children; or the representation may be realistic, for the sculptor may depict the

[98] e.g. Pheidostrate; see n. 126 below.

[99] On the identification of figures on tombstones see most recently Clairmont, *Classical Attic Tombstones*, Introd. vol., 119–21, *et passim*.

emotional attachment between the deceased owner and children who were slaves in the household. Women are portrayed in their youthful bloom, so that it is often impossible to determine whether a warrior is bidding farewell to his wife or to his mother. Artistic conventions changed over time.[100] In the fourth century the age of a female survivor may be depicted, but the dead woman continues to be idealized as youthful, as of the age of greatest fertility and sexual attractiveness.[101] In sculpture showing two people joining hands in a mutual gesture of farewell, or showing a cast of characters who do not concentrate their gaze upon one figure, it is difficult to determine which member of the family group died. The conclusion may be that no one has died, for in the memory of the immediate family dead members continue to exist and to interact with one another. The living and the dead not only look into each other's eyes, but sometimes are portrayed clasping hands and conversing.[102] Certainly in tragedy it is not bizarre for characters to address the dead with confidence that their words are being heard (e.g. Aes. *Cho.* 5, 88, 130, 139, 156, etc.). Many white-ground *lekythoi* depict women at tombs in the presence of what appears to be the dead person.[103] The preservation of a bond between living and dead may still be observed in some parts of Greece, where women visit cemeteries and talk to dead relatives. They report that they have visited these people, not that they have visited their tombs.[104]

Even when inscribed epitaphs accompany a sculptured relief, there is often a lack of correspondence between the people mentioned specifically and the visual depiction. Should the modern viewer consider the information from the two sources as complementary or conflicting?[105] Is our demand for precise correspondence between

[100] See further Marion Meyer, *Der griechischen Urkundenreliefs*, MDAI(A), 13 (Berlin, 1989), *passim*.

[101] See further Susanne Pfisterer-Haas, *Darstellungen alter Frauen in der griechischen Kunst*, Europäische Hochschulschriften, ser. 38, vol. 21 (Frankfurt, 1989), 10–15, 24, 93, with some observations on the identification of the dead person in a family portrait.

[102] e.g. monument of Aristylla: Athens, Nat. Museum inv. 766 = *IG*² 1058 = Clairmont, *Classical Attic Tombstones*, 2. 51.

[103] See further Shapiro, 'Iconography of Mourning', 652–3.

[104] See further Loring Danforth, *The Death Rituals of Rural Greece* (Princeton, 1982), ch. 5.

[105] Meyer, 'Epitaphs and Citizenship', 108–9, points out that as the classical period progressed, writing, more than visual respresentations, provided information about the dead.

image and text anachronistic? An epigram may state that a woman had three children, but the Attic stela depict her with only one or two. This limitation seems to be the result of artistic convention and the size of the stela.[106] Large family groups are shown in the course of the fourth century. Two children may also be symbolic of any number exceeding one. The viewer may wonder if, as seems to be true of some Roman sarcophagi, the stela was purchased ready-made, and the inscription added to order. Some of the epigrams are so repetitious—for example, praising a woman for the traditional virtue of *sophrosyne* ('modesty')—that they too seem to have been ready-made, just awaiting the insertion of a name of the proper metrical length.

For the family historian, conventional depictions on apparently ready-made funerary monuments are important reflections of contemporary assumptions, preoccupations, and ideology. The unique custom-made stelae and epigrams, however, which record a kaleidoscope of situations and relationships that defy expectations, exert a fascination. These monuments reveal that kinship bonds, especially those of the natal family with married women and their offspring, remain strong.

One is easily seduced into constructing a scenario, or soap opera, behind the creation of the stela of Phylonoë.[107] The relief depicts a standing woman holding a baby boy. The child is reaching towards a seated woman who appears oblivious to his gesture. The epigram mentions neither husband nor child: 'Phylonoë daughter of [. . .] lies here, modest, wise, and possessing every virtue.' Was Phylonoë a new bride whose claims on her father's affections were stronger than her claims on her husband's?[108] Did the latter predecease her, divorce her when she was pregnant, or simply refuse to pay for the monument? The information given by the epigram, as well as that of the sculpted image, demonstrates the three-generation limit on family affections.

The relief on the monument to Philocydis shows a seated woman, an elderly man, and a young man who may represent the dead woman's brother, for he appears too young to be her husband. The

[106] The stela of Phanostrate shows her with four children, but this is exceptional, and a reference to her work in obstetrics. See n. 119 below.

[107] *IG*[2] II[2] 12963 = Peek, *GV* 335. Athens, National Museum 3790 = Clairmont, *Classical Attic Tombstones*, 2. 780, *c.*380–370, Psychiko.

[108] Cf. Shaw, 'Age of Roman Girls at Marriage', 37–8 and fig. 2.1, for the burial of young brides by parents rather than husbands.

epigram, however, mentions the dead woman, her parents, and her daughter, but omits the young man: 'Philocydis, daughter of Aristocles and Timagora, farewell. Eucleia, whom you left to her grandparents, misses you.'[109]

By contrast, the husband of Polyxena is united with his parents-in-law in an expression of grief: 'Leaving grief to her wedded husband and to her mother and father who engendered her, Polyxena lies here.'[110] The stela, depicting a seated woman with her left hand around the back of a small boy whose hands are placed on his mother's thighs, and a slave who was probably a nursemaid, adds the information that Polyxena was a young mother.

The stela of Myrtis shows two women shaking hands in a gesture of farewell. The inscription states that they are Myrtis and her mother Hieroclea: 'Myrtis, daughter of Hieroclea and wife of Moschus lies here. In her ways she pleased both her husband and the children she bore very much.'[111] We can only wonder about the emphasis on the ties between a married woman and her mother in the relief, and the related use of the matronymic in the inscription. The matronymic here does not indicate illegitimacy, for surely such a status would not be announced on a tombstone. Plenty of women and men are named on tombstones without patronymics.[112] On this stela it appears that other first-degree kin of Myrtis are mentioned. Why is her father excluded?

The monument of Ampharete emphasizes ties between three generations of women: 'I hold this dear child of my daughter, whom I held on my knees when we were alive and looked with our eyes upon the light of the sun, whom now dead, I dead hold.'[113] The relief depicts a

[109] Cranbrook Academy of Art, Bloomfield Hills, Mich., 1938.27, late in the second quarter of the fourth century, unknown provenance. See further C. Clairmont, *Gravestone and Epigram* (Mainz, 1970), 169–70, appendix 2, and plate 37.

[110] *IG* II^2 12495 = Peek, *GV* 345 = Clairmont, *Classical Attic Tombstones*, 2.850, *c.*380–360, Cerameicus.

[111] *IG*^{2} 12210a = *GV* 343 = Leipzig, Archaeological Institute, S39 = Clairmont, *Classical Attic Tombstones*, 2. 434a, *c.*mid-fourth century, unknown provenance.

[112] e.g. in Clairmont, *Gravestone and Epigram*: the stela of Diphilus (Athens, National Museum 886, end of first quarter of fourth century, Piraeus), 131–2, no. 54, and plate 25 = *IG* II^2 11200 = Peek, *GV* 1779; the stela of Anthippe (Athens, National Museum 2698, *c.*380–370, unknown provenance), 132–3, no. 55 and plate 25 = *IG* II^2 10672 = Peek, *GV* 1705, *Griechische Grabgedichte*, Schriften und Quellen der Alten Welt, Bd. 7 (Berlin, 1960), 73; the stela of Phanostrate, see n. 119, below; and of Ampharete, see n. 113, below.

[113] Cerameicus, late fifth century. *IG* II^2 10650 = Peek, *GV* 1600 (104) = *GG* 96. See further Clairmont, *Classical Attic Tombstones*, 1. 660.

seated woman holding a baby in her left hand. Her cloak envelops the baby. Boys are conventionally depicted as nude; therefore the baby is probably a girl. The baby's gaze is diverted to the bird which her grandmother holds in her right hand, but Ampharete's attention is totally devoted to her grandchild. Because the seated figure does not appear grandmotherly, one may ask whether the stela was ready-made for a deceased mother and child. An Athenian grandmother, however, could have been only 30 years old, and in classical art it was not usual to show a woman's age, but rather to portray her in her youthful prime.[114] Furthermore, the indication that the baby is female makes the rendering rather specialized. Therefore we assume that Ampharete's daughter commissioned the lovely, appropriate monument.

The stela of Telemachus, a married man, gives his patronymic, and records a special bond with his dead mother:

Telemachus, son of Spoudocrates, from Phlya.
O you who for your unforgettable virtue among all your fellow-citizens have great praise and are greatly missed by your children and dear wife. At the right of your tomb, mother,
I lie, not parted from your love.
Hieroclea,
daughter of Opsiades,
from Oion.[115]

Because Telemachus's father is not mentioned, we presume that he had predeceased his son, and was buried elsewhere. Telemachus probably looked after his widowed mother.

Less surprising in view of the usual emphasis on the patriline are the monuments to father and son. The stela of Andron depicts a father with two sons. The epigram indicates that one of his sons predeceased him: 'Andron lies here. He witnessed the death of one son. Having died, he welcomes the other.'[116] The stela of Potamon depicts a father and a son who were both flautists.[117] Both men hold

[114] See n. 101 above; Clairmont, *Classical Attic Tombstones*, vol. 1. p. 406; and for general remarks on the depiction of age, ibid., introd. vol., 19–29.

[115] Athens, National Museum 1016, mid-fourth century, Piraeus. *IG* II^2 7711 = *SEG.* xxxii (1967), no. 183 = Peek, *GV* 1386 GG 86. The last three lines were added later. See further Clairmont, *Gravestone and Epigram*, 149–50, no. 74, and plate 30. Note the change from second person to first person.

[116] *IG* II^2 10665 = Peek, *GV* 336 = Clairmont, *Classical Attic Tombstones*, 2. 268, *c.*380–370, Piraeus (?).

[117] *IG* II^2 8883 = Peek, *GV* 894 = Clairmont, *Classical Attic Tombstones*, 2. 235. See further p. 147

flutes. The name of Patrocleia, wife of Potamon, was added later: 'Hellas awarded first place in the art of flute-playing to Potamon of Thebes, and this tomb received his body. The praise of his father, Olympichus, also increases in memory because he produced such a son, a standard for the skilled.'

Funerary monuments rarely allude to respectable women's work outside the home, though in the fourth century some women began to receive an education similar to that of men and to pursue careers in the liberal arts and the professions. Among the numerous gravestones commemorating virtuous wives and daughters, it is interesting to find one dedicated to one of the first female physicians in Athens:[118]

Phanostrate
of Melite
Antiphile. Phanostrate.
Phanostrate, a midwife and physician lies here.
She brought pain to no one. Dead, she is missed by all.[119]

As mentioned above, the normal number of children portrayed on Athenian gravestones was limited to two. We therefore deduce that the four children portrayed on the stela represent the many whom she had delivered. Appropriately enough, she is portrayed shaking hands with a woman.

Scenes painted on white-ground *lekythoi*, and less often on other vase shapes and on ceramic plaques, portray bereaved members of the family mourning and visiting tombs.[120] Depictions on white-ground *lekythoi* of a female mourner bringing offerings to tombs or of a woman at home with a female slave preparing such offerings begin in the 470s. Conventions of vase-painting dictate that the woman be shown as young and lovely, dressed unrealistically in transparent garments. Such vases were probably painted before purchase. If the

[118] See further Pomeroy, 'Technikai kai Mousikai: The Education of Women in the Fourth Century and in the Hellenistic Period', *AJAH* 2 (1977), 51–68, esp. 60.

[119] *IG* II² 6873 = Peek, *GV* 342 = Athens, National Museum 993 = Clairmont, *Classical Attic Tombstones*, 2. 890, mid-fourth century Menidi. See further N. Firatli and L. Robert, *Les Stèles funéraires de Byzance gréco-romaine*, Bibl. archéol. et hist. de l'Inst. franç. d'Archéol. d'Istanbul, 15 (Paris, 1964), 176.

[120] These scenes and artefacts are not uniformly popular in all parts of the classical period; for example, the production of plaques decreases after the first quarter of the fifth century, while the production of funerary vases increases during the fifth century when Solon's ban on expensive sculpted monuments is observed. See further Donna C. Kurtz, 'Vases for the Dead, an Attic Selection', in H. A. G. Brijder (ed.), *Ancient Greek and Related Pottery*, Allard Pierson Series, 5 (Amsterdam, 1984), 314–28, esp. 320.

owner and user were truly young, for whom would such a woman be mourning? For her husband? For her brother who was killed in battle? For children who died after infancy? For her husband's parents? Would a visit to her own parents' tombs be construed as an act of disloyalty to her husband's family?[121] Surely a woman would experience some losses of kinsfolk with genuine sorrow; with others, such feelings would be mixed with feelings of relief, but all would demand some public expression of concern for the dead. The vase-painters depicted various expressions, ranging from quiet fortitude to crying and gestures of lamentation. Women are more likely to display emotion than men, and in the case of death they are encouraged to do so. Furthermore, mourners brought offerings to tombs, and only women traditionally carry baskets. Some scenes may represent specific rather than generic mourners. These were probably custom-made.[122] For example, a *lekythos* from the second quarter of the fifth century shows a young girl and a boy, doubtless brother and sister, flanking a tomb.[123] The vase is small, appropriate for children.

The family's life cycle is knocked out of kilter when a baby dies at the same time as her grandmother, as in the case of Ampharete; when a child predeceases a parent, as in the case of Aristylla;[124] and when a young mother dies leaving young children needing her care. Although such events must have occurred frequently, as a result of the fragility of life in the ancient world, the losses were none the less poignant. The deaths of Philocydis, Polyxena, and Myrtis were exceptionally tragic on two counts, and the circumstances may have inspired their families to erect sculpted stelae and to commission epitaphs—not an inexpensive undertaking. In cases where adults predecease their parents, both parents and spouses may have contributed to the costs of the burial. We also note that when women die in their most fertile years (at their highest value to both their family and the larger society), they are more likely to be awarded significant commemorative monuments.

[121] For the obligations of a married woman to the dead, see above.

[122] On ready-made and custom-made tombstones see most recently Clairmont, *Classical Attic Tombstones*, Introd. vol., 71–2.

[123] The J. Paul Getty Museum, S.86. AE. 253. *ARV*², 746.5 bis and p. 1668, by the Painter of Athens 1826. See further Donna C. Kurtz, 'Mistress and Maid', *AION (archeol)* 10 (1988), 141–9, esp. 143, 149.

[124] See n. 102 above.

PUBLIC AND PRIVATE AT RHAMNOUS

Some burial precincts (or *periboloi*) at Rhamnous were extravagant enough to articulate the distinctions between public family and private family verbally, spatially, and visually. Rhamnous was a garrison deme, relatively prolific in epitaphs and deme inscriptions.[125] The presence of the soldiers drawn from other parts of Athens probably served to stimulate ostentation and economic prosperity. The principal sculpted monuments in the *peribolos* of Diogeiton from the second half of the fourth century provide a good example (see Plate 3[126]).

Left-hand stela:	Diogeiton son of Callias of Rhamnous [husband] Habro daughter of Archebius [wife] Lysimachus son of Diogeiton of Rhamnous [son] Choronice daughter of Eudoridus [daughter-in-law] Lysistratus son of Lysimachus of Rhamnous [grandson] Telestagus son of Theomnestus [?] Lysimachus son of Lysistratus [great-grandson]
Central plinth:	Glaucon son of Calliteles of Rhamnous Olbius son of Timotheus of Aphidna Andropheles son of Nicostratus of Rhamnous Pheidostrate daughter of Eucolus of Pitheis
Right-hand plinth:	Lyceas son of Cephisius of Rhamnous

Some of the dead are listed on the large stela on the left. The names and patronymics of three of the four men, Diogeiton, Lysimachus, and Lysistratus reveal that they are blood-relations. The names of men precede and outnumber those of women. The branch of the family referred to on the plinth below displays similar features.

[125] Meyer, 'Epitaphs and Citizenship', 115, and Whitehead, *Demes of Attica*, 361–2, 402, 405–6.

[126] Vasileios X. Petrakos, *Rhamnous* (Athens, 1991), 35–6, figs. 22 and 23. Petrakos (ibid. 39, 41) dates the inscriptions to the third century. Petrakos has been publishing the excavations at Rhamnous for more than twenty years, and, understandably, revising his interpretations. See the list of publications in 'Hoi anaskapheis tou Ramnountos (1813–1987)', *AE*, 126 (1987), 265–98, esp. 298. To these add: '*Το Νεμεσιον του Ραμνοῦντος*', *Mélanges Mylonas*, 2, 295–326; '*Ανασκαφὴ Ραμνοῦντος*', *PAE* (1989), 1–37, and brief annual excavation reports in *To Ergon,* and *Praktika*. There are many other bits of archaeological remains at the site, but they are too fragmentary to discuss here. According to P. M. Fraser, *Rhodian Funerary Monuments* (Oxford, 1977), 55–6, who compares the late Hellenistic and Roman multiple burials at Rhodes to those at Athens, the phenomenon does not appear elsewhere. See further above, p. 118.

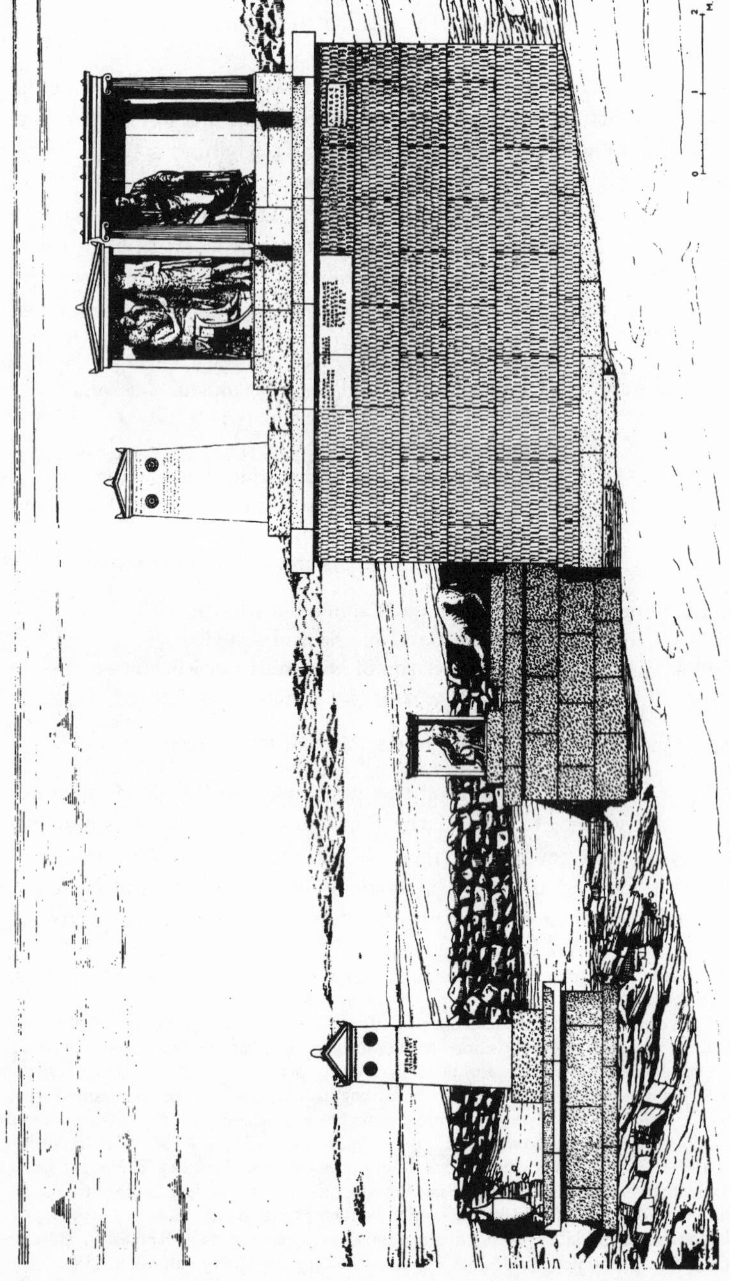

PLATE 3. Sepulchral monuments of the family of Diogeiton

The name 'Lyceas, son of Cephisius, of Rhamnous' is inscribed. His sons Cephisius and Hierocles and Callistomache, daughter of Cephisius, share a stela nearby.[127] Lyceas and at least one of his sons must have been married, for there is evidence of a descendant in 232/231;[128]

[127] Petrakos, 'Hoi anaskapheis tou Ramnountos', esp. 291.

[128] For Lyceas, son of Hierocles, see J. Pouilloux, *La Forteresse de Rhamnonte: étude de topographie et d'histoire,* Bibliothèque des Écoles françaises d'Athènes et de Rome, 179 (Paris, 1954), 130, ll. 45–6. Pouilloux (p. 131) suggests that this Lyceas is the priest of Asclepius in *IG* II^2 1534, B, l. 213 (*PA* 9192).

but their wives are buried either elsewhere or anonymously. A less likely hypothesis is that the names were inscribed at points in the family cycle when the sons had not yet married, but when the daughters were betrothed, and therefore it was expected that they would be buried elsewhere. In any case, this family is presented as predominantly male, including only a daughter, who presumably died before marriage.[129] The two stelae flank the central stela which shows an intimate group. A seated man gazes up at a younger man who is standing. The two are holding hands. We presume that the older man is the deceased.[130] A woman stands on the left, behind the seated man. She is portrayed as a new bride, making the stylized flirtatious gesture of the new bride (*anakalypteria*, 'lifting her veil'); therefore she must be his wife Habro, whose name follows his on the left-hand stela. Because of its proximity, this relief may also be related to the plinth below it which bears the names of Glaucon, Olbius, Andropheles, and Pheidostrate. As we have seen, sculpted stelae quite regularly did not serve as an exact illustration of the people named on the inscription, even if, as we suppose in the case of Diogeiton's family, the members were wealthy enough to commission the stelae, and obviously were concerned about the design of their burial precinct. Pheidostrate was a priestess of Nemesis. Because she was engaged in a public role when living, there was no reason to suppress her name. To the contrary, her kinsmen were doubtless proud of her. The sculptor, however, has depicted her as a typical woman, with her head modestly covered by a veil. The larger *naiskos* shows a mature woman with a female slave.[131]

Other major *periboloi* at Rhamnous present demographic and naming patterns similar to those of Diogeiton's family. For example, the inscription on the stela of the Menestides family from the first half of the fourth century lists only:

Menestheus son of Menestides
Menesthenes son of Menestides
Nausiptolem[i] wife of Menestides.[132]

[129] The family inscriptions reported by Fraser, *Rhodian Funerary Monuments*, 54–7, likewise list many more males than females.

[130] Petrakos, '*Ανασκαφὴ Ραμνοῦντος*', *Πρακτικά* (1975), 5–35, esp. 24–5.

[131] Clairmont, *Classical Attic Tombstones*, I. 143, who draws attention to the uniqueness and artistic quality of the monument.

[132] Petrakos, *Rhamnous*, 8, 12, Plates 3 and 4. For the tomb of Hierocles and his wife Demostrate who produced five sons see ibid., 41–2.

The stela of Euphranor from the second half of the fourth century congratulates him on living to the age of 105 and having seen three generations of children. Members of his family are listed:

Euphranor the Rhamnousian son of Euphron
Euphron the Rhamnousian son of Euphranor
Avrylla
Euthyphron the Rhamnousian son of Euphranor
Phainarete daughter of Cleophon
Phainarete daughter of Euphranor the Rhamnousian
Archedemus the Rhamnousian son of Euphranor.[133]

Gender relations in the Athenian family are manifested in several patterns. The first version, as we saw in the discussion of the phratry, is a pseudo-kin group restricted to male citizens (see Chs. 1 and 2). Families comprised of both women and men represent themselves in two ways, one oriented towards the public, the other more intimate and private. Though the first of these admits some women, men predominate. Only the private version accommodates women, though men are not necessarily excluded. Funerary practices make the distinction clear. As noted above, women are prominent at the *prothesis* ('laying out of the corpse'), which takes place in private. But only those women over the age of 60 or related to the deceased within the degree of second cousin are permitted to participate, with the latter also permitted to return to the house after the burial. There is no restriction on the attendance of distant male relatives. These men must have created an impressively masculine public spectacle as they marched in the cortège in front of the cart bearing the corpse. The several versions of the Athenian family at Rhamnous also leave no doubt that, despite the identification of women with the private sphere, in death, as in life, males are represented as dominating the family.

In the present chapter it becomes evident that the size of the Greek family was normally small, although some multiple-family households are found in Ptolemaic Egypt (see Ch. 6). The agricultural economy provided limited resources. Small families with two sons and at most one daughter were the best reproductive strategy, permitting a family to survive while maintaining its economic status. Even after the invention of coinage created an expandable *oikos*, the size of

[133] Ibid. 12–13 and Plate 5.

families did not increase. Very wealthy men, including Ischomachus, Phormio, and Pasio had only two sons each, and only Ischomachus also had a daughter. Endogamy may be explained, at least in part, as an adaptation to limited resources, for when close kin marry, property is redistributed within a small group of relatives, and bridegrooms are given preferential access to brides. The old notion that the family disintegrated progressively from a huge *genos* ('clan') is no longer acceptable. Instead, the *genos* appears to be an artificial construct (see Ch. 2). The effective kinship network rarely extended more than three degrees either horizontally or vertically, and shrank even more in the Hellenistic world, owing to migrations, wars, and the attraction of social communities other than the family. Yet the élite re-emerged in the Hellenistic world, and created funerary foundations as a means of persuading their descendants to perpetuate their memories, a grace that parents in the past had been able to assume as their due.

4

Some Greek Families at Work

All the known law codes of Greek states in the archaic period included regulations governing family relationships. The *polis* intruded into some areas that many contemporary societies consider private.[1] The tacit goal of such legislation may have been not only to produce an orderly society, but to assure the reproduction of citizens who would be able to maintain and defend the *polis*.

Solon's laws were the first in Athens to regulate families. One of his laws was that a father must teach his son a trade or give him some means of support, so that, in return, the son could look after his parents when they became old.[2] Otherwise, a son was not obliged to maintain his parents. The reward for such care was the inheritance of the patrimony at the father's retirement or death. Like so many of Solon's laws, this one codified what must have been normal behaviour not only in Athens, but throughout the Greek world—at least under the pressure of peers, or as a result of common sense.

How this intergenerational system works among families whose economy is based on agriculture is obvious. Its effects, moreover, are wide-ranging for, as Aristotle (*Pol.* 1256a38–40) states, most men made their living from farming. The ideal for the household was self-sufficiency.[3] Most farms in Attica were small;[4] yet they were large enough to supply the bulk of the family's sustenance, if not grain, at

[1] The first part of this chapter was presented at the American Academy of Religion and Society of Biblical Literature annual meeting, Kansas City, 24 Nov., 1991, and published as 'Some Greek Families: Production and Reproduction', in Shaye J. D. Cohen (ed.), *The Jewish Family in Antiquity*, Brown Judaic Studies, 289 (Atlanta, 1993), 155–63.

[2] Plut. *Sol.* 22. 1, 4 = Ruschenbusch, frs. 56–7; Galen, *Protrept.* 8; Diog. Laert. 1. 55; Aesch. 1. 28; cf. Ael., *NA* 9. 1 = Ruschenbusch, fr. 55c; Arist. *Ath. Pol.* 56. 6; Xen. *Mem.* 2. 2. 13, *Oec.* 7. 12; Dem. 57. 70; Din. 2. 17–18; Ar. *Birds* 1353–7, etc. On Solonian legislation see also Ch. 3 n. 2.

[3] See further Robert Sallares, *The Ecology of the Ancient Greek World* (Ithaca, NY, 1991), 298–9.

[4] On the size of farms see further J. K. Davies, *Wealth and the Power of Wealth in Classical Athens* (Salem, NH, 1984), 52–5.

least fruits, vegetables, and livestock. Mixed agriculture was the rule, with cultivation of cereals, vines, olives, and figs in various combinations on a single plot, and the holding of scattered pieces of land as insurance against local climatic or biological disasters.[5] Furthermore, farmers sold their products in markets at the *agora* and locally in their deme, and could use the cash to buy other necessities.

In the *Oeconomicus*, a 'Treatise on the Skills of Estate Management', Xenophon gives details about the family farm and the domestic economy.[6] Ischomachus tells his wife that children will be the support and allies of their aged parents (*Oec.* 7. 12). Furthermore, farming requires no special knowledge. Skills and traditions were passed down from one generation to the next, and were common knowledge. All a man needed to do was look around and see how his father and neighbours did it (*Oec.* 6. 9, 15. 4, 10, 16. 3). Ischomachus also learned from his father the rare skill of judging the potential of neglected land, buying it, improving it, and selling it for a profit (20. 22, 26).

Most landowners acquired their property not through purchase but by inheritance. Therefore, as they grew up, they would have become familiar with it, for all members of the family worked on the farm, especially at critical times such as harvests. The regime of partible inheritance, however, was interpreted by the heirs as they saw fit. Some brothers continued to hold inherited land in common (e.g. Lys 32. 4); in some cases they divided it eventually (e.g. Isae. 2. 28). In Athens women did not own land. The dowry constituted women's contribution to the *oikos* at the start of marriage. Through shrewd household management and work such as textile production (skills that were passed down from mother to daughter), the wife, though shielded from the public eye, could increase the family's fortune.[7]

Throughout antiquity, agriculture continued to be the basis of the Greek economy, but some large landowners turned their property over to professional managers; others farmed part-time while pursuing other lines of employment; and some people were totally dependent on the cash economy, and purchased all their food in the market.[8] In this chapter we will look more closely at some Greek families whose

[5] See further Pomeroy, *Xenophon Oeconomicus*, 54–5, and Gallant, *Risk and Survival*, 36–45.

[6] See Pomeroy, *Xenophon Oeconomicus*, 46–50.

[7] On women's contribution to the domestic economy, see Pomeroy, *Xenophon Oeconomicus*, 58–65, sects. G–H, 273–85.

[8] See ibid., 65, 71–2, 218, 241, 281, 316–17, 324, 329.

economic foundation was not agriculture, or perhaps not agriculture alone, but rather skilled labour, where children inherited from their parents the materials and tools of the trade or craft (*technē*), their reputation, and their long-time customers. In the Greek world, these practitioners of the liberal arts and skilled professions were not people at the bottom of the social and economic scale, or slaves as some of them were at Rome; but they were not usually members of the top class either.[9] Landowners were always the highest class socially and economically. Nevertheless, most of the families we will discuss here were wealthy and important enough to have left monuments bearing their names and to be mentioned in the historical records more than once.

PHYSICIANS

Families of physicians are well attested in the Greek world. Many of them are found in Cos, the birthplace of Hippocrates and a medical centre throughout antiquity. The Hippocratic oath enjoins the physician to transmit his knowledge to his sons.[10] A pupil who was not a blood-relation of his teacher swore to treat his teacher as though he were his father, to maintain him and share his life, and to teach the art of medicine to his teacher's sons, if they so wished. This prescription was not necessary. The oath, whether its exact date is late classical or Hellenistic, is more likely to have described the prevailing situation than to have instituted a radical change. A physician's son was his father's natural apprentice.[11] The Greeks had no compunctions about putting young children to work. The *Law* (ii–iii) states that training in medicine should begin in childhood. According to the *Law* (ii) and *Decorum* (iv) natural ability (physis) is essential.

[9] Some exceptions were Pheidias, who was a friend of Pericles: Plut. *Per.* 13. Cephisodotus II was eligible for liturgies: Davies, *APF*, 8334, and see below. H. Lauter, *Zur gesellschaftlichen Stellung des bildenden Künstlers in der griechischen Klassik*, Erlanger Forsch., ser. A, vol. 23 (Erlangen, 1974), 25, classifies them as 'Durchschnittsbürgers'. In contrast to the Greek world, artists and sculptors who worked in Rome were of low social status: R. R. R. Smith, 'Greeks, Foreigners, and Roman Republican Portraits', *JRS* 71 (1981), 24–38.

[10] For the text, commentary, and date see Ludwig Edelstein, *The Hippocratic Oath*, Supplements to the Bulletin of the History of Medicine, 1 (Baltimore, 1943).

[11] Plato *Laws* 720B, *Pr.* 311B. *Para tois goneusin ek paidon askoumenois*: Galen, *Anatomicarum Administrationum*, 2. 1, 280–1 (Garofalo).

Moreover, the profession was attractive, for it was prestigious and lucrative. Thus, inscriptions from Cos include physicians in lists of public benefactors.[12]

Biographical traditions about Hippocrates himself allude to a family of doctors that survived for at least seven generations. The family tree as reported by the *Suda* (Adler, s.v. Hippocrates, paras. 564–9) is given in Figure 1.[13]

According to the *Suda* (662–3, para. 564, s.v. Hippocrates [Adler]), the famous Hippocrates, the second one by this name, was the grandson of the first Hippocrates, who was a physician, and was descended from a certain Chrysus ('the Golden One') and Elaphus ('The Ivory One') who were also physicians. Hippocrates' sons Thessalus and Draco were physicians, and their sons, Hippocrates III and IV, were also physicians. Hippocrates III, son of Thessalus, is attested in two inscriptions.[14] The *Suda* (p. 663, paras. 565–7, s.v. Hippocrates) mentions three more physicians named Hippocrates who were members of the same family. Other ancient biographical sources provide a few additional details. For example, Soranus,[15] gives an abbreviated genealogy, but he does name the father, mother (Phaenarete), and sons of Hippocrates II, and adds that Hippocrates traced his ancestry back to Heracles and Asclepius. A pseudepigraphic letter

[12] See below on Hippocrates III.

[13] For source criticism see now Jody Rubin Pinnault, *Hippocratic Lives and Legends* (Leiden, 1992). See also Wesley D. Smith, 'Notes on Ancient Medical Historiography', *Bulletin of the History of Medicine*, 63 (1989), 73–109. Smith (pp. 105–6) does not totally reject the traditions about the genealogy of Hippocrates' family, but suggests that the biographies contain 'the remains of a genuine insular succession'. Because of ambiguities in the text of the *Suda*, Smith's genealogical chart differs slightly from my own. For a critical view of the biographical tradition, especially as it concerns the attribution of authorship of parts of the Hippocratic corpus to members of Hippocrates' family, see Wesley D. Smith, *Hippocrates. Pseudepigraphic Writings* (Leiden, 1990), and *idem*, *The Hippocratic Tradition* (Ithaca, NY, and London, 1979), 221–2.

[14] A man named Hippocrates lent money to Calymnus in the middle of the fourth century. *I. Cos* 10a, l. 51 (end of third century BC) records that a Hippocrates, son of Thessalus, contributed money to an emergency military fund *c.*200 BC. Louis Cohn-Haft, *The Public Physicians of Ancient Greece* (Northampton, Mass., 1956), 20 no. 58, number 5, identifies him as a physician and a descendant of Hippocrates II. Jost Benedum, 'Griechische Arztinschriften aus Kos', *ZPE* 25 (1977), 264–76, esp. 272–3, confirms Cohn-Haft's identification, and gives the text of an inscription recording honours awarded to a physician named Hippocrates, son of Thessalus, around 200 BC. See also Susan Sherwin-White, *Ancient Cos*, Hypomnemata, 51 (Göttingen, 1978), 262 n. 33, 265 n. 51, and 271 n. 83A.

[15] *Life of Hippocrates*, in J. Ilberg, *CMG* iv. 175–8.

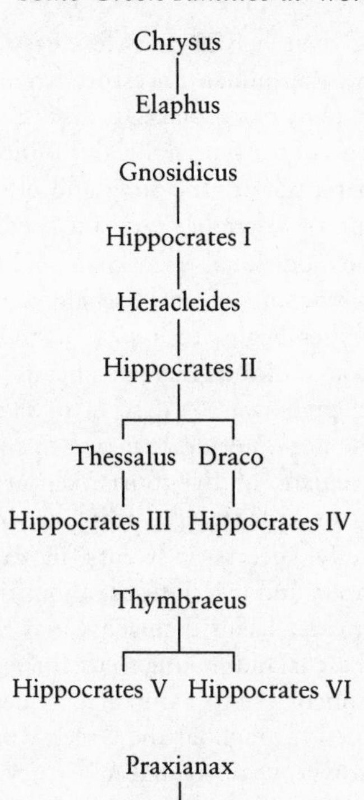

FIG. 1 The family of Hippocrates VII

declares that Hippocrates is the son of Heraclides, son of Gnosidicus, son of Nebrus, son of Sostratus, son of Theodorus, son of Cleomyttades, son of Crisamis, seventeenth from Asclepius, nineteenth from Zeus, and his mother is Phaenarete's daughter Praxithea.[16] Some sources also mention Polybus, or Polybius, a pupil and son-in-law of Hippocrates II.[17] Most ancient biographies are a blend of fact and fiction. Modern scholars may summarily reject the gods, 'the Golden One', and 'the Ivory One', although the biographers and their audience probably would have placed credence in them as they did in the

[16] Littré 9. 314 = Smith, *Hippocrates. Pseudepigraphic Writings*, 48–50, no. 2: Paitus to Artaxerxes. See also 'Embassy', attributed to Thessalus, son of Hippocrates: Littré 9. 405 = Smith, *Hippocrates. Pseudepigraphic Writings*, p. 110, 27. 1.

[17] e.g. Arist. *HA* 512b; Galen, *In Hipp. de nat. hom.* comm. ii, proem., 22 = *CMG* 5. 9. 1, p. 57 (Mewaldt), Hipp. Littré 9. 420.

mythical ancestors of their heroes. It is less easy to dismiss, or to prove the existence of, the human ancestors whom the biographers name; but this is not the proper place to discuss the details of the notorious scholarly crux of the biographical tradition of Hippocrates. Nevertheless, the general picture the *Suda* and other sources give of men in each generation of a family practising medicine is credible.

Though there is no additional data that could corroborate the reports about the physicians of the archaic period, epigraphical evidence for such families begins to appear in the fourth century.[18] An inscription of 360 BC indicates that membership in the Coan and Cnidian guild of Asclepiads was by descent in the male line.[19] The priority awarded to the notion of descent *ipso facto* suggests that the ancestors of the Asclepiads of the fourth century had themselves practised medicine for at least two preceding generations.

The theme of family succession recurs in various testimonia, including pseudepigrapha and inscriptions, about the lineage of Hippocrates and of Asclepiads.[20] This exclusivity may have been confined to the Asclepiads of these islands owing to their special privileges and prestige. It would be incorrect to assume that medical information was so jealously guarded throughout the Greek world that only sons of physicians, or men who were treated as if they were sons, could receive a proper education that would entitle them to call themselves competent physicians. Even Hippocrates II was said to have studied medicine not only with his father, but also with Herodicus the Selymbrian, who was not a relative.[21] Many physicians who were

[18] For a family of physicians in Cos, see e.g. Jost Benedum, 'Inscriptions grecques de Cos relatives à des médecins hippocratiques et Cos Astypalaia', in M. D. Grmek (ed.), *Hippocratica. Actes du colloque hippocratique de Paris* (4–9 septembre 1978) (Paris, 1980), 35–43, esp. 36–7. The list of physicians begins after 241 BC with Philistus, son of Nicarchus; Philistus, son of Moschion, attested in Cos in 218/217; Praxagoras, son of Nicarchus; and the public physician Isidorus, son of Nicarchus, honoured in Cos in the first century BC.

[19] *SEG* xvi. 94, no. 326. See further J. Bousquet, 'Inscriptions de Delphes', *BCH* 80 (1956), 547–97, esp. 579–93, who suggests (pp. 585–8) that the inscription records a reaffirmation of privileges that had been awarded to the Asclepiads earlier.

[20] e.g. Littré, 3, 4. 316 = Smith, *Hippocrates. Pseudepigraphic Writings,* 50; 'Embassy', 27.1 = Smith, *Hippocrates. Pseudepigraphic Writings,* 110; Doro Levi and G. Pugliese Carratelli, 'Nuove Iscrizioni di Iasos', *ASAA* n. s. 23–4 (1961–2), 573–632, esp. 587, no. 16 (*c.*151 BC); Galen 2. 1, 280 (Garofalo), and see Bousquet, ' Inscriptions de Delphes', 579–93.

[21] Soranus, *Life of Hippocrates*, p. 175, para. 2; *Suda* (Adler), p. 662, para. 10; Tzetz. *Chil.* 7. 155 (Kiesseling), p. 276, l. 960. For Herodicus see *Suda*, s.v. Hippocrates, p. 662. 12; Tzetz., *Chil.* 7. 155; and Plato, *Rep.* 406A–407C.

actually sons of physicians, or who claimed to be, would have existed, and surely would have enjoyed an advantage over their colleagues who lacked such affiliation.[22] There was no licensing procedure in antiquity; anyone could call himself (or, less often, herself) a physician.[23] Charlatans abounded. The patient might justly have more confidence in a physician who had served an apprenticeship with his own father, and perhaps inherited his practice. As we saw in Chapter 1, the first son is usually named for the father's father, the second son for the mother's father. In the case of the descendants of Hippocrates, the name itself must have carried so much prestige that two brothers who apparently were contemporaries, Hippocrates V and VI, used it. Whether or not the biographical traditions about the revered family of Hippocrates reflect historical truth, they demonstrate a link between family connections and professional prestige.

MUSICIANS, ACTORS, POETS, AND PHILOSOPHERS

Talent and knowledge constituted a significant patrimony in many liberal professions. For example, an epigram of *c.*370–350 refers to a father and son who were both flautists. Their stela depicts the two shaking hands. Both father and son hold flutes. The epigram states that the son won prizes for his art; his father is praised for teaching him.[24]

Dyads of father and son who were actors are common. One family of Athenian comic actors of the fourth and third centuries can be traced for three generations: all three are named Callippus.[25] Striking examples of career continuity through as many as five or six

[22] For the entrance of a complete outsider into the field of medicine, see e.g. the story about Hagnodice, the first female physician in Athens, and her studies with Herophilus: Hyg. *Fab.* 274.

[23] For female physicians see n. 22, and Ch. 3 n. 119 above.

[24] See also Ch. 3 n. 117 above.

[25] The following pairs appear in Paulette Ghiron-Bistagne, *Recherches sur les acteurs dans la Grèce antique* (Paris, 1976): Antiphanes, comic actor, son of Panaitius, comic poet (p. 309); Ararus, comic actor?, son of Aristophanes, playwright (p. 311); Aristophanes, comic actor?, son of Philip, comic poet (p. 313); Arcesilaus, tragic actor?, son of Hiero, playwright (p. 314); and the triad named Callippus (p. 335). I. E. Stefanis, *Διονυσιακοὶ Τεχνῖται* (Heraklion, 1988), claims to have corrected the prosopography of Ghiron-Bistagne. Because Stefanis lists only performers, not dramatic poets, his book is less useful for the present purpose. See Stefanis, *Διονυσιακοὶ Τεχνῖται,* 58–9 for Antiphanes, and 247–8 for the Callippi.

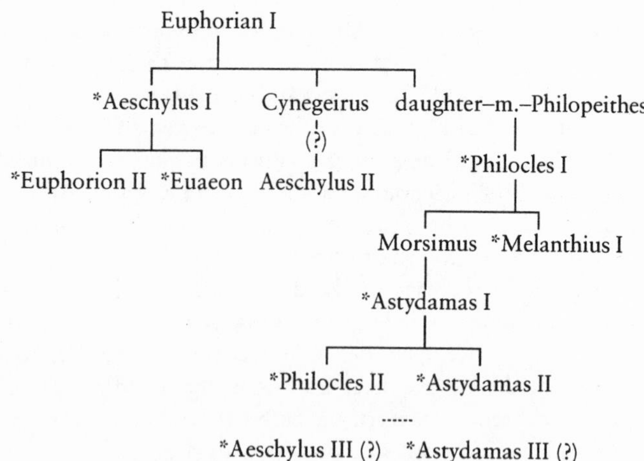

FIG. 2 The family of Aeschylus

generations appear among the families of tragic and comic poets, including Aeschylus, Sophocles, Euripides, Philemon, Diphilus, and others.[26] The work was highly specialized. There was no crossing over between genres: some families worked exclusively in tragedy, others in comedy.[27] The longest sequence appears in the family of Aeschylus. These are shown in Figure 2.[28]

In this stemma the continuity is achieved through the descendants of Aeschylus's sister. Among her descendants appear Melanthius I, who also wrote tragedy, and Aeschylus III, who was a tragic actor. Legally, children belonged to the *oikos* of their father, but the history of this family (and many others—for example, the tradition about Polybus, son-in-law of Hippocrates II, mentioned just above) illustrates that contact with the maternal family was often retained, especially when such a family had some property or renown.

Inasmuch as Plato did not have children, the leadership of the Academy passed to Speusippus who was a son of Plato's half-sister Potone (Diog. Laert. 3. 4, 4. 1).[29] She was Plato's sister by a different

[26] See further Dana Ferrin Sutton, 'The Theatrical Families of Athens', *AJP* 108 (1987), 9–26.

[27] See ibid. 26 for a possible exception in the family of the actor Eugeiton III.

[28] Sutton, 'The Theatrical Families of Athens', 14. The names of the men who were involved in the tragic theatre are preceded by an asterisk.

[29] For the genealogy see Davies, *APF*, 8792.

father, and therefore not a member of his *oikos*. The disciples of Aristippus, who was a companion of Socrates, included his daughter Arete. Arete's son and pupil, in turn, was Aristippus, who was called 'mother-taught' (*metrodidaktos*: Diog. Laert. 2. 86). Even in strongly patriarchal Athens, intellectual and vocational capital, as it were, was sometimes transmitted through women, and matrilineal naming, as the stemmata of Aeschylus and Aristippus demonstrate, advertised connections to the mother's family.

PRIESTESSES AND PRIESTS

For respectable women in classical Athens one of the very few desirable professions that provided work in the public sphere was that of priestess. The servants of Greek divinities tended to be of the same sex as the god they served. Therefore the cults of goddesses usually required the employment of priestesses. Priestesshoods, like priesthoods, of many major cults were often the hereditary preserves of particular aristocratic *gene* who traced their lineage back to heroic ancestors. Succession to hereditary priesthoods was achieved by a variety of strategems, usually involving primogeniture. Most often the oldest male in each generation acquired the office, but occasionally the succession proceeded through entire generations. For example, the priesthood of Poseidon at Halicarnassos was held by all the men of each generation before being passed down to the oldest man of the succeeding generation (see Fig. 3[30]). It was held first by Telamon, then by each of his three sons, then by his three grandsons, and then by his great-grandson, in each generation starting with the oldest.[31]

Principles of succession and inheritance in most aspects of Greek life show a preference for males over females, but in the case of priestesses it was essential that the successor be female. The succession to the priesthoods of various cults of important goddesses was usually accomplished without abandoning patrilineality. As an example, we will look at the priestesshood of Athena Polias, which

[30] Elizabeth M. Craik, *The Dorian Aegean* (London, 1980), 196.

[31] *SIG* 1020. For the genealogy of Telamon and his successors, see Craik, *The Dorian Aegean*, 196–8.

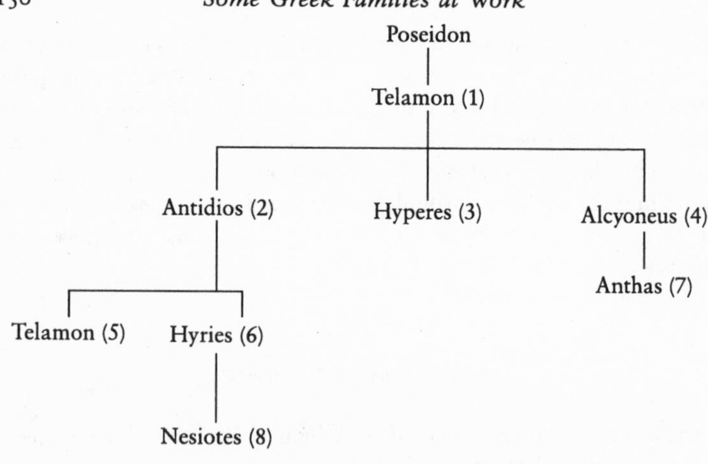

FIG. 3 The succession to the priesthood of Poseidon

was hereditary in the aristocratic Eteoboutad *genos*.[32] The names of some of the women who held the post over a period of seven centuries, starting in the fifth century BC are known. The genealogy of some of the priestesses whose names are known is shown in Figure 4.[33] When a new priestess was needed, the office passed to the oldest daughter of the oldest male. The tenure of the office by Theodote Polyeuctou II between 200 and 150 indicates that sometime between 255/254 and her inauguration into the priestesshood there were no descendants in the male line, and the office passed directly to the oldest female.

Not very many women could become priestesses. The jobs remained in the control of a limited number of families with both the requisite lineage and, usually, the financial resources. Some priesthoods did not produce much income, but, rather, required that the family of the priestess pay expenses connected with the office. We know specifically that the priestess of Demeter at Eleusis collected cash fees from each initiate, and the priestess of Athena Nike received

[32] See further Judy Ann Turner, '*Hiereiai*: Acquisition of Feminine Priesthoods in Ancient Greece (Ph.D. diss., University of California, Santa Barbara, 1983), 249–60, and Davies, *APF*, 4549.

[33] Adapted from Turner, *Hiereiai*, 250, to show only the family members effective in the transmission of the priestesshood. The names of the women who held the priestesshood are preceded by an asterisk.

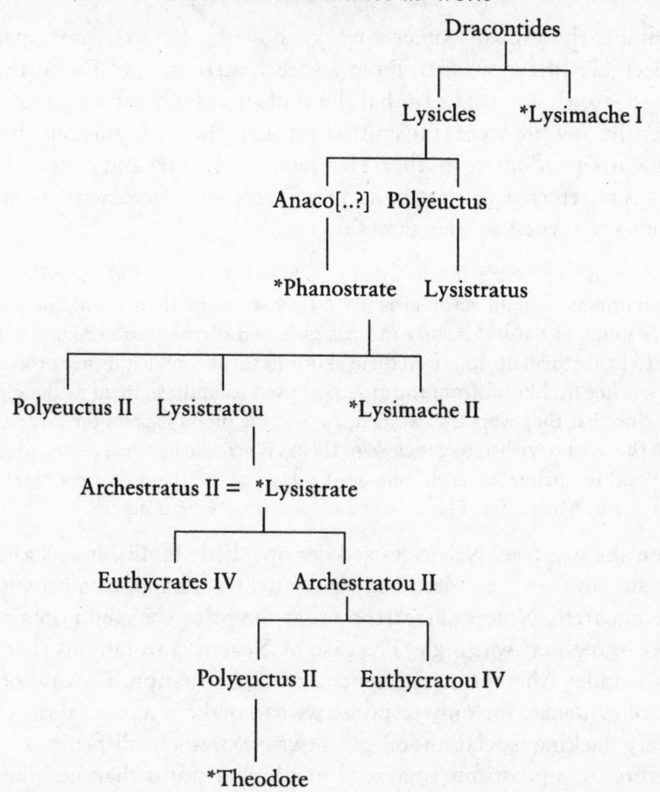

FIG. 4 The succession to the priestesshood of Athena Polias

50 drachmas annually, and took the legs and skins of sacrificial victims.[34] But certainly, all priestesses earned prestige and respect.

PROSTITUTES

In the classical period, doubtless far more women than could become priestesses followed the career of prostitution, though it is impossible to support this assertion by statistics. For a successful *hetaira* ('prostitute') such work could be extremely lucrative, indeed more

[34] *IG* I^2 24 = *GHI* 44, 450–445 BC.

profitable than most women's work, though, of course, not open to respectable citizen women. From a speech attributed to Demosthenes (59. 18–19, 50, 67) we learn that the skills necessary for working as an expensive *hetaira* were transmitted through three generations, beginning with an adoptive mother, Nicarete, who raised and trained seven girls. She referred to the young prostitutes who were actually slaves whom she owned as 'daughters':

Nicarete, who was the freedwoman of Charisius of Elis and the wife of his cook Hippias, bought seven girls when they were small children. She was an astute judge of natural beauty in little girls and furthermore she understood how to bring them up and train them skilfully, for she made this her profession and got her livelihood from the girls. She used to address them as daughters, implying that they were free women, so that she might extract the largest fees from those who wished to get close to them. When she had reaped the profit of the youthful prime of each, she sold all seven of them: Anteia, Stratola, Aristocleia, Metaneira, Phila, Isthmias, and this Neaera here.[35]

When she was free, Neaera raised her own little family. It was alleged that she, in turn, exploited her own daughter, Phano, as a prostitute. Like Nicarete, Neaera understood that the price she could obtain for a free 'daughter' was high. The case of Neaera is so famous that one may wonder whether it represents a typical situation. Because of the lack of evidence, the only response we can make is a general one. In a society lacking social mobility, it was extremely difficult for the daughter of a prostitute to ascend to a higher status than her mother. Neaera's husband was brought to trial, charged with living with a non-Athenian woman as though she were his wife, and with giving Phano in marriage to an Athenian citizen as being his own daughter born from a citizen woman.

ARTISTS AND SCULPTORS

Dyads of fathers and sons who were sculptors are not uncommon. For example, Daidalus of Sicyon, brother of Polyclitus of Sicyon[36], was a son, pupil, and collaborator of Patrocles.[37] Pantias of Chios (*c.*380)

[35] Ps.-Dem. 59. 18–19.

[36] Paus. 2. 3. 4–5, 6. 2. 8, 6. 3. 4, 7, 6. 6. 1, 8. 45. 4, 10. 9. 5–6; Pliny *NH* 34. 76. See further, Bianchi-Bandinelli, *EAA* ii. 989–90, s.v. 'Daidalos'.

[37] See further Bianchi-Bandinelli, *EAA* ii. 989–90, s.v. 'Policleto', vi. 266–75, esp. 266.

was the pupil of his father, Sostratus (Paus. 6. 9. 3). In the Hellenistic period there were several pairs of fathers and daughters whose artistic works were important enough to have been mentioned by Pliny (*NH* 35. 147).[38] These include Timarete, who was the daughter of Micon, and perhaps granddaughter of the elder Micon. Pliny (*NH* 35. 59) names both Micons in the same paragraph, but does not mention any kinship. Yet, it is difficult to believe that the names were mere coincidence. If the younger Micon was not a blood descendant of the elder, his adoption of his predecessor's name suggests that he, or his parents who named him, wanted him to be considered as a relative of the famous homonymous painter whose work was displayed in the Stoa Poicile ('Painted Stoa') in Athens.[39] As I pointed out in discussing the use of the name 'Hippocrates' by physicians, there could be much to be gained by such a fiction. Though it is likely that younger artists learned from their elders, there is not always enough evidence to demonstrate similarities in style or subject-matter between generations of artists in the same family. There are, however, some examples of the preservation of artistic traditions within families. Eirene was the daughter and pupil of Cratinus. Like her father, Eirene painted actors and entertainers (Pliny, *NH* 35. 140, 147). Aristarete was the daughter and pupil of Nearchus. Nearchus painted pictures of gods (Pliny, *NH* 35. 141): the only painting by Aristarete mentioned by Pliny was also of a god, a figure of Asclepius. Alexandra was the daughter of Nealces.[40] Helena, daughter of Timon of Egypt, is not mentioned by Pliny.[41] The works by the women artists and their fathers are not extant. Many girls—at least those who attended school—learned how to paint, for painting was part of the school curriculum (Arist. *Pol.* 8. 2. 1337b3). Such girls were only amateurs. With the exception of Olympias and Laia, or Lala, of Cyzicus, whose ancestry is not given by Pliny, all the notable women artists whom Pliny names were the daughters of artists. This

[38] For their dates see Pomeroy, 'Technikai kai Mousikai', 53.

[39] Pausanias (2. 2. 2) mentions the sculptures of an Athenian named Myron who must have worked after 384 BC when the race for foals was introduced as an event at Olympia. The *floruit* of the more famous Myron was *c.*460.

[40] Probably the same as Anaxander in Pliny, *NH* 35. 146; see Pomeroy, 'Technikai kai Mousikai', 65 n. 20.

[41] For Helena see W. Peremans and E. van 't Dack, *Prosopographia Ptolemaica*, vol. 6, Studia Hellenistica, 17 (Leuven, 1968), no. 17084.

generalization draws attention to the supreme importance of the family as the locus for professional training. Respectable women were not apprenticed out to be taught by artists who were not their kin. The only way that such women could have learned the skills essential to their work was at home, watching and helping their male relatives.[42] Men, by contrast, not only learned the craft from their father, but they could also be apprenticed to a sculptor who was not a relative or to a relative who was not a member of the nuclear family. Lucian wrote of his brief apprenticeship to a maternal uncle:

> Just after I had left school and was approaching manhood, my father and his friends considered what he should have me taught then. . . . The inspiration for the next discussion was which was the best of the crafts and easiest to learn and adequate for a freeborn man, employing supplies that were handy, and producing a sufficient income. Each man praised a different craft, according to his opinion or experience; but my father glanced at my uncle—for my mother's brother was present, a man who was considered a master sculptor—and said, 'It isn't right that any other craft should prevail while you are here. Come take this fellow,' and he pointed to me. 'Take him under your wing and teach him to be a good stone worker, mason, and sculptor, for he can do this, as you know he is naturally talented.' He judged from the way I used to play with wax, for whenever I was dismissed by my teachers, by scraping wax I would make models of cattle, or horses, or, by Zeus, men, realistic ones, my father thought. I used to get beatings from my teachers because of these, but at that time they also served as a reason to praise my talent. Considering that sculpting, there was hope that in a short time I would learn the craft. (*Somn.* 1–2)

No women sculptors are known by name. Sculptures, however, endure, especially the bases on which the artists' signatures appear. Because most signatures include the patronymic, it is possible to trace the genealogy of sculptors' families. Among sculptors we can trace the largest number of generations in a single family practising the same profession. Although the details of these stemmata are not always certain, at least they are not plagued with the historiographic problems surrounding the traditions about Hippocratics. The names of members of the family of Praxiteles, son of Cephisodotus, and the

[42] Thus in the first century AD Pamphila, daughter and wife of scholars, wrote some thirty-three books of historical materials as well as other works: Photius 175 S 119b = *FHG* iii 520–1; *Suda*, s.v. Pamphila, etc.

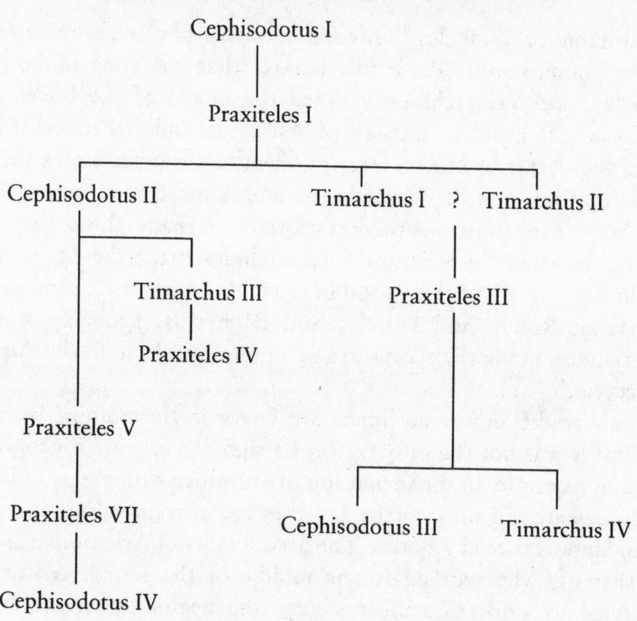

FIG. 5 The family of Praxiteles

artistic works they produced over a period of five centuries are known.[43] These appear in Figure 5.[44]

Pliny seems to have credited the success of some of the descendants to inherited talent rather than instruction, for he comments that Praxiteles' son Cephisodotus was his father's *artis heres* ('artistic heir', *NH* 36. 24). The precise dates and genealogy of the family of Polycles are not so evident as those of Praxiteles' family.[45] There are reports, however, of at least three sculptors named Polycles and two named Timarchides, in addition to another bearing the family-linked

[43] Virginia C. Goodlett, 'Rhodian Sculpture Workshops', *AJA* 95 (1991), 669–81, esp. 676 n. 29, points to the discontinuity in the evidence, and questions whether the Timarchus and Cephisodotus of the first century BC were descended from the sculptors of the fourth century.

[44] Adapted from Davies, *Athenian Propertied Families*, p. 289, to show the recurrence and relative chronology of the sculptors' names: Cephisodotus, Praxiteles, and Timarchus.

[45] It seems most likely that Polycles I and his two sons should be dated to the second century BC. For various solutions to the problem of dating the members of this family see Frazer, *Pausanias's Description of Greece*, iv. 12–15.

hybrid name of Timocles.[46] Members of this family co-operated on various commissions. Pausanias reports that the sons of Polycles, Timocles, and Timarchides sculpted the image of the boxer Agesarchus at Olympia and those of Asclepius and Athena at Elatea (6. 12. 8; 10. 34. 6, 8). An inscription on a statue at Delos records that Dionysius, son of Timarchides, and Timarchides, son of Polycles, both Athenians, worked together.[47] Perhaps these two were cousins. In a later generation a Timarchides made the sculpture of Apollo holding a lyre that stood in a temple beside the Colonnade of Octavia at Rome; and Polycles and Dionysius, probably sons of Timarchides, made the sculptures of Jupiter and Juno in the Porticus of Octavia.[48]

Family tradition was an important factor in the training of sculptors, but it was not the only factor. Its significance varied geographically. For example, in the formation of sculpture workshops at Delos, family ties are not noteworthy, but they are of tremendous and long-lasting importance at Rhodes. The descendants of Aristonidas, son of Mnasitimus, who worked in the middle of the fourth century BC, continued to work as sculptors until the beginning of the second century BC.[49] There are several other families of sculptors who worked collaboratively in Rhodes for two or more generations.

LEGACY

There are many examples of the continuity of the family, even where the principal source of income is not immovables. The family that enjoys economic success reproduces itself in each generation: the same names and the same professional activities occur. This repetition can make the primary sources difficult to interpret: for example, it is not always possible to determine to which Praxiteles, son of Cephisodotus, a particular sculpture should be attributed, because of the continuity of artistic traditions within the workshop. Sometimes people deliberately created a fictitious genealogy. Although they were not related to the famous bearers of the name, they assumed it, or

[46] Pliny, *NH* 34. 50, 52, *fl.* 372 and 156.

[47] T. Homolle, 'Statue de Caius Ofellius: sur une œuvre signée des artistes Dionysios et Polyclès', *BCH* 5 (1881), 390–6.

[48] Pliny, *NH* 36. 35. See further *EAA*, s.v. Dionysios 3 and Polycles 6.

[49] Goodlett, 'Rhodian Sculpture Workshops', esp. 673, 676.

gave it to their children, expecting to enjoy the fame and fortune of the earlier homonymous practitioner. Homonymous artists were rampant, as well as those whose name was significant in the field of sculpture—for example, Daidalus, mentioned above.[50] A name might be chosen for a girl baby too, in anticipation of the job that child was destined to perform. So, for example, some Athenian parents who expected their daughter to serve as a priestess named her Theano, after the priestess of Athena in the *Iliad* (6. 300).[51] This tendency appears to have been more pronounced in post-classical times, although the relative frequency may be merely an artefact of the increase in epigraphical evidence in the later period. We may also note, in passing, the tendency of members of neo-Pythagorean communities to name their children after the original Pythagoreans. The choice indicates that in this Hellenistic philosophical community spiritual affiliation was more important than biological descent.[52]

A name alone can create an expectation of success in a particular career. Thus the homonymous descendants of famous generals and political leaders were expected to be not inferior to the most glorious bearers of the family names. The name itself was usually an asset. For example, the distinction of Cimon's family, the Philaids, in international politics can be traced back to the archaic period, continuing through five generations.[53] Miltiades III lay the foundations for Athenian influence in the Thracian Chersonese *c.*524, and his nephew Miltiades IV ruled as a dynast there, and even married a daughter of the king (see Ch. 1). His son, Cimon II, was the most illustrious member of the family, repeatedly holding the office of general, and serving Athens in various diplomatic and political capacities. Cimon's brother Metiochus, and one of his sons, Lacedaimonius, also held military command, though Oulius, who was Lacedaimonius's twin brother, left no mark on history. After 430, for more than a century, the family was not active in politics, perhaps because they disdained participating in the radical democracy, or perhaps because their gift for that sort of activity had petered out, at least for a while. In the

[50] On homonymous artists see *EAA*, *passim*.

[51] The priestesses named Theano are mentioned in Plut. *Alc.* 22; *IG* II² 1514. 36, 1515. 30, 1516. 14, 1517B, II. 142; 1524B, II. 22; 153; 5164, 3634; and see further Blaise Nagy, 'The Naming of Athenian Girls: A Case in Point', *CJ* 74 (1979), 60–4, and Christiane Sourvinou-Inwood, 'Priestess in the Text: *Theano Menonos Agrylethen*', *Greece and Rome*, 35 (1988), 28–35.

[52] See further Pomeroy, 'Technikai kai Mousikai', 57–8.

[53] See further Davies, *APF*, 8429, and *idem*, *Wealth*, 120–2, for additional examples.

mid-fourth century the name Cimon was diffused beyond the Philaids' original deme of Laciadai, and some bearers of the name were active in Hellenistic politics and diplomacy. It is not clear, however, whether they were descendants, or even remote relatives, of the man who bore the name in the mid-fifth century, or whether through a naming fiction they were trying to establish a link with the most glorious period of Athenian history. In any event, in the fourth century political power was less likely to be passed from father to son.[54] Aristotle (*Rh.* 1390b27–30) wrote: 'if the family is noble, for some time distinguished men are born in it, and then it declines. Well-born families often degenerate towards the maniacal type, as was the case with the descendants of Alcibiades and Dionysius the elder; while those that are stable degenerate towards foolishness and sluggishness, as was the case with the descendants of Cimon, Pericles, and Socrates.'

Scattered bits of information indicate that even among more humble families, the same economic and social dynamics appear. Socrates inherited his trade from his father.[55] His abandonment of it in favour of philosophy probably precipitated his fall into poverty.[56] As Aristotle remarked, his sons were not distinguished.

Literary texts provide biographical data about Socrates. Epigraphical and papyrological evidence provides glimpses of families who practised the same trade for generations. Although the Hellenistic period is thought to be a time of innovation and individualism, the inscriptions and papyri, which are abundant in this period, show that some families retained professional traditions. This is true not only of sculptors. For example, several decrees concerning the training of ephebes at Athens give information about four members of the same family who were employed as official military instructors from 232/231 to 128/127. In this case, as in others already mentioned, succession to this position passed through a sister, from uncle to nephew (see Fig. 6).[57]

Hellenistic mercenaries bequeathed their horses and armour to

[54] So Davies, *Wealth*, 121–2; but cf. Ch. 5 on Demosthenes and his nephew Demochares.

[55] Diog. Laert. 2. 18–19; Lib. *Apol.* 17–18.

[56] By the time the second version of Aristophanes' *Clouds* was produced, he was poor (*c.*420–417 BC: see *Clouds*, 103, 175, 362).

[57] For the genealogy see Benjamin D. Meritt, 'Greek Inscriptions', *Hesperia*, 11 (1942), 275–303, esp. 300–1 and E. W. Marsden, *Greek and Roman Artillery* (Oxford, 1969), 71–2.

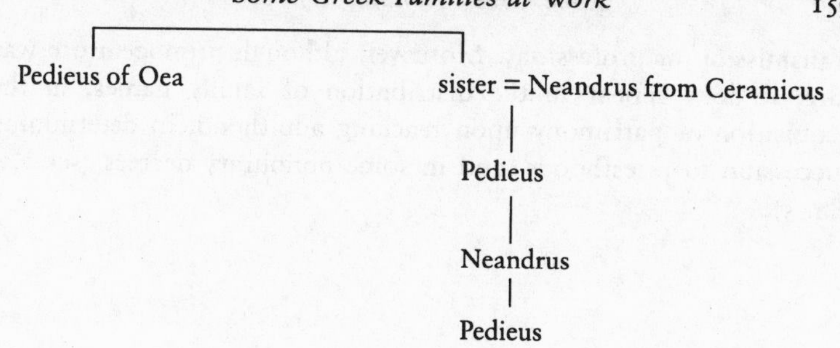

FIG. 6 The succession of four family members to the position of official military instructor

their sons.[58] In Egypt, originally only their sons could inherit their cleruchy ('land allotment') and the attendant military obligations. Sometimes the state itself obliged sons of soldiers to assume military responsibilities. Few children in such families would have had the countless options and faced the risks and pleasures that those in the modern Western world do in selecting a career. A society composed of such families would be characterized by conservatism and slow change over time, despite political changes in the larger society. On the other hand, both demographic and economic constraints, individual talent, and the vagaries of fortune make change inevitable. At least in the upper classes, it was difficult to preserve a family's financial status.[59] Furthermore, probably some 40 per cent of married couples did not have biological sons at all.[60]

Throughout this book, it has been apparent that despite the legal bias favouring the agnatic bond, and patrilocal marriage and burial, connections to the maternal line were effective and sometimes powerful forces in the choice of spouses, adoptees, and names and in the

[58] See *P. Petr.*² I 3. 75–80, 18. 11–12, 22. 23–4, 31, and Dryton's will (*P. Grenf.* I 12. 20–1, 21. 3–4 = *Select Papyri*, i. 83). See further H. Kreller, *Erbrechtliche Untersuchungen auf Grund der gräco-ägyptischen Papyrusurkunden* (Leipzig and Berlin, 1919), 12–13.

[59] According to Davies, *Wealth*, 86–7, only one family remained in the liturgical class for five successive generations, five families for four generations, sixteen families for three generations, forty-four families for two generations, and 537 for only one.

[60] See p. 122, above.

transmission of professions. Moreover, although primogeniture was rare, it does appear in the distribution of family names, in the acquisition of patrimony upon reaching adulthood, in determining succession to priesthoods, and in some honourary decrees (see e.g. Ch. 5).

5
Two Case Histories

> Happy families are all alike; every unhappy family is unhappy in its own way.
>
> Tolstoy, *Anna Karenina* (1873), trans. C. Garnett (1950), 3

Far from being grotesque or totally pathological, the families encountered in private orations can often serve as examples for the generalizations that have been made in preceding chapters about topics such as sentiment, naming patterns, demographic regimes, choice of spouses, and devolution of property. This is not the result of circular reasoning. The patterns have been detected in other pieces of evidence deriving from 'normal' families, rather than solely from those that became the fractured, fractious ones well known through litigation.

Rather than discuss families in the abstract, I have chosen to present detailed case-studies and to generalize using these examples as touchstones. I trace the life cycle in at least three generations of two well-known families, which allows us to view the changing relationships within families as men select wives, wives become widows, children become adults and marry, and patrimonies are dispersed. This provides a more complex picture of the family than would be the case with discussions of anonymous persons engaged in normal or average behaviour. The risk is that the material will seem anecdotal, and the wide range of primary sources may suggest to the reader that the families being sketched are incomparable and incommensurate. These two families, however, are representative in many respects. Demographic realities including the large age span between husband and wife, and women's death in childbirth and men's in war probably produced a society in which step-parents were not uncommon.[1] Female infanticide also created a shortage of women,

[1] According to Saller's demographic tables in *Patriarchy, Property*, 189, more than one-third of Roman children were fatherless by the time they reached puberty, and another third before the age of 25. There is no reason to believe that the situation in classical Greece was less grim, though it may not have been exactly the same: see Introduction, n. 21, and p. 102, above.

ensuring that widows of childbearing years, like Cleobule and Archippe, continued to be desirable marriage partners. We do not usually hear much about stepmothers as they quietly moved into the places vacated by their predecessors. Instead, the dynamics in the two families to be discussed created conflicts between stepfathers and stepsons which produced a spate of legal suits that record the ongoing tension between two generations of men in a single household. I hope that the vividness and nuanced detail with which these families are presented will compensate for the lack of a 'textbook' approach, which would focus upon patriarchy, iron out differences, attempt to answer all questions, and offer a polished overview.

DEMOSTHENES

Demosthenes was both the most famous orator and one of the most active politicians of the fourth century. He lived at the end of the classical period and into the first year of the Hellenistic period, though perhaps he was not aware of the definitive change. Entering the public arena at the earliest possible age and speaking on his own behalf in a private lawsuit, he remained in the public eye throughout his lifetime. He devoted most of his adult life to opposing the Macedonian conquest of Greece. Athens was decisively defeated in 322, and a Macedonian garrison was installed. This event marked the death of the independent *polis*. Demosthenes, then in exile, took his own life, in the view of his admirers both ancient and modern, a martyr in the cause of liberty.

Demosthenes' own family history is paradigmatic of the histories of many families, known through speeches written by Demosthenes himself and other classical orators. More than any other family of his time, Demosthenes' is documented by a variety of historical sources, ranging from extremely hostile to most favourable. Demosthenes is one of the few men in classical Athens about whom we have substantial verbatim autobiographical information concerning his private life and family activities. This evidence is largely limited to the period of his youth and young adulthood. Much of the testimony, is, of course, not presented frankly or dispassionately, but rather with the bias and exaggeration required to win victories in the Athenian courts and assemblies. Demosthenes' own speeches, naturally, were designed to elicit sympathy for his mother, sister, and himself.[2] In their orations rival orators and politicians sought to smear him—for example, by innuendo implying that his kinsmen were dishonourable or non-Athenian. Though the data they divulge are mainly derogatory, this hostile testimony cannot be dismissed off hand as mere lies. In addition to speech-writers, other ancient authors wrote about Demosthenes and his family. Some of their works, including those by Theopompus, and Marsyas of Pella, are no longer extant except in fragments.[3] Furthermore, there are several *Lives* necessarily based on the speeches of both Demosthenes and his enemies and on other prose texts, including some that have not survived. Among the biographies, Plutarch's, written some four centuries after Demosthenes' death, is by far the most valuable and sensible, for he presents the evidence, and tempers his report with his own comments and views on education, human virtue, and other relevant subjects, which enable the reader to place the biography in its proper context. Another, briefer *Life of Demosthenes* is found in the anonymous *Lives of the Ten Orators*, erroneously attributed to Plutarch and included in his *Moralia*.[4] Libanius's preface to his *Argumenta orationum Demosthenicarum* constitutes a biographical sketch.[5] In addition, there is a *Life* attributed to Zosimus of Ascalon and an anonymous biography.[6] Because of their brevity the *Lives* by Libanius and Zosimus lack the subtlety and alternative possibilities presented

[2] The speeches are traditionally referred to by the name of the accused; here they will be cited by number only. Thus *Aphobus* 1 = 27; *Aphobus* 2 = 28; *Aphobus* 3 = 29; *Onetor* 1 = 30; and *Onetor* 2 = 31. Anonymous speeches by Demosthenes' contemporaries included in the Demosthenic corpus are cited herein as Ps.-Dem.

[3] Theopompus in Plut. *Dem.* 4. 1, 13. 1, 14. 3, 18. 1–4, 21. 2, 25. 6–8 (*FGrH* 115, Fs. 325–30); Marsyas in Plut. *Dem.* 18. 2 (*FGrH* 135; F20), and see below.

[4] Cited in this Chapter as Ps.-Plut. *Mor.* To a large extent, it is based on a work by Caecilius, according to E. Ofenloch, *Caecilii Calactini Fragmenta* (Leipzig, 1907), pp. xxi–xxv. The fragments of the *Life of Demosthenes* that Ofenloch attributes to Caecilius are 116–27, frs. 133–47. There can be little certainty, however, about Pseudo-Plutarch's sources. On the biographical tradition see further F. Blass, *Die Attische Beredsamkeit*, 2nd edn., iii (Leipzig, 1893), 4–6, and Arnold Schaefer, *Demosthenes und seine Zeit* (Leipzig, 1885; repr. Hildesheim, 1966), i. 235–302.

[5] *Libanii Opera*, viii. 600–81, ed. R. Foerster ([1915]; repr. Hildesheim, 1963), esp. 601–5.

[6] These are printed in A. Westermann, *ΒΙΟΓΡΑΦΟΙ. Vitarum Scriptores Graeci Minores* (Braunschweig, 1845): Zosimus of Ascalon, pp. 297–302; anonymous *Life*, pp. 302–9, and in W. Dindorf, *Demosthenes*, viii (Oxford, 1851): Zosimus of Ascalon, pp. 18–22, and anonymous *Life*, pp. 23–8. Because they are repetitious, citations below from these biographies are selective.

by Plutarch and Pseudo-Plutarch. The anonymous *Life* does provide some information that is missing from other sources, but is unverifiable, such as an identification of Demosthenes' wife and an explanation of his behaviour soon after his daughter's death. As is true of many famous men, there are brief biographical remarks about Demosthenes' family life scattered in various texts, such as Dionysius of Halicarnassus, *Demosthenes*, the *Suda* (454–6 Adler), and Photius (492b–495a). Although biographies by Plutarch and others add idealizing, fictional, or unprovable elements, they do give a more balanced picture of Demosthenes' private life than the orations, not only because they were drawn from both sympathetic and hostile sources, but also because they were written hundreds of years after Demosthenes' death, when the controversies that had fuelled them were no longer vivid.

The first members of Demosthenes' direct lineage to appear in historical sources are his grandfathers, Demomeles and Gylon, and the last is his daughter who predeceased him (see Fig. 7[7]). We have noted that historical memory rarely spanned more than three generations of a family, even when, as in the case of a family such as Demosthenes', the family was both wealthy and well attested (see Ch. 3). Thus we are fortunate to have some information about Demosthenes' grandfathers and great nephew. Demomeles had three surviving children in a family of ideal size: two sons and one daughter. The order of birth was probably Demon, then the daughter, and finally Demosthenes the elder. Although the younger brother predeceased the older, Demosthenes I died of illness, not old age (Dem. 27. 4, 28. 15). As is often the case with respectable women, the names of Demosthenes' grandmothers, paternal aunt, sister, wife, and daughter are not known. The name of Demosthenes' maternal aunt, Philia, appears only on a funerary monument. Her daughter Hippoclea is named on the same monument as well as on a *horos* inscription concerning her dowry.[8] An inscription of 421 records a Demomeles

[7] Davies, *APF*, Table III (adapted). For the genealogy see Davies, *APF* 3597.

[8] The monument of Demochares' family: *IG* II^2 6737a, p. 891; the *horos* inscription: *IG* II^2 2670. See further M. I. Finley, *Studies in Land and Credit in Ancient Athens 500–200* BC (New Brunswick, NJ, 1952), J. V. A. Fine, *Horoi. Studies in Mortgage, Real Security, and Land Tenure in Ancient Athens*, *Hesperia*, Suppl. 9 (Princeton, 1951), and P. Millett, 'The Attic Horoi Reconsidered in the Light of Recent Discoveries', *Opus*, 1 (1982), 219–49. *Horoi* may also record the encumbrance of property in connection with a promised dowry: see Harrison, *Law of Athens*, i. 297–301. Like some other men in

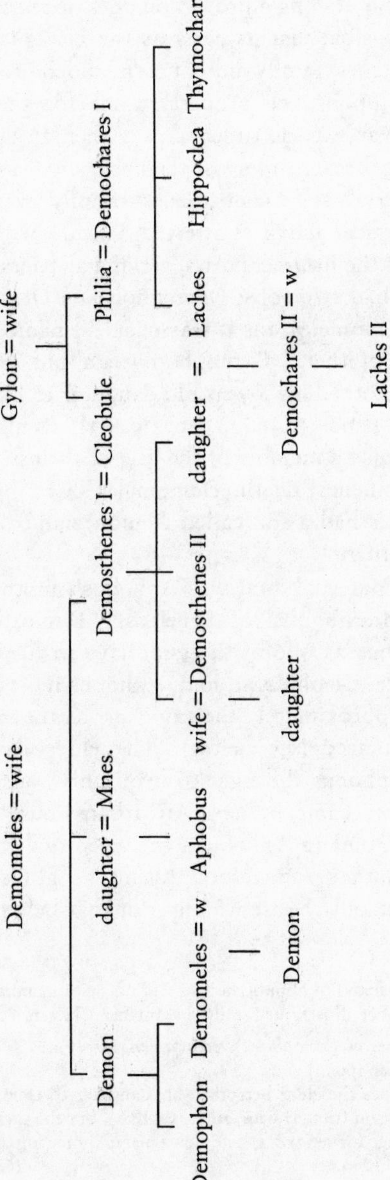

FIG. 7 The family of Demosthenes

(probably Demosthenes' grandfather) as an architect of a bridge at Eleusis. Although pursuing a profession does not necessarily preclude farming, it is possible that as early as the last quarter of the fifth century Demosthenes' family did not own landed property, or at least did not depend upon such property alone for their income. The Peloponnesian War was detrimental to Athenian agriculture. After the war, farming became more specialized and less the domain of the landed gentry.[9] Yet Demosthenes' family was wealthy, with many major liturgical activities attested. Demosthenes' uncle Demon was a member of the liturgical class, serving as trierarch in 373/2 and 366/5.[10] Demon had two sons: Demophon and Demomeles. Perhaps the elder was Demomeles, for it was usual to name the first son for his paternal grandfather.[11] Demophon was about 25 when the elder Demosthenes betrothed his 5-year old daughter to him. They were to marry ten years hence (*c.*366, Dem. 29. 43). Demosthenes' cousin Demomeles was also a member of the liturgical class.[12] At the time of the elder Demosthenes' death, Demomeles owed him 1,600 drachmas.[13] Demomeles had a son called Demon, named, in turn, for his paternal grandfather.[14]

Demosthenes' paternal aunt was Aphobus's mother; her husband was probably Mnesiboulus of Sphettos.[15] Demosthenes the elder appointed Aphobus as one of the guardians of his estate, and also betrothed his wife, Cleobule, to him. Aphobus must have been about 30 at the time, approximately the same age as the woman whom he had agreed to marry (see below). The elder Demosthenes also bequeathed to Aphobus the right to live in his house with Cleobule until Demosthenes came of age. An urban house may have been welcome at this point in Aphobus's life, even one with work-rooms and store-rooms that soon stood vacant as a result of his own depredations. The only house we know of that belonged to Aphobus

classical Athens, a husband of Hippoclea is buried not with members of his own *oikos*, but with his wife's more illustrious family. See further Ch. 3 n. 80, above.

9 See further Pomeroy, *Xenophon, Oeconomicus*, 46–55.

10 *IG* II[2] 1607, l. 26; 1609, l. 13.

11 That Demosthenes the elder betrothed his daughter to Demophon may indicate that he was the older son (thus Davies, *APF* 3597IIIA), but the fact that the girl would not be ripe for marriage for ten years, and thus a better choice for the younger son, does not support Davies's inference.

12 *IG* II[2] 1609, ll. 62, 91.

13 100 drachmas = 1 mina, 60 minas = 1 talent.

14 Davies, *APF* 3597IV.

15 Dem. 27. 4 and see Davies, *APF* 3597 V–VI.

was on a farm.[16] Aphobus paid for a trierarchy in 375, soon after Demosthenes' father died (Dem. 27. 14). That the death of Demosthenes I in 376/5 predated the attested liturgical activities of his brother Demon and his two nephews lends some support to Demosthenes' contention that his kinsmen had enriched themselves by embezzling his patrimony.[17]

The elder Demosthenes must have married early in the 380s. This date is deduced from the birthdate of his oldest child, Demosthenes, who was born in 385/4 or 384/3.[18] He was given the same name as his father. Thus we see in the same family both the pattern of using a name in alternate generations and the pattern of repeating the same name for father and son. Their deme was Paiania, but there is no indication that either father or son ever resided there. When Demosthenes did have a house outside the city centre, it was in Piraeus.[19]

Demosthenes' mother, Cleobule, was a daughter of Gylon of Cerameis. Her father had resided for a long time in the Black Sea region. Demosthenes' political rival Aeschines (3. 171–2) alleged that Gylon had been banished because he was held responsible for the loss of Nymphaion, an ally of Athens in the Tauric Chersonese (Kertch), during the Peloponnesian War. This accusation is an example of matrilineal inheritance of dishonour.[20] Gylon's punishment was probably a fine, and Demosthenes himself admits that his grandfather had once been a state debtor.[21] Gylon subsequently took up service with half-barbarian tyrants of the Cimmerian Bosporus, and was given a property in a place called Kepoi ('Gardens').[22] There, in

[16] Dem. 30.2 , 26–9. The house was probably transferred to Onetor: Dem. 31. 1–4.

[17] Aphobus served as trierarch shortly after his uncle's death: Dem. 27. 14 and Davies, *APF* 3597VI.

[18] Dem. 21. 154, 30. 15, and see Mark Golden, 'Demosthenes and the Age of Majority at Athens', *Phoenix*, 33 (1979), 25–38.

[19] Aesch. 3. 209; Din. 1. 69; Hyp. 1.17.

[20] Din. 1. 111. *Atimia* ('loss of civic rights') was inherited by direct descent. See Ch. 2 n. 63 above, and see further Louis Gernet, 'Note sur les parents de Démosthène', *REG* 31 (1918), 185–96, and Harrison, *Law of Athens*, i. 129. It is not clear when, or whether, Gylon's debt was paid. He continued to be a 'skeleton in the closet'.

[21] On Gylon see Dem. 27. 1, 28. 1–3; Aesch. 3. 171–2; Plut. *Dem.* 4. 2; Ps.-Plut. *Mor.* 844a. E. H. Minns, *Scythians and Greeks* (Cambridge, 1913), 561, argues that the loss of Nymphaeum was unavoidable, and points out that soon after Gylon surrendered the place, the Bosporan kings became friendly with Athens. Minns, however, is not convincing. Athens had not yet lost the Peloponnesian War, and such friendship was not suggested until the 390s.

[22] Aesch. 3. 171–2; Plut. *Dem.* 4; Ps.-Plut. *Mor.* 844a; Lib. *Hypoth. Dem.*

408–406 he married a wealthy wife. Kepoi was a Milesian colony.[23] Thus Gylon's wife was probably a daughter of a Greek settler, although she may not have been Athenian. Later, however, to stigmatize Demosthenes, Aeschines and other political opponents alleged that his mother was a Scythian by blood.[24] The marriage produced two daughters: Philia, and her younger sister Cleobule, who eventually became Demosthenes' mother.[25]

Cleobule was born before 403. The insinuation that his mother was not Athenian puts Demosthenes on the fringe of citizenship. After the reimposition of Pericles' citizenship law in 403, a prerequisite for citizenship was descent from parents who were both citizens, even though the rule was not retroactive.[26] To attack an opponent by casting slurs on his female kin was a common tactic.[27] As a result of the seclusion of respectable women, little was known about them—not even their names. Nor could their appearance or speech be used as evidence of ethnicity (see Chs. 1 and 2). Certainly there would have been few witnesses in Athens in the last third of the fourth century who could have testified to the lineage of a woman born in the Bosporus some seventy years earlier. Moreover, because of Gylon's dishonour, the family would have avoided mentioning him. In any case, Demosthenes never responded to the allegations about his mother and grandfather, perhaps because there was some truth in them, or because it was beneath his dignity to honour them with a response, or because he was reluctant to drag his mother's name through the Athenian courts. The charges, however, amount to a legacy of disloyalty and lack of patriotism. Perhaps Demosthenes' public career was inspired to some extent by a desire to surmount this heritage.

The elder Demosthenes had betrothed his wife and his 5-year-old

[23] C. M. Sofia Danoff, 'Kepos', in *Der Kleine Pauly*, iii (Stuttgart, 1969), col. 194.

[24] Gylon's wealth is evident in the size of Cleobule's original dowry; see also Aesch. 3. 172. For the allegation 'Scythian' see Aesch. 2. 78, 3. 172; Din. 1. 15; Zosimus of Ascalon, 146. 17, 22 (Westermann), and Ps.-Plut. *Mor.* 847f. The Scythians were 'barbarians'; the Athenian police force was composed of Scythian slaves.

[25] On Philia see Davies *APF*, 3716.

[26] Arist. *Ath. Pol.* 26. 4; Plut. *Per.* 37. 3; Dem. 57. 30, etc., and see p. 39 above.

[27] For a similar strategy see Ps.-Dem. 59 where Stephanus is attacked by means of allegations about his wife Neaera (see Ch. 4), and Dem. 57. 30–43, where Euxitheus's citizenship is questioned, in part, because of his mother's menial occupations. G. H. Macurdy, 'Apollodorus and the Speech against Neaera', *AJP* 63 (1942), 257–71, esp. 261, suggests that although Demosthenes was not the author of the speech against Neaera, he was ultimately responsible for framing the accusation against her.

daughter to his sister's son and his brother's son, respectively.[28] Such endogamous arrangements were common among propertied Athenians. Demosthenes' sister eventually married her first cousin, and his niece also married a kinsman.[29] It was not uncommon for a husband to make arrangements for his wife's subsequent marriage (e.g. Dem. 30. 7, 57. 41; Isae. 2. 7–9). Pericles had found another husband for his wife after they were divorced, and Pasio betrothed his wife to his manager Phormio. Phormio also became the guardian of Pasio's minor son, Pasicles, when his father died (Dem. 36. 8 and see below). Some husbands doubtless were motivated by protective concern for their wife's future. Moreover, an unattached widow had the potential to dishonour her family, and even to inspire doubts about the parentage of her children.[30] Therefore it was incumbent upon her male relatives to find another husband for her. It is likely that the elder Demosthenes consulted Cleobule concerning the choice of her future spouse, for they seem to have communicated well with one another. Aphobus alludes to a close relationship between them when he alleges that Demosthenes' father had hidden four talents in the ground, and that he had put Cleobule in charge of this buried treasure.[31] The elder Demosthenes also appointed Aphobus, Demophon, and his lifelong friend Therippides of Paeania as guardians of Demosthenes and his sister. According to conventional wisdom, the elder Demosthenes could scarcely have made a better choice than his kinsmen and friend. He entrusted his closest relatives and all his property to them. As events turned out, however, bonds of kinship and friendship between men did not necessarily extend to wives and children, whereas the blood tie between sisters survived their marriages (see below).

The elder Demosthenes had allocated a large dowry of two talents (i.e. 12,000 drachmas) to his daughter[32] and 8,000 drachmas to his widow.[33] As we have mentioned, the two women were to have married two of the appointed guardians. From the point of view of the ages of

[28] Dem. 27. 5, 28. 15, 29. 43. Cleobule was probably around 30 at the time of her husband's death: Davies, *APF* 3597 VIII, dates her birth between 408 and 400. For other examples of the remarriage of widows see Thompson, 'Athenian Marriage Patterns', *passim*, and n. 96 below.

[29] For other examples, see below on Apollodorus's daughter, and see further Davies, *APF* 3716B, and Thompson, 'Marriage of First Cousins'.

[30] See below on Pasicles; on Chrysilla, Ischomachus's widow, who bore a son who was at first rejected by the putative father, see Pomeroy, *Xenophon Oeconomicus*, 261–3.

[31] Dem. 27. 53.

[32] Dem. 27. 4–5, 42–5, 65; 27. 15, 19; 29. 43.

[33] Dem. 27. 4, 28. 19, 29. 43.

the spouses, the marriage arrangements were not ideal. As we saw earlier, in the upper class, the normative age at first marriage of men was 30 and of women 14 or 15.[34] Demophon was to wait until he was about 35 to marry Demosthenes' sister, and Aphobus was to marry his aunt by marriage, a woman as old as he was, even if she was still young enough for childbearing and of proven fertility. He was also to take on a ready-made family and to live in the widow's house, a situation that, though perhaps convenient, was not entirely desirable in terms of a man's self-esteem. Nowadays, in traditional Greek societies, it can be considered humiliating for a man to marry a widow, and to work on property and live in a house belonging to another man (i.e. the deceased husband, and his heir).[35] In antiquity too, it was normal for a bride to move to her husband's house. Staying in one's own house definitely gave a spouse an advantage: the slaves would be loyal, and one would avoid having to live with suspicious in-laws and hostile stepchildren. Perhaps the elder Demosthenes thought he would secure his nephews' fidelity by means of large dowries.[36] Therippides, the third guardian, was rewarded by the usufruct of 70 minas until Demosthenes came of age. The reason for the disparity in the dowries of mother and daughter may be that Cleobule's original dowry had been 5,000 drachmas. Although this was generous, to have increased it was even more generous (Dem. 27. 4, 45, 65, 69). Or the reason may have been emotional: the elder Demosthenes may have felt more expansive towards his own flesh-and-blood daughter, a pitiful 5-year old, than toward his wife. A large dowry would guarantee her marriage, whether or not she grew up to be attractive from other points of view. Practical considerations as well may have prompted the elder Demosthenes to apportion a larger dowry to his daughter, for the costs of her maintenance and education for ten years until the time of her marriage would have been paid from it (Dem. 27. 5, 11–13). Demosthenes himself was to receive the bulk of the inheritance, which totalled some fourteen talents. Inheritance was partible among males. At Athens the daughter was entitled to receive

[34] Introduction, n. 17 above.

[35] Ernestine Friedl, *Vasilika. A Village in Modern Greece* (New York, 1965), 64. On the marriage market, a widow is usually less desirable, and brings a man less prestige than a virgin: see Paul Sant Cassia and Constantina Bada, *The Making of the Modern Greek Family* (Cambridge, 1992), 192–3.

[36] The amounts allocated as dowries by Demosthenes' father constituted a larger proportion of his total estate than was common among the wealthy. See further David M. Schaps, *Economic Rights of Women in Ancient Greece* (Edinburgh, 1979), 78.

nothing more than her dowry. Favouring of sons over daughters in the distribution of the patrimony was normal practice. It is interesting to observe that the elder Demosthenes' arrangements are consistent with the patterns of *philia* ('friendship') relationships within the Greek family described by Aristotle (*Eth. Nic.* 1161b18–1162a24). The affection of parents for children is the primary bond. Fraternal affection is most reliable, and cousins and other relatives derive their relationship from the bond between brothers (similarly Dem. 36. 20). Among the basic relationships in the family, Aristotle treats that of husband and wife last, and does not consider sisters. He is doubtless not much concerned with affective relationships that do not include men. However, bonds between sisters could be quite strong (see below).

Although Demosthenes' cousins had agreed to the betrothals and appropriated the dowries, they did not marry his mother or sister. Nor did they serve as model guardians for the family and their property. Remarriage was normal for a widow or divorcée who was still capable of bearing children. Life as an unmarried woman was to be avoided.[37] Medical texts emphasize the importance of childbearing, and understand the female anatomy as designed expressly for this purpose. Marriage at the time of puberty was essential, for without defloration the menses might remain bottled up inside the body.[38] A woman's health depended upon having intercourse and producing children at regular intervals.[39] Thus it was necessary to avoid prolonged virginity or widowhood during the childbearing years.

Usually relatives looked after a widow and orphans. In this case, however, the abusers were themselves relatives. It is relevant to observe that Plutarch praises the exogamous practices of the Romans, for a wife could always turn to her blood-relations to defend her against her husband.[40] Who would guard the guards? When relatives gave a dowry, it was customary to require of the husband some security equal to the value of the dowry, such as house or land

[37] Dem. 45. 74; Hyp. *Lyc.* 13; cf. Isae. 2. 7; Lys. 13. 45.

[38] See further Ann Ellis Hanson, 'The Medical Writers' Woman', in D. M. Halperin, J. J. Winkler, and F. I. Zeitlin (eds.), *Before Sexuality* (Princeton, 1990), 309–38, esp. 318, 323–4.

[39] Otherwise her womb might dry out, become light, and wander through her body, in search of moisture. See e.g. Hippocrates, *Diseases of Women* 1. 1, 2, 6, 7, 24, 8. 62, etc., and see further Leslie Dean-Jones, 'The Cultural Construct of the Female Body', in Sarah B. Pomeroy (ed.), *Women's History and Ancient History* (Chapel Hill, NC, 1991), 111–37, esp. 121–2.

[40] *Roman Questions*, 108, and see Ch. 1 nn. 32 and 33 above.

(Harp., s.v. *apotimetai*). Those who administered the property of orphans were also required to put up security. *Horoi* inscriptions were erected on property that was encumbered as security.[41] Furthermore, a magistrate called the 'Archon Eponymos' was supposed to look after widows and orphans (Arist. *Ath. Pol.* 56. 7; Isae. 6). Nevertheless, none of these protective devices seems to have been put into effect: at least, there are no records of such activity. Cleobule was at the mercy of her ex-husband's kinsmen, because she had no brother, and owing to her father's disgrace, there apparently were no old friends of the family who were willing to champion her cause. Later, Demosthenes refers to family friends (Dem. 27. 1), and when his fortunes were restored, one old friend of the elder Demosthenes, the general Cephisodotus, paid him the special favour of sailing on the ship Demosthenes had furnished in 360/59 as trierarch (Aeschin. 3. 52). When Cleobule was desperate, however, her brother-in-law Demochares was probably her only ally.[42] Although he belonged to another *oikos*, the bonds of sentiment between the two sisters evidently were stronger than the legal divisions that separated them. Demochares was a member of the liturgical class, and the size of his daughter's dowry suggests that he was also generous.[43] So helpful was Demochares that eventually his son Laches married Demosthenes' sister, even though her dowry had been dissipated.

As the first sentence of Pseudo-Plutarch's *Life of Demosthenes* states, Demosthenes spent the period of his orphanage with his mother.[44] The word *orphania* refers to the lack of a father, whether or not there is a mother. Nevertheless, Plutarch (*Dem.* 4. 3) emphasizes Cleobule's protective influence. The *Suda* (454 Adler) and Photius (*Dem.* 495a) report that when Demosthenes was young, he often dressed in women's clothing. In any case, his stutter and his unusual youth in the presence of a strong mother and in the absence of positive male role models, lacking even male slaves, make him an obvious candidate for psycho-historical analysis—if this approach is valid for anyone in classical Athens.[45]

[41] See n. 8 above. [42] Dem. 27. 14–15, and see Davies, *APF* 3717.

[43] Dem. 28. 3. Her dowry was one talent; cf. nn. 32 and 33 above.

[44] *Mor.* 844b; cf. Plut. *Dem.* 4. 3.

[45] On the mother–son relationship see Virginia Hunter, 'Women's Authority in Classical Athens: The Example of Kleoboule and her Son (Dem. 27–29)', *EMC* 33, n.s. 8 (1989), 39–48. For a Freudian analysis of the Athenian male see Philip Slater, *The Glory of Hera* (Boston, 1968).

Without a father to teach him a profession and without a farm or a family business to inherit, but needing to earn a livelihood, Demosthenes was free, as few other upper-class youths were, to choose a career (see further Ch. 4). Indeed, his rootlessness made him vulnerable as an adult to his enemies' attacks; he was like a metic, for his mother was said to be foreign, he did not own land, and he actually charged fees for writing speeches.[46] His biographers name various sources for his inspiration and education, including Isocrates and Isaeus.[47] Because both were known as writers of speeches in cases of intrafamilial disputes over inheritance, biographical tradition will have associated Demosthenes with them, whether he actually was their pupil or not. Dionysius of Halicarnassus begins his essay on Isaeus with the statement that Isaeus was Demosthenes' teacher, and became illustrious because of it (*Isoc.* 1). Anecdotes make him a pupil of Plato and Eubulides the Eristic as well.[48] But if he was as impoverished as he claims, how could he have paid the tuition? In any case, these traditions are more dubious than those that relate Demosthenes' later opposition to the philosophers.

By contrast with other upper-class boys whose education was entrusted to male relatives or who attended school and exercised in the gymnasium, Demosthenes was brought up at home, for his mother thought him too frail to consort with boys his own age outside the house (Plut. *Dem.* 5). Perhaps it was this isolation that produced his nervous, truculent demeanour.[49] Biographers give various reports of Demosthenes' study of oratory and self-discipline. He was single-minded, if not obsessive, about restoring the family's fortune and punishing the miscreants. He is said to have subjected himself to many discomforts in order to force himself to learn oratory. Thus, he retired to a cave, shaved half his head in an unbecoming style to prevent himself from going out, and slept on a narrow bed in order to wake up early.[50] Demosthenes became a celebrated example of overcompensation for a physical handicap. He is said to have practised many exercises to improve his gestures

[46] See below, and in general Whitehead, *Ideology.*

[47] Plut. *Dem.* 5. 4; Ps.-Plut. *Mor.* 844b; Lib. 602. 7.

[48] Diog. Laert. 2. 108; Zosimus of Ascalon, 147, 39 (Westermann).

[49] e.g. Demos. 8. 68, 19. 46, 206; Aesch. 2. 34, 35.

[50] Ps.-Plut. *Mor.* 844d–e; cf. Plut. *Dem.* 7. 3; Lib. 604. 12; anon., *Life*, 154. 48 (Westermann); *Suda*, 456, etc.

and to overcome speech disabilities.[51] It is credible that an adolescent would invent bizarre devices such as dangling a spit or a dagger over his head to force himself, through fear, to stop moving his shoulder unsuitably.[52] Equally credible is the report that in order to improve his pronunciation and overcome his lisp, Demosthenes practised speaking with pebbles in his mouth, or while running or climbing steep hills (Plut. *Dem.* 11. 1–2). Even if specific details of these anecdotes are fictitious, it seems plausible that in the absence of a father or a stepfather or social peers, the young Demosthenes was free to indulge in some eccentric behaviour.

As soon as he reached maturity, in 364/3, Demosthenes launched his prosecution of his guardians for misusing and squandering his patrimony. He paints a picture not only of negligence, but of deliberate malevolence on the part of his guardians. His most severe accusations were against his cousin Aphobus. Doubtless, he overstated his case in order to win. It is more than likely that three guardians were too many. None took responsibility, for each must have expected another to do so. All were probably busy with their own affairs. Furthermore, the possession of wealth does not guarantee that a man will not seek additional wealth. Indeed, the official and private burdens that befell wealthy Athenians were substantial.[53] In the vacuum that existed after his master's death, Milyas, a slave foreman who had been freed by the elder Demosthenes, had managed the family's financial affairs (Dem. 27. 22, 29. 25–6, 29–31). The elder Demosthenes had written a will, but the actual document had vanished (27. 40). This loss was not a hindrance to Demosthenes' claim. Written evidence such as a will might be forged;[54] witnesses and a speaker's own testimony were considered at least as reliable, though it was understood that they might lie. According to Demosthenes, his father's knife factory had employed thirty-two or thirty-three slaves, and brought in 3,000 drachmas annually. His furniture factory had employed twenty slaves and had produced an income of 1,200 drachmas. In addition, his father had left raw materials for use in manufacture, equipment, a house, various sums invested in banks and in

[51] Ps.-Plut. *Mor.* 844e–f, 847e. For the nickname 'Batalus', probably a reference to his stuttering, see Aesch. 1. 131; Plut. *Dem.* 4. 3–4, etc.

[52] Ps.-Plut. *Mor.* 844e; Lib. 605. 13; Zosimus of Ascalon 148. 81–3 (Westermann).

[53] On liturgies see Pomeroy, *Xenophon, Oeconomicus*, 47, 52–3, 225–8.

[54] e.g. Dem. 45. 5–6, 11, etc., 46. 2–3, etc.; Isae. 1. 41, 4. 12–18, 7. 2, 9. 2, 22–5.

maritime loans, and, as previously mentioned, a loan to his nephew Demomeles.[55] The values he stipulates do not correspond exactly to the totals given in the speeches, but they are not far off, amounting to almost 14 talents. The guardians denied that they had ever received the cash and property that Demosthenes enumerated, and also blamed a ten-year war for the decline in the family's fortunes. Demosthenes, in turn, argued that even if his guardians had acted simply as custodians and not sought actively to increase his property, it would have grown to a value of as much as 30 talents.[56] Consequently, each of his guardians owed him 10 talents. Instead, all he had received was worth only 7,000 drachmas. In court he demanded only one-third of the value the property should have had (Dem. 28. 59). As frequently occurred in family disputes, private arbitration was attempted, but without success (Dem. 27. 1).[57] When Aphobus learned that the arbiters would give judgment against him, he withdrew from the proceedings. The dispute then came before a public arbitrator, who also judged favourably on behalf of Demosthenes, and sent the case to court. Although young, or perhaps because of his youth, Demosthenes won his case.[58] He was able to recover only a fraction of the property his father had possessed at the time of his death. Because almost all the estate consisted of moveable property and cash invested in various ways, it had been easy for the guardians to dispose of it discreetly, little by little, without leaving a trace.

Aphobus did not hesitate to take revenge. At his instigation, a certain Thrasylochus, who had been assigned a trierarchy, attempted to foist the responsibility off on Demosthenes by challenging him to an *antidosis* ('exchange of property'). By this manœuvre, Thrasylochus implied that Demosthenes could better afford the liturgy than he could. If, however, Demosthenes believed that Thrasylochus was wealthier than he himself was, then he would have been willing to exchange properties. At first Demosthenes agreed to the exchange rather than accept the liturgy, though he later reconsidered. When Thrasylochus and his brother Meidias came to look over Demosthenes' property which they would have got on an exchange, they damaged his house. By this act of violence they revealed that

[55] Dem. 27–29, *passim*.

[56] Dem. 27. 9–11; on the potential income see further J. Korver, 'Demosthenes gegen Aphobos', *Mnem.* 10 (1941–2), 8–22.

[57] Dem. 27. 1. On settlements out of court among kin see Hunter, *Policing Athens*, 43–69.

[58] He harps on his youth: e.g. Dem. 21. 78, 80.

they did not intend to make an exchange, for why would they damage property that was soon to be their own? What is even worse, they forced open the doors of the living quarters, and used foul language in the presence of Demosthenes' sister who was still unmarried (Dem. 21. 78–81, 28. 17). For men who were not kin, merely to be in the presence of respectable women was in itself a situation fraught with scandal.[59] Finally, in 363 Demosthenes undertook the liturgy, thereby demonstrating that even if he was not so wealthy, as he claimed he should have been, he nevertheless qualified as a member of the liturgical class.[60] He had to mortgage his house and other property to raise the necessary funds. The liturgy in question, a syntrierarchy, was one of the most costly, estimated at 20 minas per participant. Had he agreed to *antidosis*, Thrasylochus, a friend of Aphobus, would doubtless have dropped all charges connected with the property.

Aphobus also demanded that the old freedman Milyas be subjected to torture, as was usual for a slave before giving testimony.[61] Because at the trial a certain Phanus asserted that Milyas had been freed, and thus was not liable for torture, Aphobus sued Phanus. Demosthenes reports that Onetor (see below) helped him trump up this charge (29. 58).

The jury decided in favour of Demosthenes, and granted him the 10 talents he sought from Aphobus. According to Athenian law, the victor in a lawsuit had to execute judgment himself. To avoid paying Demosthenes, Aphobus moved to Megara, spitefully having left some of his property in Athens in a damaged condition, and having given some of it away (Dem. 29. 3). In 367/6 Aphobus married a woman who was a daughter of Philonides and sister of Onetor. She had just been divorced from Timocrates.[62] She was thus connected to two of the wealthiest families in the city, for, according to Demosthenes, Timocrates had 10 talents and Onetor more than 30 (Dem. 30. 10). Aphobus divorced her eighteen months later. When Demosthenes attempted to seize some of Aphobus's property, Onetor (now Apho-

[59] See Lys. 3. 6–7; Ps.-Dem. 47. 53; p. 80 above; and see further Pomeroy, *Goddesses, Whores*, 79–84.

[60] For Demosthenes' liturgies and other contributions see Dem. 19. 166–71, 21. 13, 78–80, 154, 156, 161, 27. 17, 28. 118, 99; Aesch. 2. 100, 3. 17, 51–2, 173; Ps.-Plut. *Mor.* 845c, f–846a, 851a–b, and see further Davies, *APF* 3597 XXII.

[61] Dem. 27. 19, 29, *passim*.

[62] Dem. 27. 56, 29. 48, 30. 15. For Onetor see Davies, *APF* 11473.

bus's ex-brother-in-law) prevented him, announcing that he had a prior claim on it for the repayment of his sister's dowry, which Aphobus had failed to return. Demosthenes asserted that the dowry had never changed hands, but was still in the possession of the sister's previous husband, Timocrates, who was paying interest on it (Dem. 30. 4, 7–8, 10). This assertion was credible, for if the dowry had been invested, it might not have been feasible to return it immediately at the time of the preceding divorce.[63] The dowry of Onetor's sister was worth 8,000 drachmas (Dem. 29. 48, 31. 6–9). Moreover, since the woman was still in her prime in 361 (Dem. 30. 33–4), she probably was at least several, and perhaps as many as ten years younger than Cleobule. Thus Aphobus succeeded in obtaining a dowry as large as Cleobule's. Moreover, he had married a woman younger than Demosthenes' mother and one from an even wealthier family, though she too had been married previously. Demosthenes charged collusion between Aphobus and Onetor, and was then forced to prosecute Onetor (Dem. 30. 5, 26, 33). He sued Onetor, claiming that the divorce had been a scam, concocted to defraud Demosthenes of the property that he had gained in his lawsuit. He was able to cite evidence of continuing friendship between Aphobus, his ex-wife, and her brother, and asserted that Aphobus and Onetor's sister were still living together, and that the divorce had been agreed upon in order to vitiate his claim on Aphobus's property (Dem. 30. 18–19). Demosthenes' statements raise a question of particular interest to the family historian: in the absence of written contracts and of licences issued by the state, what makes *sunoikein* ('living together') a marriage, and what qualifies as divorce?[64] Two steps constitute a marriage: (1) the *engue* ('pledging or promising of the bride'). The bride is not necessarily handed over at this point. She, in fact, is not present, for the *engue* is a private contract between men. (2) The *gamos* ('wedding celebration'). The *gamos* leads directly to *sunoikein*. The haste with which Onetor's sister was transferred from one husband to the next suggests that the proper steps constituting marriage had not been taken.

A sub-text in this part of the drama related by Demosthenes is that Onetor was a cad to deal so frivolously with his sister's reputation.

[63] Dem. 27. 13, 30. 12. On mortgaging land as security for dowries see n. 8, above.

[64] See p. 33, and Patterson, 'Marriage in Athenian Law'. On divorce, a simple procedure if the husband initiated it, see Harrison, *Law of Athens*, i. 39–44.

According to Demosthenes' version of events, owing to her brother's machinations, the woman had moved directly from the house of her husband Timocrates to the house of Aphobus without interval (Dem. 30. 11). She was living with Aphobus, to whom she was not properly married, not only compromising her own reputation as a respectable woman, but jeopardizing the legitimacy of any potential children, inasmuch as their father might not acknowledge them (Dem. 30. 26, 29). The production of heirs for the husband was the purpose of marriage, for the bride's father or guardian pledged her to the groom 'for the purpose of the sowing of legitimate children'. Onetor had perverted the traditional purpose of marriage. Demosthenes paints the woman as a mere pawn in the financial transactions of Aphobus and her brother, and does not give her name, as perhaps he would have if he had considered her a guilty party.[65] We may also note a slight miserliness in Onetor's allocation of a dowry to his sister, compared with the generosity of the elder Demosthenes. Whereas Demosthenes' father had bequeathed to his sister 14.3 per cent of his total estate, Onetor had given his sister only 4.4 per cent of his.

In contrast to Onetor's behaviour, we may compare Demosthenes' valiant struggle to defend his sister's honour and to regain her dowry, so that he might arrange a proper marriage for her. Demosthenes' sister was two years younger than he was. A substantial part of his charge against Aphobus in 364/3 was that she was without a dowry and at the age of 15 already an old maid (Dem. 21. 79, 27. 65–6, 28. 21–2). As we have seen, 14–15 was the normal age of first marriage for an upper-class Athenian woman.[66] The mores of Mediterranean society demanded that the male head of the household defend the honour of his family's women and secure proper marriages for them. A dowerless unmarried woman was a pitiful creature. It was incumbent upon kinsmen and family friends to supply a dowry, certainly not, as in this case, to steal the dowry.[67] The marriage of Demosthenes' sister to her maternal cousin Laches has been mentioned above. Their descendants were named according to the regular

[65] According to Cox, 'Sibling Relationships', 388, Onetor's sister was 'actively involved'. Cox cites Dem. 31. 11–12, but this passage does not corroborate her interpretation. Moreover, such a succession of husbands was not to the woman's advantage, but quite the opposite.

[66] See Introduction, n. 17 above.

[67] Lys. 19. 59. In the case of poor 'heiresses' (*epikleroi* of the thetic class) the authority of the state attempted to assure that a dowry was provided: Ps.-Dem. 43. 54; Isae. 1. 39. See further Harrison, *Law of Athens*, i. 48–9.

pattern: their son, Demochares, was named for his paternal grandfather, and their grandson, in turn, was named Laches for his paternal grandfather. Laches' last reported activity was the proposal of a decree honouring his father in 271/70 (see below). Thus we have information about five generations in this family spanning approximately a century and a half, corresponding neatly to the Greek demographic pattern of thirty years per generation.

How Demosthenes dealt with Therippides and Demophon is not known; perhaps they came to some compromise after seeing how severely he had handled Aphobus. The unity of the family was shattered: the three guardians and Demosthenes' uncle Demon, who was also implicated, testified against each other (Dem. 29. 20, 33, 36, 52). There were further lawsuits against Demomeles for recovery of the money that had been loaned by the elder Demosthenes (Dem. 27. 11) and for a cut on the head which he had inflicted on Demosthenes.[68] This was the third recorded time that Demosthenes had been the victim of violence at the hands of his relatives and their friends, though the two preceding attacks had been upon his property or property that he claimed, rather than upon his person. Demosthenes was eventually reconciled with at least some members of his family. Some of them gave him money; others he let off for the sake of good will (Ps.-Plut. *Mor.* 844d). He even wrote a speech for his uncle Demon, breaking his rule to speak only on public matters (Dem. 32. 32).

Demosthenes' own experience and education enabled him to write speeches for others. He wrote speeches dealing specifically with disputes over inheritance[69] and some on commercial subjects.[70] He wrote a speech for a man whose citizenship had been challenged on the grounds of his mother's origin and legality of her marriage.[71] He was wealthy enough to belong to the liturgical class, and it is doubtful that fees gained from speech writing and teaching rhetoric alone would have enabled him to qualify.[72] In 323 his enemies described him as the wealthiest man in Athens, but they were intimating that he

[68] Aesch. 2. 93, and schol., 3. 51; cf. Harp., s.v. *Paianieis*; anon. *Life*, 156. 96–7 (Westermann).

[69] 41 Spoudias; 38 Nausimachus; 45 Stephanus I; 36 Phormio; 39 and 40 Boeotus 1 and 2.

[70] 32 Zenothemis, 37 Pantainetus, 56 Dionysodorus.

[71] 57 Eubulides.

[72] Aeschines (1. 94, 2. 165, 180, 3. 173) and Dinarchus (1. 111) accuse him of ungentlemanly behaviour in taking money for speech writing. Aeschines (1. 117, 173, 175) insinuates that he is a Sophist.

had obtained funds illegally.[73] Indeed, all the sources of his wealth are not clear. It appears that, like his father, who had 7,000 drachmas on loan to Xouthus when he died, he invested in bottomry loans.[74] Demosthenes had also managed to obtain Aphobus's house (Dem. 31. 1).

Demosthenes married at least once, but the obscurity of respectable women makes it difficult to determine the identity of his wife.[75] The allegations about Cleobule's alien birth were revived in connection with his wife, though in a milder form, for the fathers of both women had spent a good part of their lives away from Athens. The father of Demosthenes' wife may have been an Athenian cleruch on Samos named Heliodorus.[76] They had one daughter, who was born after 347 and who died unwed, predeceasing her father.[77] So overjoyed was Demosthenes at the assassination of Philip II, who had destroyed the independence of Athens and other Greek cities, that he discarded his mourning attire and dressed in festive white at the news, despite his daughter's recent death.[78] If this anecdote is true, his behaviour at his daughter's death could be viewed in terms of the pervasive devaluation of women. Aeschines' tone (clearly hostile) suggests that Demosthenes lacked the normal human sentiments that a father should feel at a child's death, especially a first-born and only child. A dubious tradition adds that Demosthenes was also survived by two sons born of a non-citizen woman, and thus illegitimate (Ps.-Plut. *Mor.* 847c). This tradition seems yet another version of the theme of foreign women in Demosthenes' biography. Inasmuch as penalties for marrying a foreign woman were much harsher in the fourth century than they had been in the fifth, and numbers of people were expelled from the citizen body in 345, if the allegations about his children's origins were true, none of them would have been Athenian citizens, and Demosthenes himself would have been vulnerable to prosecution.[79]

[73] Din. 1. 111; Hyp. 5; Ps.-Dem. 22.

[74] High-risk, high-interest loans on cargo shipped by sea. Information on maritime loans from Hyperides (a hostile source) is not necessarily true: Hyp. 1, frs. 4.166 (Jensen); Plut. *Comp. of Demos. and Cic.* 3.6.

[75] According to the *Suda*, 456, and to anon. *Life*, 156. 99–100, he married the widow of the general Chabrius, the mother of Ctesippus. On Demosthenes' marriage and offspring see further Davies, *APF* 3597 XXIV.

[76] Cf. Plut. *Dem.* 15. 4; Ps.-Plut. *Mor.* 847c.

[77] Dem. 21. 187; Plut. *Dem.* 22. 2.

[78] Aesch. 3. 77–8; Ps.-Plut. *Mor.* 847b; anon. *Life*, 157. 39–45 (Westermann).

[79] Ps.-Dem. 59. 16; Isae. 12; Aesch. 1. 77, etc.: see most recently Lambert, *Phratries of Attica*, 27–9.

When he died, Demosthenes was a wealthy man without legitimate direct descendants. By laws governing intestacy, his fortune would have passed to his sister and her descendants.[80] In light of the problems concerning his father's testament, it seems likely that Demosthenes wrote a will favouring his maternal relatives. His political and literary heirs were his sister's son Demochares II and her grandson Laches II. As we have seen in other families, talents and professional traditions were often transmitted through the female line (see Ch. 4). When they were growing up, Demosthenes must have developed unusually close ties with his sister. Unlike other boys who went off to the gymnasium and *palaistra* and made friends with their peers, Demosthenes stayed home because of his poor health. His sister, only two years younger, must often have been his only companion. Due to her delayed marriage, they will have been together even longer than was usual for a brother and sister. Perhaps she also attended when her brother had his lessons, and was active in transmitting this knowledge to her son.

Like his uncle Demosthenes, Demochares II pursued both a literary and a political career, and his son Laches II was also active in politics. Demochares II, born to Laches and Demosthenes' sister probably between 355 and 350, was a soldier, administrator, politician, diplomat, orator, and historian.[81] As the great-grandson of Gylon and his allegedly foreign wife, he shared not only Demosthenes' heritage of anti-Macedonian sentiment, but also his unswerving ambition to devote his life to the service of Athens. Upon his request that his uncle's resistance to the Macedonians be commemorated, the Athenians granted *prohedria* ('a front seat at public events') and maintenance in the Prytaneum in perpetuity to Demosthenes' oldest descendant, and in 280/79 erected a bronze statue of Demosthenes in the *agora*.[82] The reference to the 'oldest descendant' (*ekgonon aei to presbutato*: Ps.-Plut. *Mor.* 850f) is merely formulaic; there is no indication that Demosthenes had actually adopted Demochares, or anyone else.[83] Ten years later, when Demochares had presumably died, his son, Laches, in turn, requested that Demochares and his

[80] Harrison, *Law of Athens*, i. 144–5.

[81] See further Plut. *Demetr.* 24. 11–12; H. Swoboda, *RE* iv (1901) 2863–7, s.v. Demochares 6; *RE* xii (1925), 339, s.v. Laches 6 and 7; Blass, *Die Attische Beredsamkeit*, 2nd edn., iiib. 304–9.

[82] Ps.-Plut. *Mor.* 847a, d–e, 850f–851c.

[83] An adoption would be more likely, if Demochares I had other male descendants, but there is no evidence for others.

oldest descendant be honoured perpetually by *prohedria* and maintenance in the Prytaneum, and that a statue of his father be erected in the *agora* (Ps.-Plut. *Mor.* 851d–f). Even though Demochares was not adopted by Demosthenes, tradition associated the two. Polybius (12. 13) defended Demochares against the slurs of Timaeus, in part, by citing his good breeding and birth: he does not refer to Demochares' father Laches, but rather to the fact that he was Demosthenes' nephew. Athenaeus (6.252f) identifies Demochares as Demosthenes' cousin, and Diogenes Laertius refers to Demochares as Laches' son.[84] Demochares wrote *Histories* in over twenty books about his own time, a courageous choice of subject that included criticism of his own fellow citizens, of Demetrius of Phaleron, and of Demosthenes' opponent Antipater (Cassander's son).[85] Cicero identified Demochares as his uncle's literary heir when he declared that the *Histories* belonged more to the genre of rhetoric than history (*Brut.* 286; cf. *De Or.* 2. 95). Demochares' ideals and policies in support of Athenian independence and in opposition to Macedonian domination were similar to his uncle's: these produced conflicts that eventually resulted in a long period of exile.[86] He would have been able to write his history during this time. Demochares' embassies to Lysimachus and Antipater (Cassander's nephew), *c.*286–285, were more successful than Demosthenes' journey to Philip II had been, for he returned to Athens having obtained gifts from Lysimachus worth 130 talents.[87]

[84] Diog. Laert. 7. 14, describing an atypical incident in which Demochares offered to put the Stoic Zeno in touch with Antigonus, probably so that he could exploit the relationship between philosopher and governor subsequently.

[85] Polyb. 12. 13, and for the histories see Ath. 6. 253b–d, *FGrH* ii. 75; and F. Susemihl, *Geschichte der griechischen Literatur in der Alexandrinerzeit* (Leipzig, 1891), i. 552–8.

[86] Plut. *Dem.* 24; L. C. Smith, 'Demochares of Leuconoe and the Dates of his Exile', *Historia*, 11 (1961), 114–18, argues that the exile lasted from 303 to 286/5. On politics in this period see T. Leslie Shear, Jr. *Kallias of Sphettos and the Revolt of Athens in 286 BC*, *Hesperia*, Suppl. 17; (Princeton, 1978), *passim*.

[87] Ps.-Plut. *Mor.* 851f. Helen S. Lund, *Lysimachus: A Study in Early Hellenistic Kingship* (London, 1992), 181–2, following William Scott Ferguson, *Hellenistic Athens* (London, 1911), 137, suggests that during his exile Demochares had also visited Lysimachus. Shear, *Kallias of Sphettos*, 82 n. 225, identifies this Antipater not as the son of Cassander, but as 'the Etesian', the nephew who was in exile at Lysimachus's court.

PASIO, ARCHIPPE, AND PHORMIO

The history of Pasio and Phormio illustrates the intimate connection between family and financial relationships. It also provides a case-study of the exaggerated perversion of traditional sentiments. Some of the themes reverberate with those found in the history of Demosthenes' family, and, in fact, Demosthenes himself was the author of several of the orations that deal with Pasio and Phormio. Intimate details about gender, ethnicity, and social status are divulged in a series of private orations. Thus, once again, despite the obvious bias of such material, it can be exploited as an important source of information not only about the parties to the litigation, but also about the values of the jurors who comprised the audience. The historian may then attempt not only to judge the truth and falsehood of particular assertions, but also to find corroboration in sources beyond the orations themselves. Speeches are extant from only one side in the conflicts in Demosthenes' family, but for the problems in the family of Pasio, Archippe, and Phormio there are speeches presenting multiple viewpoints. In its detailed depiction of upward social mobility in classical Athens the story of this family is unique (cf. Ch. 4).

Pasio was a freedman. He was probably born by 430. Whether Pasio had been purchased or born at home, and whether he was of foreign origin or Greek is not known. He had been a slave of the bankers Antisthenes and Archestratus, and was manumitted certainly by 394.[88] Pasio had managed the bank with great success. Banking, unlike most businesses, was thought to depend on the personal talent, experience, and trustworthy reputation of the banker. In fact, the elder Demosthenes had been one of Pasio's clients (Dem. 27. 11). Therefore, although Archestratus had a son named Antimachus, he bypassed him and turned over the management of the bank to Pasio. Having inherited neither property nor profession, in 350 Antimachus was destitute (Dem. 36. 45–6).

Pasio married Archippe (see Fig. 8). They had two sons: Apollodorus and Pasicles. Judging from the age of the first-born son,

[88] Dem. 36. 45–6; Isoc. 17, *passim*. The following discussion is consistent with the chronological sketch in Davies, *APF* 11672. Archestratus may have been the son of the banker Antimachus named in a play of Eupolis in 412 (fr. 134 Kassel-Austin), for his son is also named Antimachus (Demos. 36. 45).

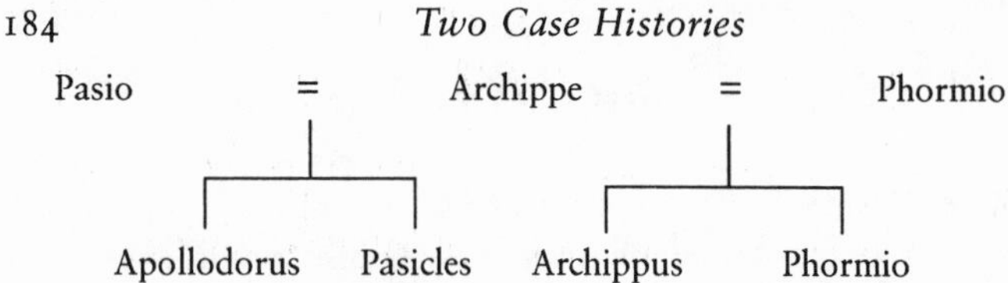

FIG. 8 The family of Pasio and Archippe

Apollodorus, the marriage must have taken place by 395.[89] Like Cleobule, Archippe was very young when she married her first husband, for after he died she was able to produce a second family. When Pasio died in 370/69 (Ps.-Dem. 46. 13), his sons were 24 and 11.

Archippe's ethnic and social origins are even more obscure than Cleobule's. Some scholars have asserted that she not only was not Athenian but, like both her husbands, had been born a slave.[90] Her second husband, Phormio, had been Pasio's slave and chief employee; Pasio freed Phormio, and arranged for him to marry Archippe after his death. Arguments that she too was of slave origin are based on the belief that no guardian would have given a citizen woman in marriage to a non-citizen who had been a slave only some five years earlier. Looking at the situation from the perspective of Archippe's welfare (and hypothesizing that her guardian did the same), I come to a different conclusion. The state of the economy and the marriage market after the Peloponnesian War are relevant to this discussion. Though there was usually a surfeit of men in Athens, after the war, which had lasted some thirty years, and the disastrous Sicilian expedition, there was a dearth of marriageable adult male citizens.[91] Moreover, the economic situation was so bleak that some citizen

[89] For details concerning Apollodorus and some revision of Davies's interpretations see Jeremy Trevett, *Apollodoros, the Son of Pasion* (Oxford, 1992).

[90] For the evidence see Dem. 46. 3. For the controversy see e.g. F. A. Paley and J. E. Sandys, *Select Private Orations of Demosthenes,* ii, 3rd edn. ([1896]; repr. Cambridge, 1979), pp. xxxviii, 144 n. 22, who concluded that she was 'most probably of foreign extraction', and Macurdy, 'Apollodorus', 263, 268, who argues that there was not a drop of Greek blood in either Pasio or Archippe. Davies, *APF* 11672II, leaves the question open. Most recently C. Carey, 'Apollodoros' Mother: The Wives of Disenfranchised Aliens in Athens', *CQ* n.s. 41 (1991), 84–9, esp. 85, asserts that Archippe was a metic, and remained so even after Pasio's enfranchisement. David Whitehead, 'Women and Naturalisation in Fourth-Century Athens. The Case of Archippe', *CQ* 36 (1986), 109–14, suggests that Archippe's status was not independent of her husband's.

[91] See further Ch. 3, n. 61 above. Probably it was due to the war that neither Cleobule nor Archippe had any close male kinsman (see below).

vomen were obliged to work outside the home at menial jobs.[92] In uch circumstances a man like Pasio, who was the proper age for narriage, would appear to be an attractive spouse, even for a citizen voman. He was an honest man with many friends both within and eyond Athens (Dem. 50. 56). Pasio was one of the wealthiest men in Athens, with more property than the elder Demosthenes, Onetor, or 'imocrates (see above). The male perspective, which gives priority to olitical and social status over considerations of personal comfort nd emotional relationships, has dominated our evaluation of the elationship between metics and citizens. For the willingness of free-orn Roman women (who were not 'given in marriage' but who xercised some choice) to marry wealthy influential slaves and freed-nen, we may cite the marriages in the *Familia Caesaris*.[93] For men ike Pasio or for slaves and freedmen of the Roman Emperor, mar-iage to a free-born woman constituted a form of social mobility, but uch a marriage could be also beneficial to the woman. During her narriage to Pasio, Archippe lived well, enjoyed the services of slaves, ossessed a significant amount of gold jewellery, knew everything that vas going on in her husband's business, and exercised authority in er household (Dem. 36. 14, 45. 27). She was able to mediate between er older son and his stepfather, Phormio, for Apollodorus did not ttack Phormio until after his mother's death (Dem. 36. 14, 18, 45. 3– , and see below). In fact, Phormio testified on behalf of Apollo-orus.[94]

After approximately 394/3 or even as late as 376, in response to his enerosity towards the state, Pasio was granted citizenship.[95] There-fter he was able to own land in Athens. An extremely wealthy man, vorth about 60 talents when he died, he bequeathed his possessions o his sons and to his wife as part of her dowry: 'Pasio of Acharnai etermined in his will as follows: I bequeath to Phormio my wife Archippe in marriage. As dowry I bequeath to Archippe one talent ue me at Peparethos [the island Scopelos], one talent due me here, n apartment house worth one hundred minae, the female slaves, gold

[92] Dem. 57. 45, a tendentious, but persuasive, passage in which the speaker asserts iat many women worked as wet-nurses and labourers in vineyards, and sold ribbons in e market, jobs not usually performed by respectable women: see further Pomeroy, *Vomen in Hellenistic Egypt*, 155.

[93] For slaves and freedmen of the Roman Emperor, see Weaver, *Familia Caesaris*, 14–36.

[94] C.362, Ps.-Dem. 49. 18, 33, 52. 7, 19.

[95] Ps.-Dem. 59. 2, 53. 18; Dem. 45. 85, 36, *passim*; Ps.-Dem. 45 *passim*, 53 *passim*, oc. 17 *passim*. On the date see, *inter alia*, Davies, *APF* 11672 II.

jewellery, and whatever else she has in the house—all these I bequeath to Archippe.'[96] Pasio's property consisted of mortgages whose value is disputed,[97] as well as real property totalling 20 talents. An Athenian wife did not inherit from a husband who died intestate, but, as we see, he could leave her a legacy. Thus, from Pasio's estate Archippe inherited cash, movables, and one multiple dwelling;[98] Apollodorus gained as an outright gift another building that was worth at least 1,600 drachmas. When Pasicles came of age, the two brothers were to divide the remainder of the property, with Apollodorus subtracting from his portion whatever he had obtained meanwhile (Dem. 36. 8, 34, 53. 13).

Like the elder Demosthenes, Pasio made arrangements for his wife's subsequent marriage in his will. Unlike Demosthenes, Pasio had been a slave. Because slaves were not permitted to marry and their parentage was dubious, they had no legal kinsmen (see below). Under the circumstances, we may suppose that Pasio considered his chief employee as something of a son and heir. Shortly before he died, he freed Phormio, and directed that Archippe was to marry him. Banking was highly professionalized and dependent upon specific skilled individuals. If the chief employee (usually a slave or freedman) was not well disposed and willing to keep a bank running successfully after the owner's death, or if he was engaged in competition, severe losses would be incurred. Thus Pasio explicitly directed that Phormio was not to engage in independent banking activities without the

[96] Dem. 45. 28. On the authenticity of the will see further Trevett, *Apollodoros*, 26–27, n. 13, 183–4. Trevett accepts the document quoted as genuine.

[97] Signe Isager and Mogens Herman Hansen, *Aspects of Athenian Society in the Fourth Century* BC (Odense, 1975), 182–3, estimate their value at 39 talents.

[98] Women could not own land in classical Athens; see Schaps, *Economic Rights*, esp. 4–6 for the apparent exceptions to this rule. The exceptions are very few. If women's ownership of real property was not restricted, one might expect to find a situation similar to that in Sparta, where women owned a substantial proportion of land (see p. 42, above). Furthermore, if Athenian women could own land, the distribution of wealth would not have been so unequal as the Solonian property classes reflect: see further Hodkinson, 'Inheritance, Marriage', 88–9. In Athens, if land that was hypothecated for dowry was seized, it must have passed between the man in the wife's natal family who was responsible for dowering her and her husband. For a restriction on women's ownership of land in Ptolemaic Egypt see Ch. 6 n. 39, below; and for the contrary in Sparta and Aristotle's consternation see p. 42 above. Therefore Archippe must have inherited the building, not the land on which it stood. In Isae. 5. 26–7 a woman's husband is given a city house in lieu of a dowry. On women's use of property, see Lin Foxhall, 'Household, Gender and Property in Classical Athens', *CQ* 39 (1989), 22–44.

permission of his sons (Dem. 45. 31). Marriage to the widow was a common means of securing ongoing managerial services. Thus Socrates and Socles, bankers who were Pasio's contemporaries, gave their wives in marriage to the freedmen who managed their bank. Strymodorus of Aegina gave his wife to his slave Hermaeus, and then, presumably because she had died, gave his daughter (Dem. 36. 28–9).

Phormio's career had been similar to Pasio's, and provides a second example of the upward social and economic mobility available to slaves in the banking profession (Dem. 45. 71–2). Phormio was a purchased slave whose native language was not Greek (Dem. 36. 1, 45. 30). He managed Pasio's bank, and was manumitted (Dem. 36. 4, 48). In 371/70, before his death, Pasio had leased his bank and shield factory to Phormio (Dem. 36. 51). It has been argued that Archippe's status was not enhanced by the grant of citizenship to Pasio, because he, in turn, arranged for her to marry a non-citizen who had been a slave.[99] Phormio was not granted citizenship until perhaps 361.[100] When Pasio died, however, Archippe already had two sons who were citizens (for they had been included in the grant of citizenship to their father),[101] and who could be expected to look after her in her old age. Therefore another marriage to a citizen offered her no additional benefits that would override other considerations. Moreover, Pasio evidently thought well of Phormio, and thus was not doing a disservice to his widow in directing that she marry him. Such a marriage would simultaneously provide a stepfather for his sons who knew how to manage their property profitably. Moreover, there were probably few other eligible husbands for Archippe, for Athenians were ethnocentric, and probably considered that Archippe's marriage to

[99] Thus Carey, 'Apollodoros' Mother'. On banking in general see most recently Edward E. Cohen, *Athenian Economy and Society. A Banking Perspective* (Princeton, 1992). Cohen (p. 77) does not persuade me that (more than other widows) the ex-wife of a banker had to be bequeathed to his successor because she knew valuable secrets about her husband's affairs. The same might be true of many women, e.g. the wife of a politician or of a man who was trying to conceal his wealth in order to avoid liturgies. A man's house was often his place of business as well (see p. 31 above), and many wives must have been privy to secrets.

[100] Dem. 45. 71–2, 36, *passim*; Ps.-Dem. 46. 13, 45 *passim*. For the grant M. J. Osborne, *Naturalization in Athens* (Brussels, 1983), iv. 55.

[101] Ps.-Dem. 59. 2, 53. 18; see further Osborne, *Naturalization in Athens*, iv. 48–9, 196.

Pasio, an ex-slave, had left her with a taint that limited her marriageability.[102]

It is interesting to note that by contrast with the attention paid to stepmothers in myth-based literature, the histories of Demosthenes and Apollodorus draw attention to problems with stepfathers. Because of the usual fifteen-year age span between husband and wife, there was a significant possibility that a young woman with children would become a widow. The laws of Athens dictated that children belonged to the *oikos* of their father. Widows such as Cleobule and Archippe, who had produced sons, could remain in their late husband's house, but it was more usual for such women to return to their natal family, and for their male kin to arrange another marriage for them.[103] Neither Cleobule nor Archippe had a close male kinsman in their natal family (Dem. 46. 19, and see above). Therefore, contrary to the expectation reflected in laws governing the *oikos*, both the elder Demosthenes and Pasio provided for their respective widows husbands who would live as stepfathers with their children. In this way, both fathers were also able to secure the continuing presence of a natural mother for their children. Moreover, by finding subsequent husbands and guardians who were much younger than they were, they might have hoped to create a stable household and prevent another sequence of bereavement, turmoil, and legal arrangements.

Though the Athenians did not practise primogeniture, Apollodorus reached maturity before his younger brother, and was able to choose among the property left by his father. Apollodorus distanced himself from Phormio, by deciding to take a shield factory, and left the bank for his brother (Dem. 36. 11). Because Pasicles was still a minor, Phormio managed the bank for him. Thus Pasicles' later support of Phormio against the accusations of his brother may derive, in part, from economic self-interest. Even after he came of age, Pasicles doubtless continued to need Phormio's expertise in managing his property. Perhaps sentiment played a part as well in Pasicles' choice to give evidence against his brother on behalf of the stepfather

[102] For an example of snobbery, as well as prejudice against 'barbaroi', see Apollodorus' invective against Phormio: Dem. 45. 30, 36, 73, 81. For bias against freedmen in general see Whitehead, *Ideology*, 114–16.

[103] For details about widows see Hunter, 'Athenian Widow', and Linda-Marie Günther, 'Witwen in der Griechischen Antike—Zwischen Oikos und Polis', *Historia*, 42 (1993), 308–25, and n. 30, above.

who had help to raise him (Dem. 36. 22; Ps.-Dem. 45. 37, 84). In choosing to support Phormio against his own brother, Pasicles failed to conform to the natural hierarchy of sentimental relationships within the Greek family as described by Aristotle[104]—that is, unless Phormio actually was his father, as Apollodorus insinuated (see below).

Like the elder Demosthenes, Pasio provided a generous dowry for his widow. In this way he was able both to secure the marriage and to assure that she would continue to live in the luxurious life-style to which she was accustomed. Phormio and a certain Nicocles were appointed guardians of Pasicles (Dem. 36. 9, 45. 3, 37, 53. 9). Archippe and Phormio were married *c.*368 while Apollodorus was away, serving as trierarch in Sicily (Dem. 45. 3; Ps.-Dem. 46. 20–1). Archippe would have been approximately 42, and Phormio may have been as much as ten years younger. When Archippe had two sons by Phormio, they were not much older than her grandchildren by Apollodorus (see below). Evidently Apollodorus was disgusted to realize that his mother was in bed with an ex-slave, having babies at an advanced age, and that there was nothing he could do about it. He considered that his mother's new husband was not good enough for her, or for him in his new guise of Athenian 'gentleman' (see below), and was annoyed that she had taken this step in his absence, inasmuch as he was her legal guardian.[105] After she died, he even went so far as to insinuate that the liaison had been adulterous, conducted while Pasio was still alive, and that his brother Pasicles was actually Phormio's son (Dem. 45. 79, 84). Because Pasicles had been born after Pasio's naturalization but before Phormio's, Apollodorus's accusation compromised his brother's citizenship. Since Pasio's bank, like many other Athenian businesses, had been located in his home, Archippe and Phormio had probably not been strangers to one another (Dem. 49. 22, 52. 8). In that case, the prospective widow probably had some influence in the selection of her future husband. Nevertheless, Apollodorus observed proper etiquette in not mentioning Archippe's name in court (Dem. 45. 27).

The marriage of Archippe and Phormio produced two boys in the eight years preceding her death in February 360 (Dem. 45. 75,

[104] See Ch. 1, above.

[105] On Apollodorus's embarrassment about his own origins, see Osborne, *Naturalization in Athens*, iv. 196.

Ps.-Dem. 50. 60). One of their sons was named Archippus,[106] and the other Phormio.[107] In the distribution of her property Archippe created an awkward situation, for she attempted to favour her two younger sons, leaving 2,200 drachmas to them, and only 2,000 drachmas to her older children.[108] Doubtless Apollodorus was enraged not only to see property originally furnished by his own father devolve upon half-brothers by a different father, but was jealous and hurt to see that his mother preferred them. This distribution of property encouraged Apollodorus to initiate a series of legal skirmishes with Phormio, culminating, *c.*350, in a serious charge of embezzlement (Dem. 36). Eventually Archippe's property was divided equally among her four sons (Dem. 36. 15, 25 32, 38). Her offspring by both husbands were wealthy. Numerous liturgies are attested for Archippus,[109] and Pasicles and Phormio were accused of trying to avoid a joint trierarchy.[110]

Like many other *nouveaux riches* social climbers, Apollodorus was accused of extravagance and conspicuous consumption (Dem. 36. 45). After his father's death he had moved away from his mother's house in the Piraeus and into his own house in the country (Dem. 53. 4). As we have mentioned, the decree granting citizenship to his father had included him. Apollodorus adopted the life-style of an old-fashioned Athenian gentleman in exaggerated form, cultivating olives, walnuts, vines, and roses (Dem. 53. 16–18). If he had had to spend his life as a metic, he would not have been able to own land. He was extremely active in politics, prosecuting some generals and playing a major role in the debate over the usurpation of the theoric fund for military purposes. Apollodorus managed to marry into the family of Deinias, who seems to have been wealthy: Deinias's sister's son was eligible for liturgies,[111] and her daughter was given a dowry of 1 talent, 4,000 drachmas (Dem. 45. 66).

Because Pasio had been a slave and of foreign birth, he was without legal father or siblings; in other words, he was the founder of his

[106] We can speculate that he was named for his maternal grandfather, and that Archippe was one of the minority of women whose names were derived from their father's: see p. 74, above.

[107] See further Davies, *APF* 11672 IX.

[108] Dem. 45. 28; Ps.-Dem. 50. 60. On the dispute see most recently Trevett, *Apollodoros*, 41–2.

[109] *IG*[2] 1623, ll. 300–1, 103–4; 2318, ll. 335–6; 1631, ll. 544–5, and see further Davies, *APF* 1167IX.

[110] Hyp. 42 and 43 (Jensen), frs. 134–7, and see further Trevett, *Apollodoros*, 49 n. 30, 151.

[111] *IG* II[2] 1632, l. 29.

lineage and his *oikos*. It is interesting to note that in naming his sons he constructed a lineage, reusing the name of his benefactor (i.e. his pseudo-father) and either the actual (or plausible) name of his wife's father. In his legal disputes, he is represented by men who are not related to him. Phormio's isolation demonstrates clearly that in Athenian society only the free-born are considered to have families. Pasio's freedman status left his sons with few kinsmen, in turn. Maternal relatives were lacking too, for in 370/69 Archippe apparently had no living male relative. Therefore Apollodorus had few kinsmen by birth, except his younger brother and half-brothers. His wife's family supplied him with kinsmen. His father-in-law Deinias served as an arbitrator in Apollodorus's and Phormio's dispute over Archippe's estate, though he would not give testimony against Phormio's agent Stephanus, who was his sister's son.[112]

The marriage of Apollodorus to Deinias's daughter produced two daughters, born by 365 and *c*.363. Like the family of Demosthenes and others of the upper class, this one practised endogamy. One daughter eventually married her uncle Theomnestus III.[113] In the late 340s Theomnestus undertook the prosecution of a political rival of Apollodorus on behalf of his brother-in-law (Ps.-Dem. 59. 1–15).

Pasicles married as well. His son Pasio was born *c*.350. That the son was named for his paternal grandfather gains special significance in the light of Apollodorus's allegations that Pasicles was really Phormio's son. The younger Pasio is attested as manumitting a slave in the late 320s.[114] Thus this saga of the establishment of a citizen family by an ex-slave comes full cycle with the younger Pasio enjoying liturgical status and himself manumitting a slave some forty years after the manumission of his own grandfather Pasio.

Cleisthenes, a founder of the Athenian democracy, had encouraged men to be loyal not only to their families, but also to pseudo-family groups through which they maintained membership in the *polis* (see further Ch. 2). Some 150 years later, at the end of the development of the democracy, the activities of Demosthenes' family reveal the continuing influence of the family in shaping the behaviour and destiny of a man who became a leading politician, and in determining the

[112] Dem. 36. 15, 17; Ps.-Dem. 45. 54–6. On reliance upon kinsmen in lawsuits see S. C. Humphreys, 'Kinship Patterns in the Athenian Courts', *GRBS* 27 (1986), 57–91.

[113] Dem. 45. 55, Ps.-Dem. 59. 1–15.

[114] *IG* II^2 1570. 43, and see Davies, *APF* 116722XIII.

allegiance of subsequent generations of his kinsmen. The family unit that is involved is not an enormous clan, but rather a close network that rarely reaches beyond first cousins. The *polis* had been defeated, but the family survived.

In the new territories acquired by Alexander's conquests, neither *polis* nor monarch exerted pressure on individuals to perpetuate their families. No longer was there a need to produce sons who as citizens would defend their homeland, for soldiers could be recruited from foreign territories with the promise of land or cash. No longer did ethnocentrism, as reflected at its most restrictive in Pericles' citizenship law, prevail in the determination of social and civic status. The assumption of Pasio and Phormio and their sons into the city body is a harbinger of the de-emphasis on lineage and direct descent from citizen parents that constitutes a major difference between the classical and Hellenistic periods. Rather, intermarriage, at least among Greeks and Macedonians, of different ethnicities begins to occur in the new cities.

In the Hellenistic world the exclusively male 'public' family begins to suffer a demise. A few women are granted citizenship, given demotics, and perhaps phratry membership (see Ch. 2). The 'private' family survived, again often through the recruitment of women, as in Epicteta's admission of women to the cult of her heroized family.[115]

In this chapter we have seen two examples of households with female heads, and of widows exercising authority in matters involving large sums of money. We have also observed in the families of Pasio and Phormio impressive examples of social mobility, with slaves and their sons rising to become masters of slaves themselves, enter the ranks of the wealthiest of citizens, and become active in politics. Despite this social ferment, as we shall see in the next chapter, Demetrius, a Peripatetic and an Athenian refugee, attempted to impose a hierarchical structure on the Hellenistic family, putting women firmly under men's authority, relegating slaves to the bottom of the social scale, and reviving some of the archaic sumptuary laws attributed to Solon.[116]

[115] See Ch. 3 nn. 30 and 31 above.

[116] See Ch. 1 nn. 109 and 110 and Ch. 3 n. 2 above.

6

Families in Ptolemaic Egypt

In this chapter, as in the rest of the book, the final chronological limit is Hellenistic: from the death of Alexander the Great to the end of the reign of Cleopatra VII.[1] I will not be examining documents from Roman Egypt. I will, however, make allusions to demographic patterns that have emerged from the study of papyri recording the Roman census, inasmuch as the demographic data from the Ptolemaic period is sparse.[2] Such allusions will be highly selective, for the demographic regime must have changed over time.[3] My purpose in writing this chapter is to expand the geographical base of my study and to discuss both Greek perspectives on the family in Egypt and specific Greek or Hellenized families. Some of this material can be compared with what is known about these subjects in other parts of the Greek world, but much of it is unique. Documents written on papyri that have been excavated in Egypt record minute details about family relationships and behaviour. Such evidence is not available from earlier periods of Greek history, pre-dating the conquest of Egypt by Alexander the Great; nor have large numbers of papyri been preserved in regions outside Egypt.

There is a tendency among ancient historians to deny that papyri can contribute substantially to the study of Greek history, for, they

[1] The material in the first section of this chapter was presented at the 20th International Congress of Papyrologists, Copenhagen, 25 Aug., 1992, and published in 'Family History in Ptolemaic Egypt', in Adam Bulow-Jacobsen (ed.), *Proceedings of the 20th International Congress of Papyrologists. Copenhagen, 23–29 August, 1992* (Copenhagen, 1994), 593–7. In this chapter citations of papyri follow the list of abbreviations in John F. Oates, Roger S. Bagnall, William H. Willis, and Klaas A. Worp, *Checklist of Editions of Greek and Latin Papyri, Ostraca and Tablets*, 4th edn. BASP Suppl. 7 (Atlanta, 1992). In order not to conceal the ethnic variety of the nomenclature in the lists in this chapter, most of the names have been transliterated, not Latinized.

[2] See further M. Hombert and C. Préaux, *Recherches sur le recensement dans l'Égypte romaine. P. Brux. Inv. E.* 7616, Pap. Lugd. Bat. V (Paris, 1952); R. S. Bagnall and Bruce Frier, *The Demography of Roman Egypt* (Cambridge, 1994); and Parkin, *Demography,* esp. 19–27.

[3] See p. 6 and below.

argue, 'Egypt was different'. Yet, like colonials in later periods of history, Greeks in Egypt strove to preserve their own traditional values, and sometimes even attempted to impose them on the subject population, at least for bureaucratic purposes.[4] Often enough, Ptolemaic Egypt can provide additional examples of a trend or institution noted in earlier periods of Greek history. Endogamy is an obvious case in point. It is also clear that the economic relationship between generations whereby parents raise children and expect that the children will care for them in old age remains unaltered throughout the history of the Greek family. Consequently, sons were always a better investment than daughters, for they were more able to support and protect their elderly parents. Yet, in the absence of sons, married daughters look after mothers (see Ch. 3). The strength of the bond between brothers, evident in the notion of *phrateres* ('the brotherhood of warriors')[5] and in joint burials in family *periboloi* (see Ch. 3), appears as well among the *frérèches* in Egypt.[6]

In classical Athens the state regulated marriage, reproduction, and sexual relations. In Ptolemaic Egypt there was less public interference in private life. It becomes evident that the family roles and values of Athenians were not universal in the Greek world, although some cities did model their laws on those of the Athenians. Monogamy did not continue to be universal.[7] Furthermore, in the absence of firm regulation, in the Hellenistic period the family became even more unstable and changeable. Sometimes the Ptolemies behaved in radically new ways, which were copied by Macedonian rulers in other regions and later by members of the upper class in Egypt as well. For example, the Ptolemies were the first to practise both bigamy and brother–sister marriage with some regularity. Therefore I believe that the social historian should not assume that the evidence from the Greeks in Egypt is exotic: rather, it is as mainstream as is the evidence from the rest of the Greek world in the mosaic of the Hellenistic period.

In Athens, as we have seen, marriage between cousins or between uncle and niece was not infrequent. Inasmuch as marriage between half-siblings was permitted in both Athens and Sparta, we may assume

[4] See Ch. 1 nn. 116 and 117 above. [5] Albeit fictitious: see Ch. 2 n. 42 above.

[6] Jean-Louis Flandrin, *Families in Former Times* (Cambridge, 1979), 72–3, describes *frérèches* in eighteenth-century Corsica as households constituted of siblings, without their ancestors. *Affratellamenti*: Christiane Klapisch-Zuber, *Women, Family and Ritual in Renaissance Italy*, trans. L. G. Cochrane (Chicago, 1985), 55, and Ch. 1 n. 18 above.

[7] nn. 35–7 below.

that this was the case throughout the Greek world. The marriage of brother and sister that appears in Ptolemaic Egypt may be simply an additional stage of endogamy. Consistent with my emphasis throughout on the family as a productive unit, as in Chapters 4 and 5, the ways in which endogamy functions not only in the selection of spouses but also in financial transactions will be examined.

Written information about families in Ptolemaic Egypt derives from basically two sources: (1) official, government records and (2) private documents. This distinction will be reflected in the following discussion.

THE ADMINISTRATIVE VIEW OF THE FAMILY

Among the papyri are official surveys of the population and lists of people who were liable for the payment of the salt tax. Both types of documents function as a kind of 'census', because the salt tax was a capitation tax, paid by both women and men.[8] For the present discussion, the demographic data and the style of representation in both are relevant. The longest published document, *P. Sorbonne* inv. 331 (= *SB* XII 10860), lists some 500 people. The other texts are much shorter.[9] They derive from various geographical locations in the

[8] I will use the word 'census' in this chapter to refer to a variety of lists designed to register or enumerate populations. On the salt tax see recently John Shelton, *P. Brook.* 32, pp. 55–7, with references to earlier bibliography. Only a few people, including teachers, priests of Dionysus, and athletic victors, were exempt, and they were not numerous enough to affect the use of tax lists as demographic data. For some other possible exemptions see F. Uebel, 'Die frühptolemäische Salzsteur', *Atti dell' XI Congresso internaz. di Papirologia* (Milan, 1966), 341–3, and *CPR* XIII, 33.

[9] Published lists that have been examined for the present study include *CPR* XIII, *passim*; *P. Lille dém.* III 99, 101; *P. Petr.* III 59c, 59d; *P. Sorb.* inv. 331 = *SB* XII 10860; *P. Tebt.* III 880–1; and Basil Mandilaras, 'A Papyrus Collection of the Greek Papyrological Society', in A. A. H. El-Mosallamy (ed.), *Proceedings of the XIXth International Congress of Papyrology, Cairo, 2–9 September 1989* (2 vols., Cairo, 1992), i. 583–602, esp. 590–602; Mandilaras published the same text with some different readings in 'A Papyrus Collection of the Greek Papyrological Society', *Επιστημονικη Επετηριδα Της Φιλοσοφικης Σχολης Του Πανεπιστημιου Αθηνων* 28 (1992), 217–40, esp. 225–8. *P. Tebt.* III 880–1, previously dated to 181/80 or 157/6 is now redated by Shelton to 223/2: see *P. Brook.* 32, p. 56. For unpublished and revised lists see Willy Clarysse, '*P. Sorb.* et autres listes de population', unpublished, 1990, and idem, 'Ptolemaic Census Lists and *P. Petrie Ashmol.* ined.' unpublished, 1990. I am grateful to Willy Clarysse for sending me these unpublished papers. For the purposes of the present discussion, the unpublished papyri reveal the same format and demographic characteristics as the published texts.

southern part of the Fayum, and were recorded at different dates between 264 and 221 BC. The documentation is too sparse to demonstrate significant local variation and change over time. Nor is it possible to detect demographic differences among the lists, whether they are written in Greek, or Demotic, or a mixture of both. Consequently, for the present purpose the population lists will be treated as a homogeneous group.

A typical full record begins with the name of a male head of household, his patronymic, and his trade. Next in the list, in descending order, are his wife and adult children, followed by his siblings and slaves. The wife of a married son follows her husband in the list. Because immature children were exempt from taxes, they are not included.[10] Some families are at points in their life cycle where they do not display simultaneously all the components I have just described in the basic complete record; and due to demographic and economic factors, some families probably never acquired all these components.[11] The reports are laconic and now mostly fragmentary. Furthermore, inasmuch as the same family groups have rarely been identified in a series of subsequent reports the records provide snapshots rather than motion pictures. For example:

Eupolemos, son of Nikon
Eiren[e], his wife
Herakl[eitos], his son
Nik[aia] (or Nik[e]), his wife

Polem[on], his son
Nauplion (?), his wife
Philoxenos, his son; total 7, of which 3 (men)[12]
sheep: 170; lambs: 25; calves(?): 1
pigs: 10
(*P. Lille dém.* III 99, col. iv, ll. 6–14, 230–228 BC)

[10] The age of maturity for men in the Ptolemaic period is not known: it may have been 14, as it was in the Roman census, or it may have been 18 or 19, as it was for ephebes at Athens. Moreover, the age may have been lower for females than for males. In the face of high infant and juvenile mortality in antiquity, it was reasonable to count the population, or tax payers, only after they had reached adulthood.

[11] I will not be concerned here with numerous individuals who are named in the lists, but not recorded as members of a family group. It is impossible to determine whether the census-takers encountered such people when they were temporarily absent from their family environment, or whether they constitute permanent single-person households.

[12] One person with a male name is a boy, not a man.

Antigonos, son of Kottion
Nikaia (or Nike), his wife
Ptolemy, his son
Theophilos, his son
[.]*llw*, his peasant
Taias (?), his sister; total 6, of which 4 (men)
(*P. Lille dém.* III 99, col. iii, ll. 16–21)

Syros
Phileas, son of Theudotos
Soteris, his wife
Zopyrion
Nikaia, mother*
Theoxenos, son of Agenor
Theodoros, his brother
Nikaia, mother*
Annas, total 9, of which 6 (men)
(*CPR* XIII 4, col. x, ll. 176–83, third century BC; * = reading me[ter] rather than ge[raia])[13]

Horos, in the household of Zenodoros
and his wife
(*CPR* XIII 12, col. ii, verso ll. 77–8, third century BC)

Spartakos, son of Eutychides
Philoxene, his wife
Ath[ ]ios, son of Salymis
Iouodeitos,[14] his wife
Alexandros, his son
Pantagathos
Sabateitis,[15] mother*
Nikanor, son of Iason
Marion, his wife
Alkaios, son of Salymis
Demetrios, son of Bios
Kleopatra, his wife
Theudoros
Thasous, mother*

[13] For the new readings see Willy Clarysse, 'Abbreviations and Lexicography', *Anc. Soc.* 21 (1990), 33–44, esp. 33–4.

[14] The conventional spelling is Ioudeithos.

[15] The conventional spelling is Sabatheitis.

(*CPR* XIII 4, col. vii, ll. 113–26; * = reading me[ter] rather than ge[raia]).[16]

The format of the lists is not the result of practical accounting considerations. Gender is the principal factor determining the rate of taxation of free adults within a household who are liable for payments. Salt tax rates changed over the years, but the rate for free men was always approximately three times that for free women.[17] Therefore it would have been more efficient to group adult males together, separately from adult females.[18] Instead, because men and women are placed in the list according to family relationships, an extra step is required to tally the total number of persons and then the total number of males. The number of men was considered of primary importance, for men are both potential soldiers and payers of the highest taxes. (See below.)

PRE-PTOLEMAIC POPULATION SURVEYS

In order to determine whether the origin of the Ptolemaic census lists and, particularly, of their design was Greek or Egyptian, it is necessary to consider Pharaonic history. According to tradition, the Ptolemies were not the first to count inhabitants of Egypt. A few earlier enumerations, beginning in 1400, are recorded.[19] During the Old Kingdom a biennial census of cattle was conducted.[20] The only possible evidence for inventories of people and property in the Middle Kingdom are some papyri from Kahun.[21] These early efforts differed from those of the Ptolemies: they were not attempts on the part of a

[16] n. 13, above. [17] See n. 8 above.

[18] This system was adopted for the US census of 1840: free white males, free white females, free coloured males, free coloured females, male slaves, female slaves. See further Margo J. Anderson, *The American Census: A Social History* (New Haven and London, 1988), 30.

[19] For a review of these registrations see Hombert and Préaux, *Recherches*, 41–4, and see now also Bagnall and Frier, *Demography of Roman Egypt*.

[20] James Henry Breasted, *Ancient Records of Egypt*, i (Chicago, 1906), 61–3, 65–6, 68–71, paras. 118, 120, 122, 124, 126, 128, 130, 132–3, 145, 147, 157, 159, 161, 166. P. 64, paras. 135, 137: numbering of gold and lands. P. 59, para. 106 gives a restoration: [Numbering of] all people.

[21] See Sir W. M. Flinders Petrie, *Illahun, Kahun, and Gurob* (London, 1891), p. 48; F. L. Griffith, *The Petrie Papyri: Hieratic Papyri from Kahun and Gurob* (London, 1898), pp. 19–28.

central government to survey the entire population of the country, but were restricted to particular localities, possessions, and professions.[22] Herodotus (2. 177) relates that Amasis II required every Egyptian to declare his source of livelihood annually to the governor of his province. Furthermore, he writes that when he visited Egypt, Solon learned of this law and adapted it for the Athenians. Diodorus Siculus (1. 77. 5) repeats Herodotus's assertion, including the reference to Solon. Such a meeting between Amasis II and Solon, with consequences for the latter's legislation, is, chronologically speaking, possible.[23] Though arguments *ex silentio* are not conclusive, there is no indication that the Pharaonic registrations continued after Amasis II. Nevertheless, it has been asserted that the Ptolemaic lists derive from the Pharaonic registrations.[24] Some of the bureaucratic apparatus for collecting taxes may well have been carried over from pre-Ptolemaic times.[25] The salt tax, which served as a head tax, however, seems to have been a Ptolemaic innovation. In fact, when discussing an analogous problem presenting a gap of more than 200 years in the evidence, John Shelton declared that the Roman salt tax was not a direct descendant of the Ptolemaic one.[26] It seems unlikely that registrations of the population were held on a regular basis throughout the Pharaonic period and continued without interruption into the Ptolemaic period.[27] In any case, the focus of the discussion here is formal representation of the family in the official Ptolemaic documents.

Like the design of many institutions of the Ptolemaic regime, that of the census declaration was, apparently, the result of Peripatetic influence. Peripatetic philosophers, including Demetrius of Phaleron, advised Ptolemy I concerning the design of the administrative structures of his new state.[28] Before coming to Egypt, probably when he

[22] On the lack of a uniform administrative system in the Pharaonic period, see Barry J. Kemp, *Ancient Egypt. Anatomy of a Civilization* (London and New York, 1991), 235.

[23] See recent discussions of Solon's chronology such as M. Chambers, *Aristoteles. Staat der Athener*, in Aristotle, *Werke*, x.1 (Berlin, 1990), 61–3, *contra* Alan B. Lloyd, *Herodotus, Book II*. Études préliminaires aux religions orientales dans l'Empire romain, 43 (Leiden, 1975–88), i. 55–7, and iii. 221, who found the chronology impossible.

[24] See Horst Braunert, 'IDIA: Studien zur Bevölkerungsgeschichte des ptolemäischen und römischen Ägypten', *JJP* 9–10 (1955–6), 211–328, esp. 294–8.

[25] See most recently Diana Delia, 'The Ptolemies and the Ideology of Kingship', in Peter Green (ed.), *Hellenistic History and Culture* (Berkeley, 1993), 192–204, esp. 193–4.

[26] *P. Brook*. 32, p. 56.

[27] Thus Hombert and Préaux, *Recherches*, 44.

[28] Ael. *VH* 3. 17 = Dem. Phal. fr. 65 (Wehrli). For a review (*exetasis*) of Athenian citizens by deme see Dion. Hal. *Isaeus*, 16.

was archon in 309/308, or in another official capacity in the preceding ten years, Demetrius had conducted a census in Athens.[29] The purpose of this Athenian census is not known. Perhaps, following the tradition of the Peripatetics, who were tireless compilers of knowledge, Demetrius simply wanted to have such information for its own sake. Or, like the Megapolitans in 318 (and the Rhodians later in 305),[30] he wanted to find out how many men were available to perform military service. We do not know whether Demetrius preceded or copied the Megapolitans. If he conducted the census early in his tenure of office, he may have been inspired by events in the Lamian War. At any rate, after he left Athens, the information was not used in any practical application. We surmise that Ptolemy, a Macedonian, upon becoming sovereign of Egypt, would have wanted to know about the population of his adoptive country, and specifically the number of taxpayers and potential soldiers.[31] Therefore he consulted Demetrius, who had recent experience in organizing such a survey.

Demetrius had classified the inhabitants of Attica according to political status: Athenians, metics, and slaves. Because the resulting total number of citizens is so small, scholars have deduced that only adult males were included.[32] In Egypt, women were definitely counted, because they were liable for the salt tax, and the inhabitants were classified into more categories than were used at Athens. Even if Demetrius was not directly responsible, there is no doubt that the categories and their sequence were inspired by traditional Greek patterns of thought concerning gender hierarchy and ideology.[33] These ideas are encapsulated in Peripatetic writings about family structure. For example, according to Aristotle (*Pol.* 1253a19–20),

[29] Ath. 6. 272c = Ctesikles, *FGrH*, 2, no. 245 (Wehrli).

[30] For these censuses see Diod. Sic. 18. 70. 1, 20. 84 . 2–3.

[31] For a Demotic copy of an order of Ptolemy II from 258 concerning a detailed inventory of the royal domain, including land, water sources, orchards, leases, payments to priests and to royal dependents, and their taxes, see Stanley M. Burstein, *The Hellenistic Age from the Battle of Ipsos to the Death of Kleopatra VII* (Cambridge, 1985), 122–3, doc. 97, trans. into English from E. Bresciani, 'La spedizione di Tolemeo II in Siria in un ostrakon demotico inedito da Karnak', in H. Maehler and V. M. Strocka (eds.), *Das ptolemäische Aegypten: Akten des internationalen Symposions, 27–29 September 1976 in Berlin* (Mainz, 1978), 31–7.

[32] On Demetrius's figures see recently Mogens Herman Hansen, *Three Studies in Athenian Demography*, Historisk-filosofiske meddelelser, 56 (Copenhagen, 1988), 10, and *idem*, *Demography and Democracy: The Number of Athenian Citizens in the Fourth Century* BC (Herning, 1985), 31–6.

[33] The bibliography on these subjects is enormous. See Ch. 1.

he state is composed of *oikoi*, or households. Each household is ;overned by a single ruler: the male rules over the female, the child, nd the slave (*Pol.* 1254b13–15, 1259a40–b4, 1260a9–11). The father s superior to the mother (*Eth. Eud.* 1244a10). Human beings rule ver animals (Arist. *Pol.* 1254b10–13). Dominance and subordination re biologically determined, and therefore inevitable. The form of the ensus, which is a vertical list, imposes a patriarchal hierarchy with a hain of being starting at the top with a male head of household, lescending through his wife, children, and slaves, sometimes down to nimals. Except for the placement of siblings and children, this order s almost invariable. The family relationships reported are those etween the male head and the other individuals in the household, ut they are not reciprocal. Thus a woman may be identified as a wife' or a 'mother', and a younger man as a 'son', but the head of ousehold is not also termed a 'husband' or a 'father'. (For examples, ee above.) Men designed the census or tax system, and asked the uestions; the male head submitted the information about other nembers of the household in terms of himself ('my wife, . . . my on'); and male scribes recorded the information. The result is a focus n the male head of the house. This emphasis is a constant feature of opulation lists in the Ptolemaic period.[34] As Aristotle (*Pol.* 1253b5–3) states, one man who heads the household plays three roles: usband, father, and master of slaves. In the classical *polis* and in tolemaic Egypt he might play the second and third role in relation to everal people. Marriage in the old Greek cities was regularly mono-;amous.[35] In Egypt, by contrast, a man might also play the role of usband simultaneously more than once. The lists give a few exam-les of bigamy.[36] Such husbands could have emulated some of the

[34] See p. 203 below.

[35] See Ch. 1. The Spartans permitted 'wife-sharing', and the Athenians (toward the nd of the Peloponnesian War) are said to have encouraged men to take a second voman for the purposes of reproduction. For the production of citizen children outside narriage as an emergency measure at Athens, see Diog.Laert. 2. 26; cf. Ath. 13. 555d–56; Aul. Gell. 15. 20 .6; and see further Pomeroy, *Goddesses, Whores*, 66–7, 81.

[36] Some examples of bigamy occur in *P. Lille dém.* III 101, col. iv, ll. 30–3 (a soldier as two wives and a 'nurse': perhaps trigamy). In *P. Sorb.* inv. 331. fr. 2, col. 1. 44–5; fr. , col. i, ll. 106–7; fr. 10, ll. 144–5; fr. 12, col. i, ll. 175–6; fr. 13, col. ii, ll. 166a–67, two vomen, both identified as 'wife' (*gune*), appear together. The possibility of bigamy is he reason for the monogamy clause in marriage contracts: e.g. *PTeb.* I 104, ll. 18–21 (92 c); *BGU* IV 1052, l. 17 (13 BC), and *PEleph.* 1, ll. 8–9 (311 BC).

Ptolemaic kings and their Macedonian predecessors. Philip II ha been extravagantly polygynous.[37] Ptolemy I, Ptolemy VIII, Philip II o Macedon, and Alexander the Great also were not monogamous. I societies that anthropologists classify as polygynous, usually only th top men can afford more than one wife. Bigamy, however, was wide spread for a time among the victorious army, and was not limited t the monarchs. In Susa in 324 Alexander celebrated mass marriages o his troops with native women. He himself married two women at tha time (Arr. *Anab.* 7. 4. 4, 8). More than 10,000 of his men marrie Asian women. Many had children by them (Arr. *Anab.* 7. 10. 3) These women were lawful wives, not concubines. According to Arria (*Anab.* 7. 12. 2), when Alexander sent his veterans back to Macedo nia, he told his men that if they had children by Asian wives, the should leave them in Asia so as not to make trouble in Macedoni between foreigners and children of foreign wives and the children an mothers they had left at home. There are a few examples fron Pharaonic Egypt as well among the Pharaohs.[38] According to Her odotus (2. 92) the Egyptians were monogamous, but according t Diodorus (1. 80. 3) they were polygynous. Diodorus may have bee thinking of the Pharaohs, rather than of commoners. Otherwise, on of these statements is incorrect, or practices changed over time. I any case, the *oikos* model easily accommodates bigamy, for bigam can be represented simply as one man playing the role of husband i relation to two women.

In the Ptolemaic documents the economy is seen through a patri archal lens. The conceptualization of gender and the sexual divisio of labour would not permit free-born women to 'work'—at least, no outside the domestic sphere.[39] In general, occupations are recorde for men, but not for women. The only major exceptions to this rul are jobs that must be filled by women, both respectable and non

[37] Ath. 13. 557b–e = *FHG* 3, p. 161, fr. 5. Amongst Alexander's successors Demetrius seems to have had the most wives: Plut. *Demet.* 14. 1–2, 27. 3.

[38] P. W. Pestman, *Marriage and Matrimonial Property in Ancient Egypt.* *Contribution to Establishing the Legal Position of the Woman*, Pap. Lugd. Bat., I (Leiden, 1961), 3, discusses bigamy briefly, and concludes that it is likely tha Herodotus is correct.

[39] Thus, another legacy of some of the older Greek cities to Ptolemaic Egypt was th prohibition on women's ownership of certain types of land. See further Pomero *Women in Hellenistic Egypt*, 148–60, and Ch. 5 n. 98 above.

respectable. In the lists there are a substantial number of nurses,[40] an occasional *hetaira*, and a female dancer whose work has something to do with religion.[41] Other documents, however, do refer to various female singers, musicians, and dancers in the service of religion, and women engaged in several forms of non-domestic labour.[42]

Usually only the occupations of heads of the household are given: for example, farmers, brewers, fullers, shopkeepers, and shepherds.[43] The rest of the male members of the household are probably engaged in the same line of work as the head, for occupations tended to be hereditary, and doubtless the women often helped too.[44] The household is the unit of economic analysis, and the men within it are considered the economic foundation of the state. No doubt, men were taxed at a higher rate because they visibly produced and controlled more wealth. In the normative view of the Greek *oikos* and *polis*, only men engage in production, and control the means of production.[45]

According to traditional Greek ideals, a woman's principal function was not production, but reproduction.[46] Therefore, within an *oikos* a woman is much more useful as a wife than as a daughter. These notions probably contributed to the rationale for the lower age of marriage for women than for men. In *CPR* XIII, for example, twenty-four people are recorded as *huios*, but only two as *thugater*.[47] Although so few women are identified as *thugater*, some 200 are listed

[40] e.g. *P. Sorb.* inv. 331, fr. 1, col. i, l. 5; *P. Lille dém.* 3. 99 recto, col. iii, l. 5; col. iv, l. 30, col. v, l. 3; col. vi, l. 17; col. vii, l. 9; *P. Lille dém.* 3. 101, recto, col. iv, ll. 16, 33, etc.

[41] For another *hetaira* see *P. Sorb.* 211–12, ined. I am grateful to Willy Clarysse for this information. For female *sompheis* ('dancers') see *P. UB Trier* SS 77–14, fr. 1, ii, l. 45 and fr. 15, l. 374, an Arsinoite census list of the second century BC. I am grateful to Professor Bärbel Kramer and Dr Reinhold Scholl for this reference.

[42] For musicians, etc., see *Pros. Ptol.* 9, Studia Hellenistica, 25 (Leuven, 1981), pp. 215–31, *passim*. For other workers: e.g. *Pros. Ptol.* 5, Studia Hellenistica, 13 (Leuven, 1963), 12954 for a linen-dealer; *P. Teb.* III 814, col. xxxxvii for a general dealer; and *SB* I 1080 and *BGU* VII 1528 for weavers of garlands and fillets.

[43] As in *P. Sorb.* inv. 331, fr. 1, col. i, ll. 4, 8, 22, 29; *P. Petr.* III 59 d; *CPR* XIII, *passim*.

[44] See further Ch. 4. Braunert, 'IDIA', 294–8, interprets the units in the lists as 'work units'. This view may be valid for some of the Pharaonic documents (p. 199, above), but is not convincing for the Ptolemaic documents, which seem first and foremost to derive from family groupings where women do not 'work'. Other documents show that women were involved in the family business: e.g. for a family of weavers see *PSI* VI 599 (+ p. xviii, *BL* VIII 399).

[45] On women's role in the *polis* and *oikos* economies see Pomeroy, *Xenophon, Oeconomicus*, chs. 4 and 5.

[46] See further Pomeroy, *Goddesses, Whores*, pp. 62–5.

[47] *CPR* XIII, p. 276, s.v. *thugater* and *huios*.

as *gune*.[48] Moreover, wives are usually listed without patronymics only by a proper name, followed by *gune*. A few wives have no personal identity at all: they are nameless, and appear generically as *gune*.[49] When her husband dies, the wife loses her position and sometimes her proper name as well: she is sent from second place on the list to the bottom, where she may be recorded simply as *meter* ('mother').[50] Her son becomes the principal taxpayer in the household, and his wife assumes the second position in the list. Because she is not reproducing, a widow is less valuable than a fertile young wife.[51] In addition, for a widow to remain at the head of the list after her husband died, appearing to exercise authority over her sons would have been abnormal. Once again we see that the male is the link between the family and the government. Aristotle (*Pol.* 1269b24–1270a15) declared that states in which women ruled men were badly governed. Of course, Ptolemaic queens began to assume the prerogatives of kings, and eventually Cleopatra VII governed Egypt; the census reports, however, pre-date this transition to female rule. In the reports, only in the few all-female households of mother and daughter does a woman appear at the top of a list.[52]

Widows and women described as *meter* appear frequently in the lists.[53] In fact, the latter are so numerous that they are often designated by an abbreviation or a ligature (*h*). Legal and demographic considerations indicate that these women too are widows, rather than divorcees. First of all, they are living with their sons, whereas if there had been a divorce, the husband would have remained in his house and continued to appear at the head of the list. Secondly, because women usually married at a younger age than men, if they survived

[48] Ibid., 276, s.v. *gune* and *thugater*. But see n. 10 above on the question of the age at which male and female children begin to be listed, and see further below.

[49] See e.g. *CPR* XIII 12, col. ii, ll. 78, 84, 89.

[50] e.g. *CPR* XIII, *passim*, and *P. Petr.* III 59 c, recto col. ii, l. 8; col. iii, l. 13; d, l. 18. Cf. Ch. 3 n. 132 above *re* the stela of the Menestides family, where the mother is listed beneath her sons. In the Catasto of Florence, a tax declaration of 1427–30, widowed mothers and grandmothers are also moved to the bottom of the list. Klapisch-Zuber, *Women, Family*, 55, notes that the Florentine patrilineal system by which property is transmitted only through males leads to the devaluation of women, which is reflected in the placement in the lists.

[51] In classical Greece, as they became older, wives suffered a loss of esteem: see Xen. *Oec.* 7. 42–3.

[52] e.g. *P. Sorb.* inv. 331, fr. 6, col. ii, ll. 85–6.

[53] *CPR* XIII 13.4, col. vii, ll. 113–26, quoted above. See also *CPR* XIII, pp. 47–8, and p. 276, s.v. *ge(raios)*, *graus*, and *meter*. *Meter* should be read for *geraia* in *CPR* XII (see n. 13, above).

the perils of childbirth, they were younger than their husbands when their children were grown. Thus, families of at least three generations are usually due to the presence of widows. Furthermore, we need not conclude that, in general, women had a longer life span than men.[54] It is more likely that when they were no longer bearing children because they had reached menopause or were divorced or widowed, they were considered 'old' and less valuable. By contrast, a man would have to be much older than a menopausal woman to be so classified. As Aristotle declares, inferior creatures, including females, reach their *telos* sooner than superior ones (*Gen. An.* 775a18–23). For women, the biological *telos* coincides with the social *telos*.

Lists of Greeks who were inscribed as new citizens at Miletus and Ilion at the end of the third and in the second century BC show some demographic features similar to those in the papyri, but the semiotic features are different.[55] At Ilion 151 males and 80 females are registered. The proportion of women who migrated to Ilion with their adult sons is remarkably high. There are twenty-three mothers with adult sons, both with and without additional members of the son's family. These unmarried mothers whose names are preceded by the pronoun *meter* are probably widows whose sons are their *kyrioi* ('guardians'). The format of the lists is similar to those found in the papyri described above; the male household head is first, and sons precede daughters. At Ilion the placement of mothers shows more variety than at Miletus and in the papyri. They invariably follow their sons, but sometimes precede, and at other times follow, the son's wife.[56] As we have observed, in the papyri, family members are recorded in vertical columns that serve as an objective correlative of

[54] According to Bagnall and Frier, *Demography of Roman Egypt*, 103–9, *et passim*, life expectancy at birth was *c.*22.5–25 years and there was not much difference between men and women. On Hellenistic life span see also Sarah B. Pomeroy, 'Infanticide in Hellenistic Greece', in A. Cameron and A. Kuhrt (eds.), *Images of Women in Antiquity* (London, 1983), 207–22, esp. 214, and Introduction, n. 21 above.

[55] For the inscriptions see A. Rehm, *Milet*, 3. *Das Delphinion in Milet. Die Inschriften* (Berlin, 1914); Wolfgang Günther, 'Milesische Bürgerrechts-und Proxenieverleihungen der hellenistischen Zeit', *Chiron*, 18 (1988), 383–419; and P. Frisch, *Die Inschriften von Ilion* (Bonn, 1975), no. 64, date Hellenistic. For interpretation see Pomeroy, 'Infanticide', and Pierre Brulé, 'Enquête démographique sur la famille grecque antique', *REA* 92 (1990), 233–58.

[56] At Ilion the mother precedes the wife in ll. 10, 27, 35, and the wife precedes the mother in ll. 7, 20. At Miletus one husbandless mother is listed below her daughter-in-law (34, col. i, ll. 9–10). Another precedes her sons who are youths: Günther, 'Milesische Bürgerrechts', 390–1, no. 3, ll. 8–9.

their placement in the intrafamilial hierarchy. By contrast, the names in the inscriptions at Ilion are usually written in continuous horizontal lines, with no implication that the persons at the top are more important than those in bottom lines. The configuration of the Milesian inscriptions is not uniform, with some family units forming a vertical sequence, and others listed horizontally. Hence, the sequence in which the names of family members are recorded is not a direct reflection of their value, and is therefore less stringent than in the papyri. In addition, the Ilion inscription has the interesting feature of listing eight unaccompanied widows as a group preceded by the rubric *Cherai* ('widows').[57] The group is inscribed at the very end of the set of family inscriptions, preceding a list of single men. At Miletus also, the names of single women, some with children, are inscribed. They are part of extended family groups. A mother of two sons is accompanied by her own father and mother, and another mother is accompanied by her adult son and his wife.[58] These women were probably widows. Single men, even groups, as migrants are a feature of Greek history traceable back to the archaic period. Migrant widows without kinsmen are a new feature of the Hellenistic period, and symptomatic of both dislocation in the traditional family and the loosening of family bonds on respectable women.

Multiple-family households are not uncommon in the population records in the papyri. We have already observed similar family groupings in classical Athens (see Ch. 1). These groups usually consist of adult siblings living together, sometimes with one or both of their parents. Mediterranean anthropologists refer to sets of siblings linked for production and living in the same house as *frérèches*.[59] Despite Aristotle's recognition of bonds between brothers (see Chs. 1 and 5), the Aristotelian model of the *oikos* does not accommodate multiple sets of spouses with their offspring living under the same roof. Thus, a uniform pattern for reporting the members of such complex households was not imposed. Primogeniture was not institutionalized in Ptolemaic Egypt, either for social or for economic purposes.[60] The

[57] Frisch, *Die Inschriften von Ilion*, no. 64, ll. 58–9.

[58] *Milet* I 3 34i, ll. 5–8, and Günther, 'Milesische Bürgerrechts', 301, no. 3, ll. 8–9.

[59] e.g. for two complex households, each including two married brothers: *P. Sorb.* inv. 331, col. i., ll. 29–35, 36–43.

[60] There are some examples of unequal distribution of property, however: e.g. in the will recorded in *P. Petr.*^{2} I 25 a father favours the oldest son over a younger son and two daughters.

verticality of the lists imposes a hierarchy that does not reflect reality. Although probably equal in status to a brother who is the designated head of the household, siblings are named in the list beneath him. Usually when one brother is married, and the others are single, the married brother is listed as the household head (*CPR* XIII 4. 144, 6. 11, etc.). The married brother is probably, but not necessarily the oldest, as in the family of Dionysius and Paesis, sons of Kephalas (see below). In some lists, despite being older than the children of the household head, siblings appear as an afterthought, beneath his children. This sequence may perhaps be due to the fact that the siblings of the household head are female, and sons are awarded precedence.[61] The variation in the order of reporting siblings and offspring may be a reflection of the statement of the head of the household to the scribe: some may have reported their siblings first, and others their offspring, arranging them not only according to gender, but following their personal priorities. Once again, men listed as brothers outnumber women listed as sisters, probably as a result of the difference in the age of marriage. But some marriages apparently are matrilocal. An extra man in the household listed without indication of his role may actually be a son-in-law living with his wife in her parents' house.[62] In the classical *polis*, unless she was an *epikleros*, a married daughter was expected to leave her parents' home and join her husband in his own home or that of his parents. Thus the *oikos* model cannot easily accommodate a son-in-law in permanent residence.

FAMILY ARCHIVES

Patriarchy shapes the evidence even of what might at first glance appear to be some of the least biased of documents: that is, lists of inhabitants liable for a tax. Other texts from Ptolemaic Egypt suggest greater diversity in family dynamics and structure. Whereas the documents discussed above originated in the Fayum, an area dominated by Greek influence and by the Ptolemaic colonial élite, the documents cited below come from a largely Egyptian or Greco-Egyptian milieu. They reveal that some of the inhabitants, at least,

[61] e.g. *P. Lille dém.* III 99, col. iii, ll. 19, 21; col. v, ll. 10, 11.

[62] Tentatively suggested by Clarysse, '*P. Sorb.*'

behaved differently, and had a different view of the family from that inscribed in the government's records. Examination of the private documents suggests that in many cases the androcentric hierarchical *oikos* model based on the nuclear family was imposed by the authorities, and reflected only in official documents. Lived reality might be quite different, often contradicting the official picture. Families that include married siblings living in the same household, women who are active in the economy, and dominant widows, in particular, do not conform to the model.[63] Many family archives from Greek and Roman Egypt have been published.[64] None of the major published archives that might provide raw data are exclusively in Greek. Because the focus of this book is the Greek family, I will confine myself to bilingual archives, for the owners of these documents were either Greek by birth or sufficiently Hellenized to make some use of the Greek legal system.

The families encountered in family archives must be cited as examples of patterns in family history; but, on the whole, these families do not represent the average family of the time. In all the papyri of Ptolemaic Egypt, and of later times as well, there is nothing comparable in bulk to the Zenon archive. In Akoris there is no archive to compare with that of Dionysius, son of Kephalas. In contrast to family archives, tax lists cut across a broader swath of society. Menander wrote: 'It is work for a poor person to find a kinsman. For if he is in need of some help, no one admits that he is related to him. The reason is that at once he expects him to be asking for something' (*Adelphoe* [Körte], fr. 4). To the truism that only the rich have families, we may add that only the rich have family archives. For example, only the well-to-do went to the trouble to write wills; the remainder of the population usually relied upon the rules of intestacy. Relatively few papyri in so-called family archives actually

[63] For such women see Pomeroy, *Women in Hellenistic Egypt*, 148–73.

[64] For a list see E. Seidl, 'Die Archive', in *Ptolemäische Rechtsgeschichte* (Gluckstadt, Hamburg, and New York, 1962), 15–35, and Orsolina Montevecchi, *La Papirologia*, rev. and corrected with addenda (Milan, 1988), pp. 247–61, 575–8. In recent years, see esp. publications of P. W. Pestman, including (with F. Boswinkel,) 'Les Archives privées de Dionysios, fils de Kephalas', n. 100, below; 'Fureter dans les Papiers de Totoes', in *Textes et études de papyrologie grecque, démotique et copte*, Pap. Lugd. Bat., XXIII (Leiden, 1985), 144–85; 'Nahomsesis, una donna d'affari di Pathyris', in E. Bresciani, G. Geraci, S. Pernigotti, and G. Susini (eds.), *Scritti in onore di Orsolina Montevecchi* (Bologna, 1981), 295–315; *L'Archivio di Amenothes Figlio di Horos (P. Tor. Amenothos)*, (Catalogo del Museo Egizio di Torino, 1st ser., vol. 5 (Milan, 1981), 2, an Egyptian family.

offer a wide range of information about affective relationships of the sort that family historians might employ, such as personal letters or autobiographical accounts. Many archives are limited to a small number of texts, most of which record the financial transactions of the archive's owner with people who are apparently not his or her own kin, or related to one another.

When families with archives are represented in genealogical charts, they certainly look different from those in the census lists. After the parents' names are supplied from patronymics and matronymics, the genealogical tables are created, largely, from what we may call 'effective kin'—that is, kin who are mentioned in the documents of an archive because they are involved with one another. We must be aware that the tables are created by combining information garnered from documents in an archive that may encompass several generations. The charts in this chapter (see below) may give the reader the erroneous impression that all the people named in it knew one another personally. In many cases, the most that could have been known were anecdotes about deceased relatives. Genealogical charts eliminate family dynamics and the life cycle. Furthermore, historians and papyrologists have sometimes done violence to the evidence of the private documents by continuing to impose the model of the Aristotelian *oikos* on them automatically, as though they thought it was standard in Ptolemaic Egypt. So, for example, an archive in which a wife and her female kin are at least as active as a husband and his relatives may be presented as the 'Archive of Dryton, son of Pamphilus' or the 'Archive of Melas, son of Apollonius'.[65]

One of the richest archives is that of Dryton and Apollonia.[66] Wills, marriage documents, and records of business transactions among kin make it possible to trace the vicissitudes of this family and their financial and emotional interrelationships for more than

[65] So Carol A. R. Andrews, *Catalogue of Demotic Papyri in the British Museum*, IV. 1: *Ptolemaic Legal Texts from the Theban Area* (London, 1990), 81–8, cat. nos. 35–9. To the documents published by Andrews add *P. BM* 10394 (226 BC) = Pestman, *Recueil de Textes*, no. 7, a post-nuptial agreement in favour of Senobastis.

[66] On the archive of Dryton and Apollonia see Pomeroy, *Women in Hellenistic Egypt*, 103–24, 210; Willy Clarysse, 'Le Mariage et le testament de Dryton en 150 avant J.-C.', *CE* 61 (1986), 99–103; R. K. Ritner, 'A Property Transfer from the Erbstreit Archives', in *Festschrift E. Lüddeckens* (Würzburg, 1984), 171–87; and Reinhold Scholl, 'Dryton's Tod', *CE*, 63 (1988), 141–4. According to Willy Clarysse, in a personal communication of 18 May, 1992, Dryton's archive continued for two more generations than were previously known. The last person to keep it and to add a few items was an Egyptian soldier who was married to one of Dryton's granddaughters.

three generations. Apollonia was one of four sisters, and she and Dryton were parents of five daughters. The extensive financial activities of the women in this family are particularly noteworthy in Ptolemaic Egypt, where men controlled more capital and were more dominant than women in business and commerce. Because in both generations the sisters were joint owners of property that was not readily divisible and lived in proximity to one another, they acted as a female corporation on principles similar to those of the *frérèches* that will be examined below.

Zenon

The archive of Zenon is the largest corpus of related private documents from Ptolemaic Egypt. It is composed of contracts, accounts, petitions, correspondence, literary texts, and other documents scattered among collections in museums and universities in Egypt, Europe, and North America. The vast majority are written in Greek, but there are some in Egyptian (written in Demotic). Approximately 1,800 have been published so far, and secondary literature is plentiful. Most of the archive is concerned with the financial transactions of Zenon and his associates.[67] The earliest mention of Zenon appears in a document of 260 BC (*P. Cair. Zen.* 5. 59801). The last dated letter addressed to Zenon was probably written in 240 BC.[68]

Zenon came to Egypt from Caunos in Caria, doubtless attracted, as were other young men, by the economic opportunities. His career, however, is not an example of dramatic social mobility. Allusions in the archive suggest that his family in Caunos had enjoyed some wealth and prestige. Their status doubtless improved as a result of Zenon's activities, but they did not start from the lowest echelons of society. Zenon had been fairly well educated. His letters are grammatical and well written, and he owned some books. One of his brothers was literate enough to serve as a scribe (see below.)

For most of the time covered by the archive, Zenon was employed by Apollonius, *dioiketes* ('chief financial officer') of Ptolemy II.[69] He worked first as a secretary and financial agent. In this period he

[67] Viz. the subtitle of *P. Col. Zen.*: *Business Papers of the Third Century* BC *Dealing with Palestine and Egypt*.

[68] *P. Cair. Zen.* 3. 59371; see Pap. Lugd. Bat., XXI, p. 250.

[69] Note that this Apollonius is not Zenon's brother who bore the same name: see n. 73 below.

travelled to Palestine and Syria, arranging for imports of slaves, horses, wheat, luxury goods, and other items. He also travelled through the Delta. From 256 to 248 Zenon managed the large estate in the Fayum near Philadelphia that Ptolemy had granted to Apollonius. The vast bulk of the archive dates from the period of Zenon's stewardship. Much less is known of his life preceding and following his association with Apollonius.

Unfortunately for the family historian, the indefatigable Zenon apparently did not marry; nor does he discuss his family. He does seem to have saved every piece of correspondence, including ephemera such as brief invitations to parties. Zenon was also immensely fond of his hound Tauron, and engaged an Alexandrian poet to write learned epigrams about him.[70] Thus, at the risk of arguing *ex silentio*, we may conjecture that his interest in family matters was minimal in comparison with his zeal for administrative and financial pursuits. It is plausible, however, that the papyri do not reflect all his personal inclinations, inasmuch as written documentation was essential for the latter pursuits, while family matters might have been confined to conversations and private thoughts. In any event, examination of the huge archive yields some data which reveal familial and pseudo-familial relationships.

In 1957 Anna Swiderek published an article about Zenon's family.[71] Her work pre-dated not only the subsequent publication of some of the documents in the past thirty-five years and the careful analysis of the archive and reconsideration of some of the texts by P. W. Pestman,[72] but it was also written before the modern studies of the Mediterranean family by historians and social anthropologists. Thus, Swiderek's brief, though careful, study now seems quaint. One of the principal aims of the present chapter, by contrast, is to assess whether Greek and Hellenized families in Ptolemaic Egypt followed the patterns that have been identified as 'Mediterranean', or whether they corroborate the ancient tradition, initiated by the 'Father of History', Herodotus, and accepted by many modern historians, that Egypt was 'different' (see Introduction and above).

Because many names were popular and were used by several

[70] *P. Cair. Zen.* 4. 59532; R. A. Pack, *The Greek and Latin Literary Texts from Greco-Roman Egypt*, 2nd edn. (Ann Arbor, 1965), no. 1761.

[71] Anna Swiderek, 'Zenon fils d'Agréophon de Caunos et sa famille', *Eos*, 48/2 (1956); repr. in *Symbolae R. Taubenschlag*, ii (Warsaw, 1957), 133–41.

[72] In Pap. Lugd. Bat., XX and XXI.

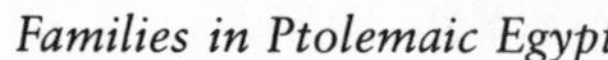

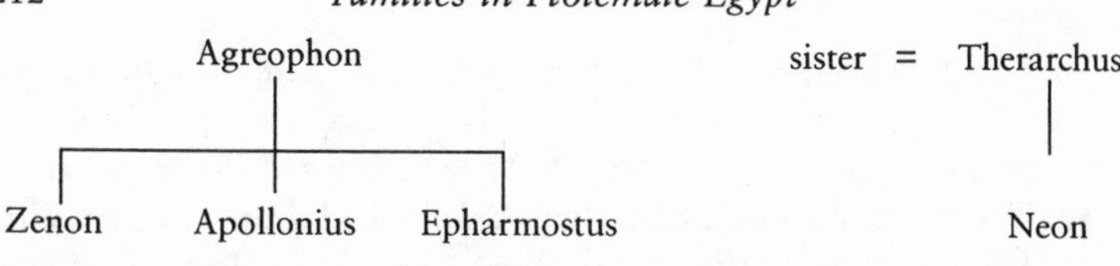

FIG. 9 The family of Zenon

different people encountered in the archive, it is necessary to be extremely cautious in reconstructing the family of Zenon and of other people encountered in the archive (see Fig. 9).[73]

The effective kin of Zenon are all male, and related to him in the male line. The name of Zenon's father, Agreophon, appears frequently in the archive as a patronymic, and he is referred to occasionally as an individual. The name of Zenon's mother is not known. This omission is probably not due to the traditional Greek reluctance to give the name of a respectable woman while she was alive. Because she is never alluded to at all, not even by a pronoun, she is probably dead. No direct correspondence between father and son is extant, despite the fact that they spent so many years apart after Zenon migrated to Egypt. Instead, we know of Agreophon's activities from

[73] See the prosopography in Pap. Lugd. Bat., XXI. However, even this perpetuates at least one dubious identification. In 1931, in *P. Mich. Zen.*, in the introductions to documents 10 and 78, pp. 70 and 176, Edgar raised the possibility that Zenon and a certain Ariston were related, but he did not offer a reason for his conjecture. Swiderek, 'Zenon', 139–40, also identified a certain Ariston as a relative of Zenon. Her identification is cited in Pap. Lugd. Bat., XXI, p. 299, s.v. Ariston, 6. Claude Orrieux, *Les Papyrus de Zénon, L'horizon d'un Grec en Egypte au iii° siècle avant J.-C.* (Paris, 1983), 54, likewise believed that Ariston was doubtless one of Zenon's relatives. (Similarly, with no justification, Orrieux conflated Epharmostus's pedagogue Styrax with other men of the same name.) No document, however, records any kind of kinship relation between Ariston and Zenon. An Ariston is listed in one document along with Zenon's brothers Epharmostus and Apollonius (*P. Cair. Zen.* 3. 59341b, ll. 13–14, 247). Proximity on the list may be the reason why Edgar, the editor, comments that Ariston must certainly have been a relative or a member of his Carian circle. However, Ariston journeys to Arsinoë in Pamphylia, which is not exactly around the corner from Zenon's native Caunus in Caria (*P. Cair. Zen.* 1. 59052). For the identification of Arsinoë, which may be identical with Korakesion, see Roger S. Bagnall, *The Administration of the Ptolemaic Possessions outside Egypt* (Leiden, 1976), 113–14. T. C. Skeat also seems to accept the identification of an Ariston as Zenon's friend or relative, for in *P. Lond.* 7. 2141 (not dated), p. 236 n. 4, he identifies the Ariston who appears in l. 4 with the Ariston of *P. Cair. Zen.* 4.59672 l. 5. He goes on to express uncertainty regarding whether this Ariston, in turn, is the friend, relative, or brother of Zenon who is mentioned in *P. Cair. Zen.* 1. 59341(b), l. 13, and *P. Mich. Zen.* 10, l. 8.

reports in letters written to Zenon by third parties. In 257 a certain Apollodotus sent a letter to Zenon from Caria, in which he reported that he had seen Agreophon and his sons in Caunos.[74] Zenon docketed the letter 'Apollodotos. Philanthropon peri tou patros' ('an expression of good will from Apollodotus about father'). On 2 January, 252, Zenon received a letter informing him that his father, accompanied by Acrisius, the city treasurer of Calynda in Caria, had arrived safely home in Kaunos after their visit to Egypt.[75] Zenon would have been concerned about their safety because of his father's age, and the hazards of a sea voyage in winter. Zenon evidently had provided cushions and leather pillows to enhance his father's comfort on the ship, but these items had been seized by customs, and he had had to make the journey without them.

Beyond Zenon's immediate family the only relatives who are known are Therarchus, the husband of Zenon's aunt, and Neon, their son, who lived in Calynda. This aunt is his father's sister; her name is not given. Neon wrote to request that a certain Damonicus speak to Zenon on his behalf, and mentioned that he had asked (his cousins) Apollonius and Epharmostus to remind Zenon to do him a favour. In 247 Zenon wrote to the authorities, using his influence to request that his cousin Neon be granted the same exemption as Therarchus (who was now dead) had enjoyed from certain payments imposed by the government for the maintenance of soldiers and cavalry (*P. Cair. Zen.* 3. 59341).

Zenon had at least two brothers. The family member who is mentioned most frequently in the archive is Epharmostus, Zenon's 'little brother' (*P. Cair. Zen.* 3. 59474, l. 3). Epharmostus's age must be inferred from his activities. He probably came to Egypt in early adolescence, as soon as he was old enough for Zenon to enrol him in school in Alexandria. We deduce that there was a very large age difference between the two brothers. Agreophon doubtless saw Epharmostus there when he visited Egypt. There is very little correspondence between the two brothers. Zenon's friends often report on Epharmostus's activities, perhaps because the youth himself did not write home. In 257, however, he wrote to Zenon about some *astragaloi* ('knucklebones' used as dice: *PSI* 4. 331). Moreover, when

[74] *P. Cair. Zen.* 1. 59056. *P. Lond.* 7. 2096 is a fragment addressed to Zenon, referring to 'your father'.

[75] *P. Lond.* 7. 1979. On this voyage and the correspondence see Hans Hauben, 'Les Vacances d'Agréophon (253 av. J.-C.)', *CE*, 60 (1985), 102–8.

Epharmostus was an adult, he lived with Zenon, so there was little need for writing. Zenon listed the books which he probably sent to Epharmostus (*P. Col. Zen.* 2. 60, with *BL* III, p. 44). The list, which is now fragmentary, mentions a collection of works by Callisthenes and a collection 'On Embassies' by an author whose name is not extant.[76] These works do not appear to have been 'light reading'. Like other affluent Greek men in Ptolemaic Egypt, Epharmostus could both read and write at a mature level. His cursive is small and neat.[77]

Epharmostus was alive in September 243 when *P. Mich. Zen.* 67 was written. The recto of *P. Cair. Zen.* 3. 59362 was written 5 November, 243; on the verso Zenon refers to payment for funeral rites for Epharmostus.[78] In the light of this premature death (perhaps in his late twenties), the many references to the health of Epharmostus in Zenon's correspondence seem more than merely conventional. Hierocles who managed an Alexandrian palaestra (*P. Cair. Zen.* 2. 59148), and Ctesias, his brother (*P. Lond.* 7. 1961, 256 BC; *P. Cair. Zen.* 2. 59181, 255 BC), specifically state that 'Epharmostus is well'. Hierocles makes this remark in a letter addressed not to Zenon, but to a doctor, Artemidorus.[79]

As a young adult, sometime between 255 and 250, Epharmostus joined Zenon in Philadelphia. He was involved in viticulture[80] and raised goats and pigs.[81] He also engaged in some financial transactions, probably as Zenon's agent. It is not clear whether Epharmostus's entrepreneurial activities were connected with the estate of Apollonius or whether they were private enterprises for his brother and himself. In any case, Epharmostus was on Zenon's payroll,[82] and received the same food rations as his brothers and other privileged employees.[83] Zenon doubtless established Epharmostus in his various

[76] Lionel Pearson, 'Callisthenes in the Zenon Papyri', *CP* 44 (1949), 200–2.

[77] Skeat, *P. Lond.* 7. 2033.

[78] See Pestman, Pap. Lugd. Bat., XXI, p. 110.

[79] For Artemidoros see Pap. Lugd. Bat., XXI, p. 302, no. 13. See also *P. Cair. Zen.* 4. 59474, ll. 2–3, after 256 BC, for a reference to the health of 'your father and of your little brother Epharmostus'.

[80] *P. Cair. Zen.* 3. 59352, *c.*243; 59504; *P. Lond.* 7. 2062.

[81] *P. Mich. Zen.* 67; *P. Cair. Zen.* 3. 59305, 250; 59346, 245; 59362, 342.

[82] Claude Orrieux, 'Les Comptes privées de Zénon', *CE*, 56 (1981), 314–40, has distinguished Zenon's personal payroll from the accounts he kept for Apollonius.

[83] He receives an adult ration of wheat in 248 (*P. Cair. Zen.* 3. 59333), but is allocated the ration of a young man in 246/5 (*P. Cair. Zen.* 4. 59569). Tony Reekmans, *La Sitométrie dans les Archives de Zenon* (Brussels, 1966), 79–80, *et passim*, explains that privileged recipients of the *sitometria* might convert their allocation to better-quality or different products, so that the quantity recorded for them is not necessarily commensurate with their age, sex, and job, as it is for lower-class recipients.

businesses. Zenon himself was involved in all the same activities as Epharmostus and many others as well, so that when he left the employ of Apollonius, he was in very comfortable financial circumstances.

In addition to Epharmostus, Zenon had at least one other brother. Apollodotus had seen the brothers in Caunos (*P. Cair. Zen.* 1. 59056), in 257. Epharmostus and another brother had joined Zenon in Egypt. If this family followed the usual pattern, probably one brother remained in Caunus to look after Agreophon and the family property. At any rate, if three, or even four, brothers had remained to share their patrimony, the family's economic status would have been diminished. Instead, the men in this family followed their kin in successive migrations, and bonds linking the brothers survived the vicissitudes of geographical and social mobility.[84] Thus we have yet another example of the powerful bond between brothers that is characteristic of the Greek family. In several documents, Zenon's associates refer to the brothers as a group, without distinguishing them as individuals. Sometime during the reign of Ptolemy III, Zenon received an invitation to come to a party with his brothers (*P. Ryl.* 4. 568, ll. 16–17). In a memorandum to Zenon, Petacus beseeches him by the health of his brothers (*PSI* 4. 416). The only person in the archive who calls Zenon 'brother' is Apollonius.[85] The term 'brother' may connote emotional closeness rather than actual kinship.[86] But even if the letter-writer actually was Zenon's brother, it is still not an easy matter to identify him, inasmuch as the name 'Apollonius' was very common. There are at least thirty-seven entries for this name in the prosopography of the archive.[87] The Apollonius who was Zenon's brother is doubtless the one who is listed in close proximity to Zenon and Epharmostus in the accounts of grain rations and who receives the allocation of those of privileged status.[88] Zenon's brother Apollonius is also probably

[84] Anthropologists in the twentieth century have traced the pattern of kin-linked migration among Greeks from many areas. Like Zenon and his brothers, the first migrants are predominantly unmarried males. The families of origin are sufficiently prosperous to be able to make the investment in educating and equipping the prospective migrants. See e.g. Ernestine Friedl, 'Kinship, Class, and Selective Migration', in J. G. Peristiany (ed.), *Mediterranean Family Structures* (Cambridge, 1976), 363–88.

[85] *P. Col. Zen.* 2. 81; similarly *P. Cair. Zen.* 3. 59391 restored (see *P. Col. Zen.* 2. 81, p. 70 n. 1).

[86] Cf. below on Cleon.

[87] See Pap. Lugd. Bat., XXI, pp. 292–5.

[88] *P. Cair. Zen.* 4. 59569, ll. 6–8, 112–13, 246/5; *P. Col. Zen.* 2. 77, ll. 29–31; *P. Lond.* 7. 2149; *P. Cair. Zen.* 3. 59341, ll. 14–15, 247 BC.

identical with the scribe of the same name.[89] In 248 Zenon retired from managing the properties in Philadelphia, and after 240/239 he turned over the archive to his brother.[90] Zenon's leadership among the brothers and the fact that he retired before Apollonius strongly suggest that he was the oldest of the three.

Zenon's coterie of friends and associates with whom he participated in the cultural and social life of Alexandria constituted a pseudo-extended family. These friendships continued even after his brothers came to Egypt. Many letters reveal a surprising degree of frankness and intimacy among the men in the group. Zenon and some of his friends were interested in young male athletes and musicians, and subsidized their training and education. In a letter addressed to Artemidorus, one member of his circle described himself as *philoneios* ('lover of youths'), and mentions the procurement of a *paidarion* ('young male slave').[91] By contrast, in a letter to Zenon, Artemidorus writes of his pleasure in wine and *pornai* ('prostitutes': *PSI* 4. 352, l. 4). Homosexuality, or bisexuality, was an acceptable characteristic of Hellenistic life, and is reflected in literary sources from the earliest times.[92]

The archive indicates that homosexual relationships in Ptolemaic Egypt were conducted according to different rules than had prevailed among the privileged classes in earlier periods of Greek history. In classical and archaic Athens, older men had been entrusted with the education of youths as part of a carefully regulated *rite de passage*, with full knowledge of the families of both men. As is true among the circle of Zenon, the older man was not a blood-relation of the youth, or at least not a close one. The situation in Alexandria that we glimpse through Zenon's archive, however, is far more chaotic than it had normally been in Athens, and the younger men are more vulnerable. The ostensible purpose is still the education of youths in the gymnasium and palaestra;[93] but the youths involved do not seem to have had families to supervise the relationship, and had to apply to Zenon and his circle for protection and support. Why these favours were granted, and how they were repaid, is not spelled out, but may be inferred. From the archive we learn about a certain

[89] See Pap. Lugd. Bat. XXI, pp. 292–3, s.v. Apollonios, nos. 10, 14.

[90] For the chronology see Pap. Lugd. Bat., XXI, pp. 175, 182 n. 11.

[91] *PSI* 4. 340, ll. 15, 24, 257/6 BC and see below. See *LSJ*, s.v. *philoneos*.

[92] See further K. J. Dover, *Greek Homosexuality* (London, 1978).

[93] *PSI* 4. 3340 refers to the instruction of a *paidarion*.

Heracleotes, a young musician, who was bequeathed a musical instrument by his teacher Demeas, head of the palaestra. This instrument had been seized as security for a loan, and Heracleotes beseeches Zenon to have it returned to him or to provide a replacement. His support had also been entrusted to Zenon and a second guardian, Nestos.[94] Such obvious payment could have been a cause for allegations of prostitution in classical Athens, and could have resulted in dishonour and loss of citizenship. The youths in Alexandria were evidently the male counterparts of the free-born, young women who flocked to Egypt in the early Ptolemaic period.[95] Lacking male kinfolk and dowries, these women became involved in sexual liaisons with men, often with unfortunate results, as we may deduce from situations described by Hellenistic poets.[96] Unlike the women, who can supply only sex and companionship, the youths can also promise glory in athletic or musical competitions to the men who support them. There was no attempt to be discreet about the patron's reward: the arrangement was clearly a source of *philotimia* ('glory') through competition. Thus young Pyrrhus, who was training in the palaestra, assures Zenon that he will be crowned through him (*P. Cair. Zen.*, 3. 59060, l. 7, 257 BC). Hierocles refers to Epharmostus and *ta paidaria* ('the youths') in a single phrase (Pap. Lugd. Bat., XX. p. 51, l. 4, 257 BC). Zenon evidently has no compunctions about sending Epharmostus to be educated in the same milieu as the other young men. He provides a pedagogue named Styrax, who would have been charged with guarding the boy's chastity. Styrax must have done his job well enough to merit Zenon's gratitude. When Epharmostus was an adult, Styrax moved with him to Philadelphia (*P. Lond.*, 7. 2042, l. 12).

In addition to the reasons usually offered to explain the occurrence of homosexuality in the Greek world, we may add the skewed sex ratio in Hellenistic Greece, produced by female infanticide and neglect of women (see below). Furthermore, as already noted, the first waves of Greek immigrants to Egypt were predominantly male. Greek tradition, as well as the laws of some of the older Greek cities, discouraged intermarriage. Only beginning in the second century, and

[94] *P. Cair. Zen.* 3. 59440; *P. Lond.* 7. 2017; *PSI* 9. 1011.

[95] See further, Pomeroy, *Women in Hellenistic Egypt*, 72–8.

[96] For unaccompanied widows migrating to Ilion see n. 57, above.

generally among the lower classes, did some intermarriage occur.[97] As far as we can tell, none of Zenon's brothers and few of his friends married. The rations each received were sufficient for only one person. As in classical Athens, homosexual relations did not preclude heterosexual liaisons or marriage. Zenon apparently engaged in a heterosexual relationship, at least briefly. He had a son named Cleon. This son is known only from two undated notes that Cleon addressed to father Zenon (*Z[eno]ni to patri*: *P. Cair. Zen.* 3. 59457; *PSI* 5. 528).[98] Of course, it is possible that Zenon was not Cleon's biological father, either because Cleon's mother had had more than one sexual partner, or because the Greeks sometimes used kinship designations such as 'father' to connote closeness rather than actual kinship. The paucity of information about Cleon, by comparison with what is known about Epharmostus, indicates that Zenon was not particularly interested in Cleon, whether he was his son or a young friend. Cleon addresses Zenon as 'father' three times in the two short documents totalling some thirty lines. Perhaps he needed to call Zenon's attention to this relationship. In fact, both letters from Cleon to Zenon are reminders to send him his food allowance; in the letters he also requests the allowance due to his mother. She is owed 3 drachmas, 6 obols, of the total monthly allowance of 12 drachmas claimed by Cleon. Similarly, in a memorandum to Zenon, Pyrrhus, the youth whose training in the palaestra was being subsidized by Zenon, mentions the allowance due to his mother (*P. Cair. Zen.* 3. 59507, ll. 22–6). It is not clear whether the mothers of Cleon and Pyrrhus were doing some work for Zenon, or whether his payments to them were a simple courtesy, an example of the generosity expected of a Greek gentleman. Cleon's handwriting is certainly inferior to Epharmostus's, possibly an indication that he was not so well educated as his uncle. By contrast with Epharmostus, Cleon never appears in the company of Zenon. He was probably illegitimate, perhaps the child

[97] See further J. Mélèze Modrzjewski, 'Un aspect du "couple interdit" dans l'antiquité: les mariages mixtes dans l'Égypte hellénistique', in Léon Poliakov (ed.), *Le Couple interdit: entretiens sur le racism*, Actes du colloque tenu en mai 1977 au Centre culturel international de Cerisy-la-Salle (Paris, 1980), 53–73. W. Peremans, 'Les Mariages mixtes dans l'Égypte des Lagides', in E. Bresciani *et al.* (eds.), *Scritti in onore di Orsolina Montevecchi* (Bologna, 1981), 273–81 and *P. Petr.*², p. 36.

[98] In addition, *P. Cair. Zen.* 4. 59580, an undated fragment, is addressed to *[Z]enoni to patroi*.

of a slave.[99] However, in light of Cleon's request for his mother's maintenance, unless she was a freed slave, it seems more likely that his mother was a free-born member of the *demi-monde* who lacked a male kinsman who would have prevented her from bearing and raising an illegitimate child, and instead, have provided a dowry and found her a husband. In the Ptolemaic period, those who were not Greek by birth could be Hellenized by education. If Cleon were the child of a foreign slave, he could nevertheless have become a Greek by acculturation. Nevertheless, whether he was Greek by birth or by education, his social status was not the same as that of a son born to a Greek wife. Thus, although Zenon had no other children, he never admitted Cleon into the inner circle of his family and friends.

Dionysius, Son of Kephalas

The Greeks in Zenon's archive were from another walk of life, a different geographical area, and a time period preceding that of the people whose archives we shall examine next. Families like the following ones constitute another segment of the varied population of Ptolemaic Egypt.

Dionysius, son of Kephalas, was an inhabitant of Akoris, in Middle Egypt in the last third of the second century.[100] He lived in a Graeco-Egyptian milieu, and could write both Greek and Demotic well. Because it was more rare for a Greek to learn to write Demotic than for an Egyptian to write Greek, it seems that Dionysius was probably Egyptian by birth, although the majority of the documents in his archive are in Greek.[101] The fact that both his father and his paternal grandfather bore Greek names, however, suggests an alternative scenario of intermarriage between a Greek man and an Egyptian woman in an earlier generation and gradual Egyptianization of

[99] Edgar suggests that Cleon was either Zenon's son by a *paidiske* ('female slave') or not his son at all, but just another youth being trained in the palaestra (*P. Cair. Zen.* 3, p. 179). The latter hypothesis seems unlikely in view of Cleon's repeated use of the word 'father', though, as mentioned above, in papyri people sometimes address one another as relatives, to indicate intimacy when they may be neither biologically nor legally related.

[100] F. Boswinkel and P. W. Pestman, 'Les Archives privées de Dionysios, fils de Kephalas' (Pap. Lugd. Bat., XXII (Leiden, 1982)). In the following discussion all references to document numbers refer to the numbering in this publication.

[101] So ibid. p. 4.

the family. Or, as I have demonstrated elsewhere, gender and ethnicity intersect and influence each other: in Graeco-Egyptian families the men tend to be more Hellenized and the women more Egyptia-nized.[102] This, however, is a tendency, not a rule. In a Demotic document Kephalas is known only by a Greek name, while his brothers are known only by Egyptian names (doc. 9). In addition to his Greek name, Dionysius bears two Egyptian names, and with the noteworthy exception of his father and grandfather, most of his family and associates named in the archive have both a Greek and an Egyptian name.

Dionysius left a bilingual archive comprised of eight Demotic and 35 Greek documents, including some that are fragmentary. The ear-liest document, a petition from Dionysius's father, is dated to 13[illegible] (doc. 9). Then there is a gap. The other papyri span a period of only twelve years, from 116 to 104. None of the documents deals specifi-cally with family life. There are no wills or private letters or marriage contracts.[103] What can the family historian deduce from this archive? A few of the documents are official petitions or complaints; the vast majority refer to loans of grain. The editors of the archive have explicated much of the material, especially chronological, economic and military matters, but something remains to be said about the evidence which this archive contributes to Mediterranean family history.

Frérèches appear in both generations of the family (see Fig. 10[104]). Brothers remain in close proximity. In the only document in which Kephalas appears, he acts in unison with his three brothers and mother. In the next generation, even after marriage, the three broth-ers remain a loose unit. They store some of their documents and other possessions in each other's houses (doc. 10), and become victims of the same criminal acts (docs. 9 and 10). Some of Diony-sius's possessions, including a tunic, a plough, and a yoke, were stolen from a house in the countryside belonging to his brother (doc. 10).

The effective kin are multi-generational: both Kephalas and Dio-nysius have a widowed mother with whom they engage in financial and legal activities in the public sphere. Because Dionysius always serves as his mother's *kyrios* ('guardian'), and because she often act

[102] See further Pomeroy, *Women in Hellenistic Egypt*, 121–4.

[103] Pestman, 'Nahomsesis', 299, makes the attractive suggestion that wives, rather than husbands, stored marriage contracts, keeping them safe from their husbands.

[104] Adapted from Boswinkel and Pestman, 'Les Archives privées de Dionysios', p. [illegible]

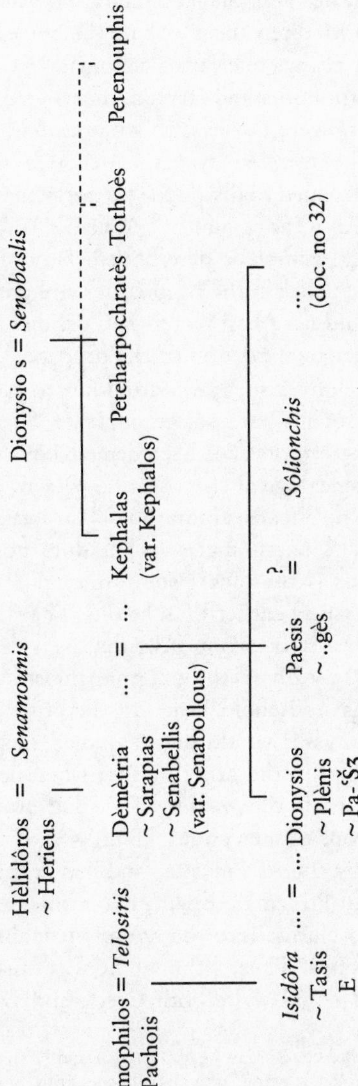

FIG. 10 The family of Dionysius

together with her son or daughter-in-law, and is the potential victim of the same injustice as he is (docs. 11 and 12), we may deduce that the widow lived with her son. Such cohabitation was the rule in the family in the eastern Mediterranean, where the household, or, better, the 'housefull' is not always nuclear or conjugal.[105] Consideration of the large archive of Apollonia and Dryton, mentioned above, suggests that economic factors were, at least to some extent, responsible for the endurance of the *frérèche* system. Although inheritance was partible, the sisters declined to divide the property they had inherited, but instead managed it as a unit.[106] Whether they were bound together by sentiment cannot be determined. Doubtless, as a group they enjoyed more influence in the community and greater bargaining power than they would have had if they had divided their assets and each had managed her own portion of the property.

The genealogical chart also draws attention to naming patterns. Dionysius is named for his paternal grandfather. Such alternation is the most common pattern that has been detected in the Greek world, but a survey of the genealogical charts in the present chapter demonstrates that it is by no means ubiquitous. The fact that Dionysius bears his grandfather's name suggests, but does not prove beyond doubt, that Dionysius is the oldest son, although Paesis joined the army and perhaps married earlier than he did. That Dionysius serves as his mother's *kyrios* also does not prove that he is the eldest son, for a younger son may stay on in the paternal house, care for elderly parents, and serve as household head. In the absence of Paesis on military service, Dionysius would have assumed such responsibility. Dionysius was enrolled in the army in 106, when he was about 30. Not only the name, but the *métier* of soldier was passed down through the generations of men about whom we are informed. Paesis served in the cavalry, but Dionysius and his father were in the infantry. The army in Ptolemaic Egypt, like armies in other periods and places, served to elevate into the dominant mainstream recruits from subordinate groups. Thus, although he was raised in a Graeco-Egyptian milieu and could write both Greek and Demotic, Diony-

105 See Ch. 1 n. 14 above. For Roman Egypt, Bagnall and Frier, *Demography*, 67–9 found a variety of households, ranging from a single person to complex and extended family groups. Marriages, at least at first, were not neo-local: the couple lived with the parents of one spouse.

106 See n. 66 above. See Ch. 1 n. 18 on the partitioning or preservation of the father's *oikos* by the sons and heirs.

sius's Hellenism, evidenced by his use of his Greek name, came to the fore after he began to serve in the army.[107]

Some information about the role of women in the family can be teased out of the documents. Interestingly, only the women are known by both patronymics and matronymics (doc. 3). Dionysius married in 108 at the age of about 28, as was normal for men in Ptolemaic Egypt. The women in this family married at a much younger age than the men, and survive them as widows. Thus Kephalas and Demetria were married sometime after 142, probably by *c*.140, for in 109 their son Paesis is approximately 30. Kephalas is dead by 113/112, but his widow is active throughout the period encompassed by the archive. When it breaks off in 104, she is probably in her mid-fifties. In the previous generation, in 139, Senobastis, Dionysius's paternal grandmother joined her three sons in a petition (doc. 9. l.19). Senobastis was probably a widow too, for her son is her guardian in the one document in which they both appear. In the next generation Demetria is evident as a busy, domineering widow with property. She is also mother of three sons, one of whom, Dionysius, serves as her legal guardian. Isidora, Dionysius's wife, like her mother-in-law, has property, for both women act as recipients or guarantors for some of the loans (docs. 3, 20, 24, 25). Isidora has been a member of the family since 108, and is probably young. Both women must have had enough property to make them credible as guarantors of Dionysius's loans. Isidora appears in the documents only when acting in unison with her mother-in-law. In one of the documents they declare that they 'are two women speaking with one mouth' (doc. 3, l. 7). We suspect that it is the mother-in-law's mouth that is meant. Demetria appears in many more documents than Dionysius's wife,[108] and acts not only with her daughter-in-law,[109] but also with her son. Thus she is a good example of the widow who exercises some authority both within her family and in the larger society, and who is more free than younger women to be active in the public sphere.[110]

Unlike the census records, private documents show that plenty of widows wielded authority, probably frequently because they were the principal beneficiaries of their husbands' wills. Some examples are

[107] See further Boswinkel and Pestman, 'Les Archives privées de Dionysios', p. 5.
[108] Docs. 3, 11, 12, 16, 20, 23–5, 27, 28, 30, 31.
[109] Docs. 3, 20, 24, 25, 30, 31.
[110] On widows see Bremmer, 'Old Women', esp. 196, and Ch. 5 n. 103 above.

the mother and grandmother of Dionysius, son of Kephalas.[111] The wife is most often the principal beneficiary in the large collection of wills in the Petrie papyri, dating from 238–26.[112] Female slaves, who may well have been like wives in some ways, and who were to care for the testators until death, also appear as beneficiaries.[113] This group of testators were well-to-do soldiers and cleruchs. They probably did not have other kin in Egypt amongst whom they might have distributed their property. Some of the testators were elderly, and had few children, or none at all, at least at the time when they drew up their will.[114] Hence the focus of these wills is on the conjugal unit or nuclear family. In any event, widows were certainly legally capable of managing, or alienating, their property, though for large transactions they would have needed the approval of their *kyrios*. When a widow and child are joint legatees, they evidently declined to divide the inheritance. Unlike the Athenians, who bequeathed the major portion of their property to their sons, and distributed a fraction as dowry to their daughters, and perhaps gave a dowry or bequest to their widows (see Ch. 5), the cleruchs were extremely generous to their widows. These considerations, not to mention those of sentiment or peer pressure, ensured that children would treat their widowed mothers with deference and respect, and that sons would be eager to act as their mothers' *kyrios* in their business transactions.

DAUGHTERS AND SONS

Diodorus Siculus drew attention to an unusual custom of the Egyptians: owing to the ease of finding sustenance, they raised all their children.[115] By defining the 'other' herein, Diodorus has characterized

[111] See also the mother and grandmother of Senobastis, wife of Melas, n. 65 above.

[112] *P. Petr.*², pp. 36–7, 170. See also the illuminating remarks in John F. Oates, review of *The Petrie Papyri*, 2nd edn., I, ed. W. Clarysse, *BASP* 29 (1992), 191–8, esp. 196–7.

[113] *P. Petr.*² 3, ll. 19–20, 45–6. The testator in the first will has a legitimate wife and sons, but also promises freedom after his death to a female slave and her son, whose paternity he acknowledges. In the second document there appears to be no legitimate wife: Semele and her children are to be freed after the testator's death.

[114] e.g. *P. Petr.*² 1: beneficiaries are two women, not evidently his relatives; 17. 25 the testator is 65, and his beneficiaries include his wife and his future children.

[115] 1. 31. 6–9. Interestingly, modern census data reporting shortages of women in China, India, and other developing countries now show Egypt as having an actual male to female sex ratio of 1.047. The expected sex ratio is calculated at 1.20. China, the country which shows the most extreme skewing, has a ratio of 1.066, with an expected ratio of 1.010. See further Kristof, 'Stark Data on Women'.

his own society, or those of his historian predecessors (including Herodotus, Hecataeus, and Polybius), as not raising all their children. He has shown himself a precursor of Malthusianism in relating population growth to economic circumstances. The census lists and the genealogical charts do not at first glance corroborate Diodorus's statement beyond doubt in so far as it applies to girls. It must be admitted, however, that the sex ratios are not so skewed as they are in the cemeteries of the older Greek cities (see Ch. 3). Moreover, the data are ambiguous. Despite the low rate of taxes, we must speculate that few people were enthusiastic about paying them. For this reason we cannot ignore the possibility that some men and women managed to avoid being listed; there is not much reason to suppose that one sex would escape more often than the other, except that in general men are more mobile than women. Furthermore, the total numbers of men and women recorded in the census are not so clear as they might be in a modern population survey, owing to the fragmentary condition of the documents, to the fact that some Egyptian names were borne by both men and women, and, most importantly, to the rule that young children were not counted, and that we do not know the age at which they begin to enter the records.[116] As mentioned above, in *CPR* XIII, for example, people listed as 'sons' far outnumber those listed as 'daughters'. Even allowing for the change of role from daughter to wife at a young age, males still outnumber females. Yet, if the age of maturity was the same for boys and girls, we would expect approximately equal numbers, and if the age was tied to puberty and girls entered the lists at a younger age than boys, we would expect women to outnumber men. The age of menarche was 13–14, and the age of puberty for boys was 14–16, with adulthood at approximately 18.[117] In *P. Lille* 1.10, fr. 2, which lists taxpayers in three areas of the Arsinoite *nome* (254–234), there are 3,418 men, and 54 young men, giving a total of 3,472 males and 3,147 females. In *P. Petr.* III 93, col. vii, ll. 10–12 (after 234), which gives the total number of taxpayers in an unidentified location that includes, however, Persea and Psenuris in the Heracleides Meris, there are 5,352 males and 5,067 females.[118] On

[116] See n. 10, above.

[117] See Introduction, n. 17 above. Arist. *HA* 581A and E. Eyben, 'Antiquity's View of Puberty', *Latomus*, 31 (1972), 677–97.

[118] D. W. Rathbone, 'Villages, Land, and Population in Graeco-Roman Egypt', *PCPS* 216 (1990), 103–42, esp. 130–1. The number of adult males exceeds the number of females in every village listed in table 2, although Rathbone points out (p. 133) that in *P. Lille* 1. 10, frs. 5 and 6, females outnumber males. Though 'young' men are counted separately from adult men, Rathbone does not discuss the definition of 'young'.

the other hand, there is also evidence for a surplus of women, at least sometimes in some places. The two women listed as *thugater* in *CPR* XIII may have been spinsters.[119] The existence of households with female heads and the few cases of bigamy (and possibly one of trigamy) also suggest that there was no shortage of women. At Athens, by contrast, a household with a female head was anomalous, and cause for intense distress (see Ch. 5).

Apart from the numerical totals in the population lists, there is almost no evidence for exposure of infants in Ptolemaic Egypt.[120] Legislation of the city of Ptolemaïs Hermiou requires a period of purification after child exposure. Ptolemaïs Hermiou was a Greek city founded by Ptolemy I. The notion of exposure was doubtless a legacy of the older Greek cities, whose laws served as the model for the laws of the Greek cities in Egypt. The existence of such a law does not necessarily attest to the actual practice of exposure at Ptolemaïs Hermiou.[121] The wills of well-to-do Greeks that are preserved in *P. Petr.*^{2} indicate that if girls had been exposed, they would not have been turned over to wet-nurses and raised to be slaves. Admittedly this is an argument *ex silentio*, but it is corroborated by other evidence. None of the slaves in the Petrie wills have Egyptian names.[122] That they all bear Greek and Syrian names suggests, but does not prove conclusively, that they were purchased from abroad. In fact, there are very few slaves in the census documents in general.[123] There was no shortage of workers, because the Egyptians reared all their children. The attitude of Greek men, at least, concerning raising daughters evidently changed once they were well-to-do landowners in Egypt. The wills of Greek soldiers in *P. Petr.*^{2} indicate that such men

[119] See n. 47 above.

[120] Sarah B. Pomeroy, 'Copronyms and the Exposure of Infants in Egypt', in Roger Bagnall and William Harris (eds.), *Studies in Roman Law in Memory of A. Arthur Schiller* (Leiden, 1986), 147–62; Abstract in *Atti del XVII Congresso Internazionale di Papirologia* (Naples, 1984), 1341.

[121] See further Pomeroy, *Women in Hellenistic Egypt*, 136–7.

[122] *P. Petr.*^{2}, p. 40. See also the comments on slave names in the Petrie wills in Reinhold Scholl, *Corpus der Ptolemäischen Sklaventexte* (Stuttgart, 1990), i. nos. 28–33.

[123] Cf. *P. Lille dém.* I 101 for approximately one slave per family. On the relatively small role of slavery in Ptolemaic Egypt see Pomeroy, *Women in Hellenistic Egypt*, 125–8. On slaves' names see Reinhold Scholl, *Sklaverei in den Zenonpapyri*, Trierer historische Forschungen, 4 (Trier, 1983), 136–7.

consented not only to raise daughters, but also to bequeath substantial amounts of wealth to them.[124]

The genealogical charts, as well, do not supply straightforward evidence on reproduction. Kephalas, father of Dionysius, is one of four brothers, and Dionysius is one of three brothers. They probably had some sisters. Like so many women, sisters enter the historical documentation less frequently than brothers, because they are less active in the public sphere, or, like Zenon's aunt and mother, they appear as ciphers. If there are sisters, they may be married and living with their husband's family, like the wives who are named on the chart of the family of Kephalas. In fact, genealogical charts of families coming from milieux similar to that of Dionysius do not support an argument that female infanticide was practised.[125] All the men in the family who have wives who might be mentioned in the documents actually have such wives. Wives are not recorded for the three brothers of Kephalas, simply because the men are named only in one document, a petition where it was not necessary to include wives.

In contrast to the men in the archive of Dionysius, no wives or sisters at all are recorded for Zenon and his brothers. As already noted, the documentation from the purely Greek circle of Zenon and his friends shows a paucity of wives, sisters, and daughters. This skewing of the sex ratio was the result of several factors, including the predominance of men in the first generation of immigrants to Egypt and the practice of female infanticide in the older Greek cities.[126] Zenon's parents in Caria may have practised it, for the evidence for female infanticide among Greeks living outside Egypt during the Hellenistic period is substantial. For example, a glance at the lists of new citizens at Miletus and Ilion, referred to above, shows a paucity of children: adults outnumber children, and among the children sons outnumber daughters by far.[127] Coming from that Greek world, Demetrius of Phaleron and Ptolemy I may have believed that it was necessary to encourage reproduction, so that there would be more taxpayers and more potential soldiers. Exempting children

[124] Nos. 7, 14, 16. 79 (with n.), 22, 25, 28. Female beneficiaries in nos. 1 and 2 may be the daughters of the testator, although the relationship is not stated.

[125] For similar evidence see the sex ratios in the archives of Apollonia and Dryton, analysed in Pomeroy, *Women in Hellenistic Egypt*, 111, and those in Andrews, *Catalogue of Demotic Papyri*, IV.

[126] Ch. 3 nn. 61–3 above.

[127] See the tabulation in Angeliki Petropoulou, *Beiträge*, 177–99, and see further Pomeroy, 'Infanticide in Hellenistic Greece', and Brulé, 'Enquête démographique'.

from taxes could have been part of a pro-natalist policy.[128] Ptolemy's distribution of land to soldiers as cleruchies certainly was a step in the same direction of population increase.[129]

Census records indicate that the government regarded the conjugal couple, or nuclear family with children, as the norm, though bigamy, and perhaps trigamy, are found. The documents emanating from the population add some alternative family structures and multi-family units. Most remarkable are the relationships with siblings. In the Ptolemaic period, these relationships appear to be limited to siblings of the same gender, but this practice changed. Although the Romans themselves were more exogamous than the Greeks, and did not countenance marriage between uncle and niece, let alone between half-siblings, there is good historical evidence from Roman Egypt for brother–sister marriages.[130] Because women's lineages do not usually appear in the Ptolemaic tax lists, as they do in the Roman census documents, sibling marriages among commoners cannot be documented for the earlier period.

As mentioned, the evidence for female infanticide in Ptolemaic Egypt is far weaker than it is for the older Greek cities. There is, however, plenty of documentation for the practice of brother–sister marriage in Roman Egypt.[131] Are we merely seeing the effect of some as yet unidentified change in historical documentation? It is true that the Roman census papyri give more detailed information about parentage than the Ptolemaic lists, but other documents, such as wedding invitations and marriage contracts, that give parents' names should give the same sort of information for both periods. Did drastic social and economic crises and changes occur under Roman domination, thereby introducing two significant changes in family behaviour: exposure of infants and brother–sister marriage among commoners? Are infanticide and brother–sister marriage related? Did the former create a shortage of women, for which the latter compensated by giving siblings access to spouses who were previously denied to them? Or were Greeks who married siblings and practised infanticide

[128] Cf. In contrast to the Roman exclusion of children only up to the age of 3: *The Gnomon of the Idios Logos*, sect. 63.

[129] Ptolemy I settled 8,000 soldiers captured at Gaza in 312 in the nomarchies: Diod. Sic. 19. 85. 3–4, and see further Roger S. Bagnall, 'The Origins of Ptolemaic Cleruchs', *BASP* 21 (1984), 7–20. Adam Smith saw the relationship between the prosperity of a country and the increase of the number of inhabitants: *The Wealth of Nations* (1776; repr. London, 1910), i. 72, 149.

[130] Bagnall and Frier, *Demography*, 127–34.

[131] Ibid., 92–5, 151–3.

adopting a new life-style or following a fad? Did sibling marriage simply trickle down the social scale in Roman Egypt?[132] Can historians justifiably discuss 'Graeco-Roman' Egypt as an undifferentiated whole, in the light of such significant differences in the history of the family under Greek and Roman domination?[133] One conclusion is obvious: the range of human behaviour we have examined in this study of the family is enormous. Human beings are infinitely resourceful and all-inventive (Soph. *Ant.* 360).

Families in Ptolemaic Egypt, even more than families discussed in previous chapters, defy generalization.[134] In the classical period, the laws and customs of the homogeneous populations of city-states had imposed a uniformity on the marriage practices of their citizens. By contrast, the heterogeneous population in Egypt, a fluid mix, including Greeks from diverse areas, Macedonians, Egyptians, Jews, and others, embraced diverse family structures, and were permitted to use different legal systems. Liaisons between soldiers and slaves and mixed marriages between Greeks and Egyptians, each well attested, but for different social classes, time periods, and locations, further complicate the picture. It is easier to generalize about family life in modern London or New York than to describe the realities underlying the appearance of a uniform family structure in the Ptolemaic administrative documents.

[132] So Joseph Modrzejewski, 'Die Geschwisterehe in der hellenistischen praxis und nach römischem Recht', *ZRG* 81 (1964), 52–82.

[133] Naphtali Lewis, '"Greco-Roman Egypt": Fact or Fiction?', in D. H. Samuel (ed.), *Proceedings of the XIIth International Congress of Papyrology, Ann Arbor, 13–17 August 1968*, Am. Stud. Pap., 7 (Toronto, 1970), 3–14, lists economic and administrative changes from the Greek to the Roman period, and refers to increased stress and economic decline. His plea to differentiate the period of Greek domination from the Roman and his view of economic decline in the latter period, however, were not accepted. Cf. e.g. Ann Ellis Hanson, 'The Keeping of Records at Philadelphia in the Julio-Claudian Period and the "Economic Crisis under Nero"', in Basil Mandilaras (ed.), *Proceedings of the XVIIIth International Congress of Papyrology*, ii (Athens, 1988), 261–77.

[134] Because new documents are constantly being published, any generalizations in this field, even more than elsewhere in ancient history, are at high risk of being contradicted.

Bibliography

With a few obvious exceptions, journal titles are abbreviated according to the form in *L'Année philologique*. Accepted abbreviations will be used for standard works. Lists of such abbreviations may be found in reference books such as the *Oxford Classical Dictionary*, 2nd edn., and in the major Greek and Latin dictionaries. Citations of papyri follow the list of abbreviations in John F. Oates, Roger S. Bagnall, William H. Willis, and Klaas A. Worp, *Checklist of Editions of Greek and Latin Papyri, Ostraca and Tablets*, 4th edn., BASP suppl. 7 (Atlanta, 1992).

ALEXIOU, MARGARET, *The Ritual Lament in Greek Tradition* (Cambridge, 1974).

AMUNDSEN, D. W., and DIERS, C. J., 'The Age of Menarche in Classical Greece and Rome', *Human Biology*, 41 (1969), 125–32.

ANDERSON, MARGO J., *The American Census: A Social History* (New Haven and London, 1988).

ANDREWES, ANTHONY, 'Philochoros and Phratries', *JHS* 81 (1961), 115.

ANDREWS, Carol A. R., *Catalogue of Demotic Papyri in the British Museum. IV: Ptolemaic Legal Texts from the Theban Area* (London, 1990).

ANDRIOMENOU, A. K., 'La Nécropole classique de Tanagra', in *La Béotie antique, Lyon-Saint-Étienne, 16–20 mai 1983*. Coll. intern. du CNRS (Paris, 1985), 109–30.

ANGEL, J. LAWRENCE, 'The Bases of Paleodemography', *American Journal of Physical Anthropology*, 30 (1969), 427–38.

—— 'The Length of Life in Ancient Greece', *Journal of Gerontology*, 2 (1947), 18–24.

—— 'Paleoecology, Paleodemography and Health', in Steven Polgar (ed.), *Population, Ecology and Social Evolution* (The Hague, 1975), 167–90.

ASHERI, DAVID, 'Laws of Inheritance, Distribution of Land and Political Constitutions in Ancient Greece', *Historia*, 12 (1963), 1–21.

—— 'Supplementi coloniari e condizione giuridica della terra nel mondo greco', *RSA* 1 (1971), 77–91.

Bacchylides. The Poems and Fragments, ed. Richard C. Jebb (Cambridge, 1905; repr. Hildesheim, 1967).

BACHOFEN, J. J., *Das Mutterrecht* (Stuttgart, 1861).

BAGNALL, ROGER S., *The Administration of the Ptolemaic Possessions outside Egypt* (Leiden, 1976).

—— 'The Origins of Ptolemaic Cleruchs', *BASP* 21 (1984), 7–20.

—— and Frier, Bruce, *The Demography of Roman Egypt* (Cambridge, 1994).

Benedum, Jost, 'Griechische Arztinschriften aus Kos', *ZPE* 25 (1977), 264–76.

—— 'Inscriptions grecques de Cos relatives à des médecins hippocratiques et Cos Astypalaia', in M. D. Grmek (ed.), *Hippocratica. Actes du colloque hippocratique de Paris (4–9 septembre 1978)* (Paris, 1980), 35–43.

Billigmeier, Jon-Christian, 'Studies on the Family in the Aegean Bronze Age and in Homer', *Trends in History*, 3, 3–4 (1984), 9–18.

Bingen, J., 'Le Papyrus du gynéconome', *CE* 32 (1957), 337–9.

Bisel, S. C., and Angel, J. L., 'Health and Nutrition in Mycenaean Greece', in N. C. Wilkie and W. D. E. Coulson (eds.), *Contributions to Aegean Archaeology. Studies in Honor of W. A. McDonald* (Minneapolis, 1985), 197–210.

Blass, F., *Die Attische Beredsamkeit*, 2nd edn., iii (Leipzig, 1893).

Boswinkel, F., and Pestman, P. W., 'Les Archives privées de Dionysios, fils de Kephalas', Pap. Lugd. Bat., XXII (Leiden, 1982).

Bourriot, Felix, *Recherches sur la nature du genos. Étude d'histoire sociale athénienne. Périodes archaïque et classique* (Thèse de Lille; Paris, 1976).

Bousquet, J., 'Inscriptions de Delphes', *BCH* 80 (1956), 547–97.

Boyaval, B., 'Remarques sur les indications d'âges de l'épigraphie funéraire grecque d'Égypte,' *ZPE* 21 (1976), 217–43.

Boylan, Michael, 'The Galenic and Hippocratic Challenges to Aristotle's Conception Theory', *Journal of the History of Biology*, 17/1 (1984), 83–112.

Bradeen, Donald W., *The Athenian Agora*, 17. *Inscriptions: The Funerary Monuments* (Princeton, 1974).

Bradley, Keith, 'Writing the History of the Roman Family', *CPh* 88 (1993), 237–50.

Brandes, Stanley, 'Reflections on Honor and Shame in the Mediterranean', in David D. Gilmore (ed.), *Honor and Shame and the Unity of the Mediterranean* (Washington, DC, 1987), 121–34.

Braunert, Horst, 'IDIA: Studien zur Bevölkerungsgeschichte des ptolemäischen und römischen Ägypten', *JJP* 9–10 (1955–6), 211–328.

Breasted, James Henry, *Ancient Records of Egypt*, i (Chicago, 1906).

Bremmer, Jan, 'The Importance of the Maternal Uncle and Grandfather in Archaic and Classical Greece and Early Byzantium', *ZPE* 50 (1983), 173–86.

—— 'The Old Women of Ancient Greece', in Josine Blok and Peter Mason (eds.), *Sexual Asymmetry* (Amsterdam, 1987), 191–215.

Brenne, Stefan, 'Cleisthenes' Name System and Names on Ostraka', in *Abstracts of the 95th Annual Meeting of the Archaeological Institute of America* (Washington, DC, 1993), 3.

BRESCIANI, E., 'La spedizione di Tolemeo II in Siria in un ostrakon demotico inedito da Karnak', in H. Maehler and V. M. Strocka (eds.), *Das ptolemäische Aegypten: Akten des internationalen Symposions, 27–29 September 1976 in Berlin* (Mainz, 1978), 31–7.

BRONEER, OSCAR, 'Notes on the Xanthippos Ostrakon', *AJA* 52 (1948), 341–3.

BRUCK, B., *Totenteil und Seelgerät im griechischen Recht*, Münch. Beiträge zur Papyrusforschung und ant. Rechtsgesch., 9 (Munich, 1926).

BRULÉ, PIERRE, 'Enquête démographique sur la famille grecque antique', *REA* 92 (1990), 233–58.

BURKERT, W., *Greek Religion* (Oxford, 1984). Originally published as *Griechische Religion der archaischen und klassischen Epoche* (Stuttgart, 1977).

BURSTEIN, STANLEY M., *The Hellenistic Age from the Battle of Ipsos to the Death of Kleopatra VII* (Cambridge, 1985).

CAREY, C., 'Apollodoros' Mother: The Wives of Disenfranchised Aliens in Athens', *CQ* n.s. 41 (1991), 84–9.

CARTLEDGE, P. A., *Agesilaos and the Crisis of Sparta* (London, 1987).

—— 'Hoplites and Heroes: Sparta's Contribution to the Technique of Ancient Warfare', *JHS* 97 (1977), 11–27.

—— and HARVEY, F. D. (eds.), *Crux: Essays Presented to G. E. M. de Ste. Croix on his 75th Birthday = HPTh* 6 (London, 1985).

—— and SPAWFORTH, ANTONY, *Hellenistic and Roman Sparta. A Tale of Two Cities* (London and New York, 1989).

CENIVAL, FRANÇOISE DE, *Papyrus démotiques de Lille*, III, Memoires publiés par les membres de l'Institut français d'archaeologie orientale (Cairo, 1984).

CHAMBERS, M., *Aristoteles. Staat der Athener*, in Aristotle *Werke* x.1 (Berlin, 1990).

CHARLIER, M. T., and RAEPSET, G., 'Étude d'un comportement social, les relations entre parents et enfants dans la société athénienne à l'époque classique', *AC* 40 (1971), 589–606.

CLAIRMONT, C., *Classical Attic Tombstones*, Introd. vol., vols. i–vi, and plates (Kilchberg, 1993).

—— *Gravestone and Epigram* (Mainz, 1970).

CLARYSSE, WILLY, 'Abbreviations and Lexicography', *Anc. Soc.* 21 (1990), 33–44.

—— 'Le Mariage et le testament de Dryton en 150 avant J.-C.', *CE* 61 (1986), 99–103.

—— '*P. Sorb.* et autres listes de population', unpublished, 1990.

—— 'Ptolemaic Census Lists and *P. Petrie Ashmol.* ined.', unpublished, 1990.

—— (ed.), *The Petrie Papyri.*, 2nd edn., i: *The Wills*, Collectanea Hellenistica, 2 (Brussels, 1991).

COHEN, EDWARD E., *Athenian Economy and Society. A Banking Perspective* (Princeton, 1992).

COHN-HAFT, LOUIS, *The Public Physicians of Ancient Greece* (Northampton, Mass., 1956).

COLE, SUSAN G., 'The Social Function of Rituals of Maturation', *ZPE* 55 (1985), 233–44.

COLLIGNON, MAX, 'Matrimonium 1. Grèce', *Dar.-Sag.* (Paris, 1877–1919), ii, pt. 2, 1639–54.

COX, CHERYL ANN, 'Incest, Inheritance and the Political Forum in Fifth-Century Athens', *CJ* 85 (1989), 34–46.

—— 'Sibling Relationships in Classical Athens: Brother–Sister Ties', *Journal of Family History*, 13 (1988), 377–95.

—— 'Sisters, Daughters and the Deme of Marriage: A Note', *JHS* 108 (1988), 185–8.

CRAIK, ELIZABETH M., *The Dorian Aegean* (London, 1980).

DANFORTH, LORING, *The Death Rituals of Rural Greece* (Princeton, 1982).

DANOFF, C. M. SOFIA, 'Kepos', in *Der Kleine Pauly*, iii (Stuttgart, 1969), col. 194.

DAVID, EPHRAIM, 'Laughter in Spartan Society', in A. Powell (ed.), *Classical Sparta: Techniques behind her Success* (Norman, Okla., and London, 1988), 1–25.

DAVIES, J. K., *Athenian Propertied Families* (Oxford, 1971).

—— 'Religion and the State', in *Cambridge Ancient History*, 2nd edn., iv (Cambridge, 1988), 368–88.

—— *Wealth and the Power of Wealth in Classical Athens* (Salem, NH, 1984).

DEAN-JONES, LESLIE, 'The Cultural Construct of the Female Body,' in Sarah B. Pomeroy (ed.), *Women's History and Ancient History* (Chapel Hill, NC, 1991), 111–37.

DELIA, DIANA, 'The Ptolemies and the Ideology of Kingship', in Peter Green (ed.), *Hellenistic History and Culture* (Berkeley, 1993), 192–204.

DINDORF, W., *Demosthenes*, viii (Oxford, 1851).

DODDS, E. R., *The Greeks and the Irrational* (Berkeley and Los Angeles, 1951).

DOVER, K. J., *Greek Homosexuality* (London, 1978).

EDELSTEIN, LUDWIG, *The Hippocratic Oath*, Supplements to the Bulletin of the History of Medicine, 1 (Baltimore, 1943).

ENGELS, FRIEDRICH, *Der Ursprung der Familie des Privateigentums und des Staates* (Zurich, 1884).

ERSKINE, ANDREW, *The Hellenistic Stoa* (Ithaca, NY, 1990).

EYBEN, E., 'Antiquity's View of Puberty', *Latomus*, 31 (1972), 677–97.

FARAONE, CHRISTOPHER A., and OBBINK, DIRK (eds.), *Magika Hiera* (New York, 1991).

FERGUSON, WILLIAM SCOTT, *Hellenistic Athens* (London, 1911).

FIGUEIRA, THOMAS J., 'Population Patterns in Late Archaic and Classical Sparta', *TAPhA* 116 (1986), 165–213.

Fine, J. V. A., *Horoi. Studies in Mortgage, Real Security, and Land Tenure i Ancient Athens*, *Hesperia* Suppl. 9 (Princeton, 1951).

Finley, M. I., *Ancient History, Evidence and Models* (New York, 1987).

—— *Studies in Land and Credit in Ancient Athens 500–200* BC (Nev Brunswick, NJ, 1952).

Firatli, N., and Robert, L., *Les Stèles funéraires de Byzance gréco-romaine* Bibl. archéol. et hist. de l'Inst. franç. d'Archéol. d'Istanbul, 15 (Paris 1964).

Flandrin, Jean-Louis, *Families in Former Times* (Cambridge, 1979).

Flower, M. A., '*IG* II² 2344 and the Size of Phratries in Classical Athens', *CQ* 35 (1985), 232–5.

Foxhall, Lin, 'Household, Gender and Property in Classical Athens', *CQ* 3 (1989), 22–44.

—— and Forbes, H. A., '*Σιτομετρεία*: The Role of Grain as a Staple Food i Classical Antiquity', *Chiron*, 12 (1982), 41–90.

Fraser, P. M., *Ptolemaic Alexandria* (Oxford, 1972).

—— *Rhodian Funerary Monuments* (Oxford, 1977).

Frazer, J. G., *Pausanias's Description of Greece* (London, 1898, repr. Nev York, 1965).

Friedl, Ernestine, 'Kinship, Class, and Selective Migration', in J. G. Peri stiany (ed.), *Mediterranean Family Structures* (Cambridge, 1976), 363–88

—— *Vasilika. A Village in Modern Greece* (New York, 1965).

Frisch, P., *Die Inschriften von Ilion* (Bonn, 1975).

Fuks, A., 'Agis, Cleomenes and Equality', *CPh* 57 (1962), 161–6; repr. in M Stern and M. Amit (eds.), *Social Conflict in Ancient Greece* (Jerusalem an Leiden, 1984), 250–5.

—— *The Ancestral Constitution* (London, 1953).

—— 'Patterns and Types of Social-Economic Revolution in Greece from th Fourth to the Second Century BC', *Anc. Soc.* 5 (1962), 51–81; repr. in M Stern and M. Amit (eds.), *Social Conflict in Ancient Greece* (Jerusalem an Leiden, 1984), 9–39.

Fustel de Coulanges, Numa Denis, *The Ancient City* (Baltimore and London 1980) originally published as *La Cité antique* (1864).

Gager, John, *Curse Tablets and Binding Spells from the Ancient World* (Nev York, 1992).

Gallant, T. W., *Risk and Survival in Ancient Greece* (Stanford, Calif., 1991)

Garland, R., 'A First Catalogue of Attic Peribolos Tombs', *ABSA* 77 (1982) 125–76.

—— *The Greek Way of Death* (London, 1985).

—— 'The Well-Ordered Corpse: An Investigation into the Motives behin Greek Funerary Legislation', *BICS* 36 (1989), 1–15.

Gernet, Louis, *Droit et Société dans la Grèce ancienne* (Paris, 1955).

—— 'Note sur les parents de Démosthène', *REG* 31 (1918), 185–96.

GHIRON-BISTAGNE, PAULETTE, *Recherches sur les acteurs dans la Grèce antique* (Paris, 1976).

GLOTZ, G., *La Solidarité de la famille dans le droit criminel en Grèce* (Paris, 1904).

GOLDEN, MARK, *Children and Childhood in Classical Athens* (Baltimore, 1990).

—— 'Demosthenes and the Age of Majority at Athens', *Phoenix*, 33 (1979), 25–38.

—— '"Donatus" and Athenian Phratries', *CQ* 35 (1985), 9–13.

—— 'The Exposure of Girls at Athens', *Phoenix*, 35 (1981), 316–31.

—— 'Names and Naming at Athens: Three Studies', *EMC* 30 (1986), 245–69.

GOODLETT, VIRGINIA C., 'Rhodian Sculpture Workshops', *AJA* 95 (1991), 669–81.

GOULD, JOHN, 'Law, Custom, and Myth: Aspects of the Social Position of Women in Classical Athens', *JHS* 100 (1980), 38–59.

GREEN, PETER, 'Philosophers, Kings, and Democracy, or How Political Was the Stoa?', *Ancient Philosophy*, 14 (1994), 147–56.

GRIFFITH, F. L., *The Petrie Papyri: Hieratic Papyri from Kahun and Gurob* (London, 1898).

GRMEK, MIRKO D., 'Ideas on Heredity in Greek and Roman Antiquity', *Physis*, n.s. 28 (1991), 11–34.

GÜNTHER, LINDA-MARIE, 'Witwen in der Griechischen Antike—Zwischen Oikos und Polis', *Historia*, 42 (1993), 308–25.

GÜNTHER, WOLFGANG, 'Milesische Bürgerrechts- und Proxenieverleihungen der hellenistischen Zeit', *Chiron*, 18 (1988), 383–419.

HAJNAL, JOHN, 'European Marriage Patterns in Perspective', in D. V. Glass and D. E. C. Eversley (eds.), *Population and History: Essays in Historical Demography* (London, 1965), 101–43.

HAMILTON, RICHARD, *Choes and Anthesteria. Athenian Iconography and Ritual* (Ann Arbor, 1992).

—— 'Sources for the Athenian Amphidromia', *GRBS* 25 (1984), 243–51.

HANSEN, MOGENS HERMAN, *Apagoge, Endeixis and Ephegesis against Kakourgoi, Atimoi and Pheugontes* (Odense, 1976).

—— *The Athenian Democracy in the Age of Demosthenes* (Oxford and Cambridge, Mass., 1991).

—— *Demography and Democracy: the Number of Athenian Citizens in the Fourth Century* BC (Herning, 1985).

—— *Three Studies in Athenian Demography*, Historisk-filosofiske meddeleser 56 (Copenhagen, 1988).

—— BERTRUP, LARS; NIELSEN, THOMAS HEINE; RUBINSTEIN, LENE; and VESTERGAARD, TORBEN, 'The Demography of Attic Demes. The Evidence of the Sepulchral Inscriptions', *Analecta Romana*, 19 (1990), 25–44.

HANSEN, P. A. (ed.), *Carmina Epigraphica Graeca*, ii (Berlin, 1989).

HANSON, ANN ELLIS, 'Conception, Gestation, and the Origin of Female Nature in the *Corpus Hippocraticum*', *Helios*, 19 (1992), 31–71.

—— 'The Keeping of Records at Philadelphia in the Julio-Claudian Period and the "Economic Crisis under Nero"', in Basil Mandilaras (ed.), *Proceedings of the XVIIIth International Congress of Papyrology*, 2 (Athens, 1988), 261–77.

—— 'The Medical Writers' Woman', in D. M. Halperin, J. J. Winkler, and F. I. Zeitlin (eds.), *Before Sexuality* (Princeton, 1990), 309–38.

HARRAUER, HERMANN, *Corpus Papyrorum Raineri*, XIII, Griechische Texte, IX (Vienna, 1987).

HARRISON, A. R. W., *The Law of Athens* (2 vols., Oxford, 1968, 1971).

HARVEY, F. D., 'Laconica: Aristophanes and the Spartans', in A. Powell and S. Hodkinson (eds.), *The Shadow of Sparta* (London, 1994), 35–58.

HAUBEN, HANS, 'Les Vacances d'Agréophon (253 av. J.-C.)', *CE*, 60 (1985), 102–8.

HAVELOCK, CHRISTINE, 'Mourners on Greek Vases: Remarks on the Social History of Women', in N. Broude and M. D. Garrard (eds.), *Feminism and Art History* (New York, 1982), 44–61.

HEDRICK, CHARLES W., JR., *The Decrees of the Demotionidai*, American Classical Studies, 22 (Atlanta, 1990).

—— 'Phratry Shrines of Attica and Athens', *Hesperia*, 60 (1990), 241–68.

HERLIHY, DAVID, and KLAPISCH-ZUBER, CHRISTIANE, *Tuscans and their Families* (New Haven, 1985). Originally published as *Les Toscans et leurs familles* (Paris, 1978).

HODKINSON, S. J., '"Blind Ploutos"? Contemporary Images of the Role of Wealth in Classical Sparta', in A. Powell and S. Hodkinson (eds.), *The Shadow of Sparta* (London, 1994), 183–222.

—— 'Inheritance, Marriage and Demography: Perspectives upon the Success and Decline of Classical Sparta', in A. Powell (ed.), *Classical Sparta: Techniques behind her Success* (Norman, Okla., and London, 1988), 79–121.

—— 'Land Tenure and Inheritance in Classical Sparta', *CQ* n.s. 36 (1986), 378–406.

HOEPFNER, WOLFRAM, and SCHWANDNER, ERNST-LUDWIG, *Haus und Stadt im Klassischen Griechenland*, Wohnen in der klassischen Polis, i (Munich, 1986).

HOLST-WARHAFT, GAIL, *Dangerous Voices. Women's Laments and Greek Literature* (London, 1992).

HOMBERT, M., and PRÉAUX, C., *Recherches sur le recensement dans l'Égypte romaine. P. Brux. Inv. E. 7616*, Pap. Lugd. Bat., *V* (Paris, 1952).

HOMOLLE, T., 'Statue de Caius Ofellius: sur une œuvre signée des artistes Dionysios et Polyclès', *BCH* 5 (1881), 390–6.

HOPKINS, KEITH, *Death and Renewal: Sociological Studies in Roman History*, ii (Cambridge, 1983).

—— 'Graveyards for Historians', in F. Hinard (ed.), *La Mort, les morts et l'au-delà dans le monde romain* (Caen, 1987), 113–26.

HOUBY-NIELSEN, SANNE, '"Burial Language" in Archaic and Classical Kerameikos', *Proceedings of the Danish Institute at Athens*, 1 (1995), 131–91.

—— 'Gender Roles and Conventional Values in Hellenistic Athens', paper delivered at conference on 'Conventional Values of the Hellenistic Greeks', sponsored by Danish Research Council for the Humanities, Copenhagen, 26 Jan., 1995.

HRDY, SARAH BLAFFER, 'Fitness Tradeoffs in the History and Evolution of Delegated Mothering with Special Reference to Wet-Nursing, Abandonment, and Infanticide', *Ethology and Sociobiology*, 13 (1992), 409–42.

HUMPHREYS, S. C., *Anthropology and the Greeks* (London, 1978).

—— 'Family Tombs and Tomb Cult in Ancient Athens—Tradition or Traditionalism?', *JHS* 100 (1980), 96–126; repr. in *The Family, Women and Death* (London, 1983), 79–130.

—— *The Family, Women and Death: Comparative Studies* (London, 1983).

—— 'Kinship Patterns in the Athenian Courts', *GRBS* 27 (1986), 57–91.

—— (with A. Momigliano), *Anthropology and the Greeks* (London, 1978).

HUNTER, VIRGINIA, 'The Athenian Widow and her Kin', *Journal of Family History*, 14/4 (1989), 291–311.

—— *Policing Athens. Social Control in the Attic Lawsuits, 420–320 BC* (Princeton, 1994).

—— 'Women's Authority in Classical Athens: The Example of Kleoboule and her Son (Dem. 27–29)', *EMC* 33, n.s. 8 (1989), 39–48.

ISAGER, SIGNE, and HANSEN, MOGENS HERMAN, *Aspects of Athenian Society in the Fourth Century* BC (Odense, 1975).

ITO, SADAO, 'The Enrolment of Athenian Phratries', *Legal History Review*, 31 (1981), 35–60, with English summary, 7–8.

—— 'Phrateres as Athenian Citizens', *JCS* 31 (1983), 1–18, with English summary, 149–50.

JAMESON, MICHAEL, 'Private Space and the Greek City', in Oswyn Murray and Simon Price (eds.), *The Greek City: From Homer to Alexander* (Oxford, 1990), 171–95.

JEFFERY, L. H., review of P. A. Cartledge, *Sparta and Laconia;* L. F. Fitzhardinghe, *The Spartans;* and T. A. Boring, *Literacy in Ancient Sparta*, *JHS* 101 (1981), 190–2.

KEARNS, EMILY, 'Change and Continuity in Religious Structures after Cleisthenes', in P. A. Cartledge and F. D. Harvey (eds.), *Crux* (London, 1985), 189–207.

KEMP, Barry J., *Ancient Egypt. Anatomy of a Civilization* (London and New York, 1991).

KITTO, H. D. F., *The Greeks* (Harmondsworth, 1951; rev. 1957).

KLAPISCH-ZUBER, CHRISTIANE, *Women, Family and Ritual in Renaissance Italy*, trans. L. G. Cochrane (Chicago, 1985).

KORVER, J., 'Demosthenes gegen Aphobos', *Mnem.* 10 (1941–2), 8–22.

KOVACSOVICS, WILFRIED K., *Kerameikos XIV: Die Eckterrasse an der Gräberstrasse des Kerameikos* (Berlin, 1990).

KRELLER, H., *Erbrechtliche Untersuchungen auf Grund der gräco-ägyptischen Papyrusurkunden* (Leipzig and Berlin, 1919).

KRISTOF, NICHOLAS D., 'Stark Data on Women: 100 Million Are Missing', *New York Times*, 5 Nov., 1991, C1, C12.

KUNSTLER, BARTON LEE, 'Women and the Development of the Spartan Polis' (Ph.D. diss., Boston University, 1983).

KURTZ, DONNA C., 'Mistress and Maid', *AION Archeol* 10 (1988), 141–9.

—— 'Vases for the Dead, an Attic Selection', in H. A. G. Brijder (ed.), *Ancient Greek and Related Pottery*, Allard Pierson Series, 5 (Amsterdam, 1984), 314–28.

—— and BOARDMAN, JOHN, *Greek Burial Customs* (London, 1971).

LACEY, W. K., *The Family in Classical Greece* (Ithaca, NY, and London, 1968).

LAMBERT, S. D., *The Phratries of Attica* (Ann Arbor, 1993).

LAUM, B., *Stiftungen in der griechischen und römischen Antike. Ein Beitrag zur antiken Kulturgeschichte* (2 vols., Leipzig and Berlin, 1914).

LAUTER, H., *Zur gesellschaftlichen Stellung des bildenden Künstlers in der griechischen Klassik*, Erlanger Forsch., ser. A, vol. 23 (Erlangen, 1974).

LEDL, A.,'Das attische Bürgerrecht und die Frauen, I', *WS* 29 (1907), 173–227.

LEDUC, CLAUDINE, 'Marriage in Ancient Greece', in Pauline Schmitt Pantel (ed.), *A History of Women in the West*, vol. 1 (Cambridge, Mass., 1992), 235–94.

LEVI, DORO, and PUGLIESE CARRATELLI, G., 'Nuove Iscrizioni di Iasos', *ASAA* n.s. 23–4 (1961–2), 573–632.

LÉVI-STRAUSS, CLAUDE, *The Elementary Structures of Kinship* (London, 1969), trans. J. H. Bell and J. R. von Sturmer from *Les Structures élémentaires de la parenté*, 2nd edn. (Paris, 1967).

LEWIS, D. M., 'Notes on Attic Inscriptions (II)', *ABSA* 50 (1955), 1–36.

LEWIS, NAPHTALI, '"Greco-Roman Egypt": Fact or Fiction?', in D. H. Samuel (ed.), *Proceedings of the XIIth International Congress of Papyrology, Ann Arbor, 13–17 August 1968*, Am. Stud. Pap., VII (Toronto, 1970), 3–14.

Libanii Opera, viii, ed. R. Foerster ([1915]; repr. Hildesheim, 1963).

LLOYD, ALAN B., *Herodotus, Book II.* Études préliminaires aux religions orientales dans l'Empire romain, 43 (Leiden, 1975–8).

LORAUX, NICOLE, *The Children of Athena. Athenian Ideas about Citizenship and the Division between the Sexes*, trans. Caroline Levine (Princeton, 1993). Originally published as *Les Enfants d'Athéna: Idées athéniennes sur la citoyenneté et la division des sexes* (Paris, 1984).

—— *The Invention of Athens: The Funeral Oration in the Classical City* (Cambridge, Mass., 1986).

LUND, HELEN S., *Lysimachus: A Study in Early Hellenistic Kingship* (London, 1992).

MACDOWELL, DOUGLAS M., 'The *Oikos* in Athenian Law', *CQ* 39 (1989), 10–21.

—— *Spartan Law* (Edinburgh, 1986).

MCLENNAN, JOHN, *Primitive Marriage* (Edinburgh, 1865).

MACURDY, G. H., 'Apollodorus and the Speech against Neaera', *AJP* 63 (1942), 257–71.

MAINE, H. S., *Ancient Law* (London, 1861).

MAITLAND, JUDITH, 'Dynasty and Family in the Athenian City State: A View from Attic Tragedy', *CQ* 42 (1992), 26–40.

MALKIN, IRAD, *Myth and Territory in the Spartan Mediterranean* (Cambridge, 1994).

MANDILARAS, BASIL, 'A Papyrus Collection of the Greek Papyrological Society', *Επιστημονικη Επετηριδα Της Φιλοσοφικης Σχολης Του Πανεπιστημιου Αθηνων*, 28 (1992), 217–40.

—— 'A Papyrus Collection of the Greek Papyrological Society', in A. A. H. El-Mosallamy (ed.), *Proceedings of the XIXth International Congress of Papyrology, Cairo, 2–9 September 1989* (2 vols., Cairo, 1992), 583–602.

MARCHANT, E. C., *Xenophon in Seven Volumes*, VII: *Scripta Minora* (London and Cambridge, Mass., 1971).

MARSDEN, E. W., *Greek and Roman Artillery* (Oxford, 1969).

MEIER, C., *Die Entstehung des Politischen bei den Griechen* (Frankfurt, 1980).

MERITT, BENJAMIN D., 'Greek Inscriptions', *Hesperia*, 11 (1942), 275–303.

MEYER, E. A., 'Epitaphs and Citizenship in Classical Athens', *JHS* 113 (1993), 99–121.

MEYER, MARION, *Der griechischen Urkundenreliefs*, MDAI(A), 13 (Berlin, 1989).

MIKALSON, J. D., *Athenian Popular Religion* (Chapel Hill, NC, 1983).

—— 'Religion and the Plague in Athens, 431–423 BC', in K. J. Rigsby (ed.), *Studies Presented to Sterling Dow*, Greek, Roman, and Byzantine Studies Monograph, 10 (Durham, NC, 1984), 217–25.

MILLETT, P., 'The Attic Horoi Reconsidered in the Light of Recent Discoveries', *Opus*, 1 (1982), 219–49.

MINNS, E. H., *Scythians and Greeks* (Cambridge, 1913).

MODRZJEWSKI, J. MÉLÈZE, 'Die Geschwisterehe in der hellenistischen praxis und nach römischen Recht', *ZRG* 81 (1964), 52–82.

—— 'Un Aspect du "couple interdit" dans l'antiquité: les mariages mixtes dans l'Égypte hellénistique', in Léon Poliakov (ed.), *Le Couple interdit: entretiens sur le racism*, Actes du colloque tenu en mai 1977 au Centre culturel international de Cerisy-la-Salle (Paris, 1980), 53–73.

MONTEVECCHI, ORSOLINA, *La Papirologia*, rev. and corrected with addenda (Milan, 1988).

MORETTI, L., *Iscrizioni Agonistische Greche* (Rome, 1953).

MORGAN, GARETH, 'Euphiletos' House: Lysias I', *TAPhA* 112 (1982), 115–23.

MORRIS, IAN, *Burial and Ancient Society. The Rise of the Greek City-State* (Cambridge, 1987).

—— *Death-Ritual and Social Structure in Classical Antiquity* (Cambridge, 1992).

MOSSÉ, CLAUDE, 'Women in the Spartan Revolutions of the Third Century', in Sarah B. Pomeroy (ed.), *Women's History and Ancient History* (Chapel Hill, NC, 1991), 138–53.

NAGY, BLAISE, 'The Naming of Athenian Girls: A Case in Point', *CJ* 74 (1979), 60–4.

NEVETT, LISA, 'Separation or Seclusion? Towards an Archaeological Approach to Investigating Women in the Greek Household in the Fifth to Third Centuries BC', in Michael Parker Pearson and Colin Richards (eds.), *Architecture and Order. Approaches to Social Space* (London and New York, 1994), 98–112.

NIELSEN, THOMAS HEINE; BJERTRUP, LARS; HANSEN, MOGENS HERMAN; RUBINSTEIN, LENE; and VESTERGAARD, TORBEN, 'Athenian Grave Monuments and Social Class', *GRBS* 30 (1989), 411–20.

OAKLEY, JOHN H., and SINOS, REBECCA H., *The Wedding in Ancient Athens* (Madison, 1993).

OATES, JOHN F., review of *The Petrie Papyri*, 2nd edn., I, ed. W. Clarysse, *BASP* 29 (1992), 191–8.

—— BAGNALL, ROGER S.; WILLIS, WILLIAM H.; and WORP, KLAAS A., *Checklist of Editions of Greek and Latin Papyri, Ostraca and Tablets*, 4th edn., *BASP* Suppl. 7 (Atlanta, 1992).

OFENLOCH, E. *Caecilii Calactini Fragmenta* (Leipzig, 1907).

OGDEN, DANIEL, *Greek Bastardy in the Classical and the Hellenistic Periods* (Oxford, 1996).

OLLIER, F., *Le Mirage Spartiate* (2 vols., Paris, 1933, 1943).

ORRIEUX, CLAUDE, 'Les Comptes privées de Zénon', *CE*, 56 (1981), 314–40.

—— *Les Papyrus de Zénon. L'horizon d'un Grec en Égypte au iii° siècle avant J.-C.* (Paris, 1983).

OSBORNE, M. J., 'Attic Epitaphs—A Supplement', *Anc. Soc.* 19 (1988), 5–60.

—— *Naturalization in Athens* (4 vols., Brussels, 1981–3).

OSBORNE, ROBIN, *Demos: The Discovery of Classical Attika* (Cambridge, 1985).

PACK, R. A., *The Greek and Latin Literary Texts from Greco-Roman Egypt*, 2nd edn. (Ann Arbor, 1965).

PALEY, F. A., and SANDYS, J. E., *Select Private Orations of Demosthenes*, ii, 3rd edn. ([1896]; repr. Cambridge, 1979).

PARKER, ROBERT, *Miasma. Pollution and Purification in Early Greek Religion* (Oxford, 1983).

PARKIN, TIM G., *Demography and Roman Society* (Baltimore, 1992).

—— review of B. Rawson (ed.), *Marriage, Divorce and Children in Ancient Rome;* S. Dixon, *The Roman Family*; etc., *JRS* 84 (1994), 178–85.

PATTERSON, CYNTHIA, 'Hai Attikai: The Other Athenians', *Helios,* 13/2 (1987), 49–67.

—— 'Marriage and the Married Woman in Athenian Law', in Sarah B. Pomeroy (ed.), *Women's History and Ancient History* (Chapel Hill, NC, 1991), 48–72.

—— *Pericles' Citizenship Law of* 451–50 BC (Salem, NH, 1981).

PEARSON, LIONEL, 'Callisthenes in the Zenon Papyri', *CPh* 44 (1949), 200–2.

PEEK, W. *Griechische Grabgedichte*. Schriften und Quellen der Alten Welt, vii (Berlin, 1960).

—— *Griechische Vers-Inschriften* (Berlin, 1955).

PEMBERTON, ELIZABETH G., 'The *Dexiosis* on Attic Gravestones', *Mediterranean Archaeology*, 2 (1989), 45–50.

PEREMANS, W., 'Les Mariages mixtes dans l'Égypte des Lagides', in E. Bresciani, G. Geraci, S. Pernigotti, and G. Susini (eds.), *Scritti in onore di Orsolina Montevecchi* (Bologna, 1981), 273–81.

—— and VAN'T DACK, E., *Prosopographia Ptolemaica,* 5, Studia Hellenistica, 17 (Leuven, 1963).

—— —— *Prosopographia Ptolemaica*, 6, Studia Hellenistica, 17 (Leuven, 1968).

—— —— *Prosopographia Ptolemaica*, 9, Studia Hellenistica, 25 (Leuven, 1981).

PESTMAN, P. W., 'Fureter dans les Papiers de Totoes', in *Textes et Études de papyrologie grecque, démotique et copte*, Pap. Lugd. Bat., XXIII (Leiden, 1985), 144–85.

—— *A Guide to the Zenon Archive*, Pap. Lugd. Bat., XXI (2 vols., Leiden, 1981).

—— *Marriage and Matrimonial Property in Ancient Egypt. A Contribution to Establishing the Legal Position of the Woman*, Pap. Lugd. Bat., IX (Leiden, 1961).

—— 'Nahomsesis, una donna d'affari di Pathyris. L'archivio bilingue di Pelaias, figlio di Eunus', in E. Bresciani, G. Geraci, S. Pernigotti, and G. Susini (eds.), *Scritti in onore di Orsolina Montevecchi* (Bologna, 1981), 295–315.

—— and BOSWINKEL, F., 'Les Archives privées de Dionysios, fils de Kephalas', Pap. Lugd. Bat., XXII (Leiden, 1982).

—— *L'Archivio di Amenothes Figlio di Horos (P. Tor. Amenothos)*, Catalogo del Museo Egizio di Torino, 1st ser., v (Milan, 1981).

PETRAKOS, VASILIOS X., '*Ανασκαφή Ραμνοῦντος*', *Πρακτικα'* (1975), 5–35, (1976), 5–60.

—— '*Οι ανασκαφὲς του Ραμνοῦντος*' (1813–1987)', *AE* 126 (1987), 265–98.

—— '*Το Νεμέσιον του Ραμνοῦντος*', *Mélanges Mylonas*, ii (Athens, 1989), 295–326.

—— '*Ανασκαφὴ Ραμνοῦντος*', *PAE* (1989), 1–37.

—— *Rhamnous* (Athens, 1991).

PETRIE, SIR W. M. FLINDERS, *Illahun, Kahun, and Gurob* (London, 1891).

PETROPOULOU, ANGELIKI, *Beiträge zur Wirtschafts- und Gesellschaftsgeschichte Kretas in hellenistischer Zeit*, Europäische Hochschulschriften, ser. 3, Gesch. und ihre Hilfswissenschaften, 240 (Frankfurt, 1985).

PFISTERER-HAAS, SUSANNE, *Darstellungen alter Frauen in der Griechischen Kunst*, Europäische Hochschulschriften, ser. 38, Archäol., 21 (Frankfurt, 1989).

PINNAULT, JODY RUBIN, *Hippocratic Lives and Legends* (Leiden, 1992).

POMEROY, SARAH B., 'Copronyms and the Exposure of Infants in Egypt', in Roger Bagnall and William Harris (eds.), *Studies in Roman Law in Memory of A. Arthur Schiller* (Leiden, 1986), 147–62. Abstract in *Atti del XVII Congresso Internazionale di Papirologia* (Naples, 1984), 1341.

—— 'Family History in Ptolemaic Egypt', in Adam Bulow-Jacobsen (ed.), *Proceedings of the 20th International Congress of Papyrologists. Copenhagen, 23–29 August 1992* (Copenhagen, 1994), 593–7.

—— 'The Family in Classical and Hellenistic Greece', *Trends in History*, 3, 3–4 (1984), 19–26.

—— *Goddesses, Whores, Wives, and Slaves* (New York, 1975).

—— 'Infanticide in Hellenistic Greece', in A. Cameron and A. Kuhrt (eds.), *Images of Women in Antiquity* (London, 1983), 207–22.

—— 'Marriage: Greece', in Michael Grant and Rachel Kitzinger (eds.), *Civilization of the Ancient Mediterranean* (New York, 1988), 1333–42.

—— review of Mark Golden, *Children and Childhood in Classical Athens*, *Classical News and Views*, 36 (1992), 73–6.

—— 'Some Greek Families: Production and Reproduction', in Shaye J. D. Cohen (ed.), *The Jewish Family in Antiquity*, Brown Judaic Studies, 289 (Atlanta, 1993), 155–63.

—— 'The Study of Women in Antiquity: Past, Present, and Future', *AJP* 112 (1991), 263–8.

—— 'Technikai kai Mousikai: The Education of Women in the Fourth Century and in the Hellenistic Period', *AJAH* 2 (1977), 51–68.

—— *Women in Hellenistic Egypt from Alexander to Cleopatra*, with a new foreword and addenda (Detroit, 1989).

—— 'Women's Identity and the Family in the Classical Polis', in R. Hawley and B. Levick (eds.), *Women in Antiquity: New Assessments* (London, 1995), 111–21.

—— *Xenophon Oeconomicus. A Social and Historical Commentary* (Oxford, 1994).

POUILLOUX, J., *La Fortresse de Rhamnonte: étude de topographie et d'histoire*, Bibliothèque des Écoles françaises d'Athènes et de Rome, 179 (Paris, 1954).

RATHBONE, D. W., 'Villages, Land, and Population in Graeco-Roman Egypt', *PCPS* 216 (1990), 103–42.

RAUBITSCHEK, A., 'The Ostracism of Xanthippos', *AJP* 51 (1947), 257–62.

REEKMANS, TONY, *La Sitométrie dans les Archives de Zenon* (Brussels, 1966).

REHM, A., *Milet*, 3. *Das Delphinion in Milet. Die Inschriften* (Berlin, 1914).

RHODES, P. J., *A Commentary on the Aristotelian Athenaion Politeia* (Oxford, 1981).

RIDDLE, JOHN M., *Contraception and Abortion from the Ancient World to the Renaissance* (Cambridge, Mass., 1992).

RITNER, R. K., 'A Property Transfer from the Erbstreit Archives', in *Festschrift E. Lüddeckens* (Würzburg, 1984), 171–87.

ROBINSON, DAVID M., *Excavations at Olynthus*, xi: *Necrolynthia* (Baltimore, 1942).

ROSE, H. J., 'The Religion of a Greek Household', *Euphrosyne*, 1 (1957), 95–116.

ROSIVACH, VINCENT, 'The Distribution of Population in Attica', *GRBS* 34 (1993), 391–407.

ROUSSEL, DENIS, *Tribu et Cité*, Annales Littéraires de l'Université de Besançon, 23 (Paris, 1976).

RUBINSTEIN, LENE, *Adoption in iv. Century Athens* (Copenhagen, 1993).

—— BJERTRUP, LARS; HANSEN, MOGENS HERMAN; NIELSEN, THOMAS HEINE; and VESTERGAARD, TORBEN, 'Adoption in Hellenistic and Roman Athens', *C&M* 42 (1991), 139–51.

RUSCHENBUSCH, E., *ΣΟΛΟΝΟΣ ΝΟΜΟΙ Die Fragmente des solonischen Gesetzeswerkes mit einer Text- und Überlieferungsgeschichte*, *Historia*, Einzelschr. 9 (Wiesbaden, 1966).

STE. CROIX, G. E. M. DE, 'Some Observations on the Property Rights of Athenian Women', *CR* 20 (1970), 273–8.

—— 'Roman Heirship Strategies in Principle and in Practice', in David I. Kertzer and Richard P. Saller (eds.), *The Family in Italy* (New Haven and London, 1991), 26–47.

SALLER, RICHARD P., '*Patria Potestas* and the Stereotype of the Roman Family', *Continuity and Change*, 1 (1986), 7–22.

—— *Patriarchy, Property and Death in the Roman Family* (Cambridge, 1994).

SANT CASSIA, PAUL, and BADA, CONSTANTINA, *The Making of the Modern Greek Family* (Cambridge, 1992).

SCHAEFER, ARNOLD, *Demosthenes und seine Zeit* (Leipzig, 1885; repr. Hildesheim, 1966).

SCHAPS, DAVID M., *Economic Rights of Women in Ancient Greece* (Edinburgh, 1979).

SCHMITT-PANTEL, PAULINE, 'Évergétisme et mémoire du mort. À propos des fondations de banquets publics dans les cités grecques à l'époque hellénistique et romaine', in G. Gnoli and J. P. Vernant (eds.), *La Mort, les morts dans les sociétés anciennes* (Cambridge and Paris, 1982), 177–88.

SCHOLL, REINHOLD, *Corpus der Ptolemäischen Sklaventexte* (3 vols., Stuttgart, 1990).

—— 'Dryton's Tod', *CE*, 63 (1988), 141–4.

—— *Sklaverei in den Zenonpapyri*, Trierer historische Forschungen, 4 (Trier, 1983), 136–7.

SCHWEIGERT, E., 'The Xanthippos Ostracon', *AJA* 53 (1949), 266–8.

SEALEY, R., *The Athenian Republic. Democracy or the Rule of Law?* (University Park, Pa., 1987).

—— 'The Entry of Pericles into History', *Hermes*, 84 (1956), 234–47; repr. in *Essays in Greek Politics* (New York, 1967), 59–74.

SEIDL, E., *Ptolemäische Rechtsgeschichte* (Gluckstadt, Hamburg, and New York, 1962).

SHAPIRO, H. A., 'The Iconography of Mourning in Athenian Art', *AJA* 95 (1991), 629–56.

SHAW, BRENT, 'The Age of Roman Girls at Marriage: Some Reconsiderations', *JRS* 77 (1987), 30–46.

SHEAR, T. LESLIE, JR., *Kallias of Sphettos and the Revolt of Athens in* 286 BC, *Hesperia*, Suppl. 17 (Princeton, 1978).

—— 'Koisyra. Three Women of Athens', *Phoenix*, 17 (1963), 99–112.

SHELTON, J., 'A Note on O. *Oslo* 1', *ZPE* 73 (1988), 204.

SHERWIN-WHITE, SUSAN, *Ancient Cos*, Hypomnemata, 51 (Göttingen, 1978).

SIMON, BENNETT, *Tragic Drama and the Family: Psychoanalytic Studies from Aeschylus to Beckett* (New Haven and London, 1988).

SLATER, PHILIP, *The Glory of Hera* (Boston, 1968).

SMITH, ADAM, *The Wealth of Nations* (2 vols., 1776; repr. London, 1910).

SMITH, L. C., 'Demochares of Leuconoe and the Dates of his Exile', *Historia*, 11 (1961), 114–18.

SMITH, RICHARD C., 'The Clans of Athens and the Historiography of the Archaic Period', *EMC* 29 (1985), 51–61.

SMITH, R. R. R., 'Greeks, Foreigners, and Roman Republican Portraits', *JRS* 71 (1981), 24–38.

SMITH, WESLEY D., *Hippocrates. Pseudepigraphic Writings* (Leiden, 1990).

—— *The Hippocratic Tradition* (Ithaca, New York, and London, 1979).

—— 'Notes on Ancient Medical Historiography', *Bulletin of the History of Medicine*, 63 (1989), 73–109.

SNOWDEN, FRANK M., JR., *Blacks in Antiquity: Ethiopians in the Greco-Roman Experience* (Cambridge, Mass., 1970).

SOKOLOWSKI, F., *Lois sacrées des cités grecques* (Paris, 1969).

SOURVINOU-INWOOD, CHRISTIANE, 'Further Aspects of Polis Religion', *AION (archeol.)* 10 (1988), 259–74.

—— 'Priestess in the Text: *Theano Menonos Agrylethen*', *Greece and Rome*, 35 (1988), 28–35.

SPYRIDAKIS, STYLIANOS V., and NYSTROM, BRADLEY P., *Ancient Greece: Documentary Perspectives* (Dubuque, Ia., 1988).

STADTER, PHILIP A. (ed.), *Plutarch and the Historical Tradition* (London and New York, 1992).

STEFANIS, I. E., *Διονυσιακοὶ Τεχνῖται* (Heraklion, 1988).

STENGEL, P., '*Γαμηλία*', RE vii.1 (Stuttgart, 1910), cols. 691–2.

STRAUSS, BARRY S., *Athens after the Peloponnesian War* (Ithaca, NY, 1987).

—— *Fathers and Sons in Athens. Ideology and Society in the Era of the Peloponnesian War* (Princeton, 1993).

SUSEMIHL, F. *Geschichte der griechischen Literatur in der Alexandrinerzeit* (Leipzig, 1891).

SUTTON, DANA FERRIN, 'The Theatrical Families of Athens', *AJP* 108 (1987), 9–26.

SUTTON, ROBERT F., JR., 'On the Classical Athenian Wedding: Two Red-Figure Loutrophoroi in Boston', in Robert F. Sutton, Jr. (ed.), *Daidalikon. Studies in Memory of Raymond V. Schoder, S.J.* (Wauconda, Ill., 1989), 331–59.

SWIDEREK, ANNA, 'Zenon fils d'Agréophon de Caunos et sa famille', *Eos*, 48/2 (1956); repr. in *Symbolae R. Taubenschlag*, ii (Warsaw, 1957), 133–41.

SWOBODA, H., *RE* iv (1901), 2863–7, s.v. Demochares 6.

—— *RE* xii (1925), 339, s.vv. Laches 6 and 7.

TALBERT, RICHARD J. A., *Plutarch on Sparta* (London, 1988).

THOMAS, ROSALIND, *Oral Tradition and Written Record in Classical Athens* (Cambridge, 1989).

THOMPSON, WESLEY E., 'Athenian Marriage Patterns: Remarriage', *CSCA* 5 (1972), 211–25.

—— 'Harpokration on *γεννῆται*,' *Hermes*, 11 (1983), 118–21.

—— 'The Marriage of First Cousins in Athenian Society', *Phoenix*, 21 (1967), 273–82.

—— 'Some Attic Kinship Terms,' *Glotta*, 48 (1970), 75–81.

TOD, M. N., 'Greek Record-Keeping and Record-Breaking', *CQ* 43 (1949), 105–12.

TODD, S. C., *The Shape of Athenian Law* (Oxford, 1993).

TOLSTOY, COUNT LEO, *Anna Karenina*, trans. C. Garnett ([1873], NY, 1950).

TREVETT, JEREMY, *Apollodoros, the Son of Pasion* (Oxford, 1992).

TURNER, JUDY ANN, '*Hiereiai*: Acquisition of Feminine Priesthoods in Ancient Greece' (Ph.D. diss., University of California, Santa Barbara, 1983).

UEBEL, F., 'Die frühptolemäische Salszteur', in *Atti dell'XI Congresso internaz. di Papirologia* (Milan, 1966), 341–3.

University of Texas at Austin, *The Pantanello Necropolis 1982–1989* (Austin, 1990).

VERMEULE, EMILY, *Aspects of Death in Early Greek Art and Poetry* (Berkeley, 1979).

VERNANT, JEAN-PIERRE, *Mythe et pensée chez les Grecs*, rev. edn. (Paris, 1985).

VESTERGAARD, TORBEN; BJERTRUP, LARS; HANSEN, MOGENS HERMAN; NIELSEN, THOMAS HEINE; and RUBINSTEIN, LENE, 'A Typology of the Women Recorded on Gravestones from Attica', *AJAH* 10 (1985), 178–90.

WALKER, SUSAN, 'Women and Housing in Classical Greece: The Archaeological Evidence', in Averil Cameron and Amélie Kuhrt (eds.), *Images of Women in Antiquity* (London and Canberra, 1983), 81–91.

WEAVER, P. R. C., *Familia Caesaris* (Cambridge, 1972).

WENTZEL, ASTRID, 'Studien über die Adoption in Griechenland', *Hermes*, 65 (1960), 167–76.

WEST, M. L., *Hesiod. Works and Days* (Oxford, 1978).

WESTERMANN, A. *ΒΙΟΓΡΑΦΟΙ Vitarum Scriptores Graeci Minores* (Braunschweig, 1845).

WHITEHEAD, DAVID, *The Demes of Attica 508/7–ca.250 BC* (Princeton, 1986).

—— *The Ideology of the Athenian Metic* (Cambridge, 1977).

—— 'Women and Naturalisation in Fourth-Century Athens. The Case of Archippe', *CQ* 36 (1986), 109–14.

WILHELM, A., 'Zum Ostrakismos des Xanthippos, des Vaters des Perikles', *AAWW*, 86 (1949), 237–44.

WILSON, NIGEL G., *Prolegomena de Comoedia Scholia in Acharnenses, Equites, Nubes*, 1B: *Scholia in Aristophanis Acharnenses* (Groningen, 1975).

WINTERS, T. F., 'Kleisthenes and Athenian Nomenclature', *JHS* 113 (1993), 162–5.

WITTENBURG, ANDREAS, *Il Testamento di Epikteta* (Trieste, 1990).

WYSE, WILLIAM, *The Speeches of Isaeus* (Cambridge, 1904).

Index